Worlds Apart?

Worlds Apart?

Disability and Foreign Language Learning

Edited by

TAMMY BERBERI *University of Minnesota, Morris*

ELIZABETH C. HAMILTON *Oberlin College*

IAN M. SUTHERLAND *Gallaudet University*

Foreword by

SANDER L. GILMAN

Yale University Press New Haven and London

Set in New Aster by Duke & Company, Devon, Pennsylvania.
Printed in the United States of America.

Library of Congress Cataloging-in-Publication Data
Sutherland, Ian M., 1956–
   Worlds apart? : disability and foreign language learning / edited by Tammy Berberi, Elizabeth C. Hamilton, Ian M. Sutherland ; foreword by Sander L. Gilman.
      p.   cm.
   Includes bibliographical references and index.
   ISBN 978-0-300-11630-4 (pbk. : alk. paper)   1. Language and languages—Study and teaching.   2. Students with disabilities.   I. Berberi, Tammy, 1969–   II. Hamilton, Elizabeth C., 1965–   III. Title.
   P53.818W67 2008
   418.0071—dc22

                                             2007024027

A catalogue record for this book is available from the British Library.

The paper in this book meets the guidelines for permanence and durability of the Committee on Production Guidelines for Book Longevity of the Council on Library Resources.

10 9 8 7 6 5 4 3 2 1

For teachers and students

Partout je rencontrais des contraintes, nulle part la nécessité.

Everywhere I encountered limits, nowhere necessity.

—SIMONE DE BEAUVOIR, *Mémoires d'une jeune fille rangée*

Ich [habe] weder Blick noch Schritt in fremde Lande getan als in der Absicht, das allgemein Menschliche, was über den ganzen Erdboden verbreitet und verteilt ist, unter den verschiedensten Formen kennen zu lernen und solches in meinem Vaterlande wiederzufinden, anzuerkennen, zu fördern.

I have never looked at foreign countries or gone there but with the purpose of getting to know the general human qualities that are spread all over the earth in very different forms, and then to find these qualities again in my own country and to recognize and to further them.

—JOHANN WOLFGANG VON GOETHE, letter to Johann L. Büchler

Homo sum: humani nil a me alienum puto.

I am a human being; I consider nothing human alien to me.

—TERENCE, *Heauton Timoroumenos*

Contents

Technology

Disabilities Abroad

Foreword

Who is different? Well, in real terms, everyone. Who is seen as different? Now that is a very different question. Norms in society are always compromises between perceived extremes. In the world of Disability Studies, where such compromises are studied, they are revealed to be fluid and dynamic. They reflect changing assumptions about physical and mental difference in the culture(s) in which they arise. Scholars of Disability Studies deal with representations of difference as well as with the very mechanisms of perception and articulation that make such representations possible. In other words, images of difference are generated and studied through precisely the same lens or paradigms or mechanisms as "foreign" languages. And yet, it is really only with this book that the links between the pedagogical, social, cultural, and psychological aspects of "foreign" language learning and Disability Studies have come to the fore as a serious topic of investigation by the leaders in each field. Approaches such as those described in Katharina Heyer's "No One's Perfect: Disability and Difference in Japan" show how texts representing disability can be used in the "foreign" language classroom to introduce a language and a culture different from the culture in which the learner lives. All of the chapters in this brilliant collection reveal intersections between the pragmatic and the analytic, between the teaching of language and the teaching of culture(s), between the world of Disability Studies and that of "foreign" language learning.

Those of you who are close readers will have noticed something in the above paragraph: "foreign" is in scare quotes; disability is not. Disability Studies has a long history, beginning with the social service structures that developed in the eighteenth century in Europe to provide a pragmatic education to (at least initially) the blind and the deaf. Those who worked in these structures were eventually educated in programs grounded upon a social service or medical model in schools of social work or of medicine. Beginning about a generation ago, these programs were expanded to include people with disabilities as advocates and specialists. The entire field was reshaped, including its service component, to be both a field for advocacy and the space for a critical analysis of difference. Those humanists and social scientists who took part in this restructuring in turn introduced Disability Studies into humanities and social sciences curricula.

All of these projects retained the term "disability." It was rehabilitated in much the same way that "queer" (as in Queer Studies) was rehabilitated: to be a term that stresses its break with past societal models and illustrates its continuities with those so labeled in the past. Disability cultures exist now in self-conscious ways that belie many of the earlier models of dependency and paternalism, but they continue to reflect earlier thinkers' principled commitment to both "theory" and "praxis." Interestingly, this quality of the integration of theory and practice is also a hallmark for language teaching and learning.

Yet one realm in the university into which the new image of "disability" seemed to have difficulty gaining entrance was "foreign" language study, which is strange, given the recent emphasis on the learning of languages being simultaneous with the learning about cultures. The "theory" and "praxis" divide that rarely haunts Disability Studies came to be rejected in the realm of language/culture learning. To no little extent the battle in North America over "foreign" languages during the past few decades was fought to normalize the notion that American, Anglophone students lived in a multilingual context in which at least one language—Spanish—was not foreign but native. The truth of the matter is that North America (including Canada and Mexico) is composed of nations that to a greater (Quebec) or lesser (Chiapas) degree were self-consciously multilingual states. The range of languages spoken today in Toronto or New York or Los Angeles is staggering—with their speakers no longer seen as "foreign" but regarded as established or new or potential citizens. The many languages spoken in the United States and Canada are no longer "foreign." They are now part of the world in which we, as North American educators, function. No language is "foreign" to us in the sense of not belonging to the realm of our experience, in spite of the insistence of "English-only" (or in Mexico "Spanish-only," in Quebec "French-only") advocates.

While the culture of multiethnic awareness permeated the teaching of languages during the 1980s and 1990s, the one population group that was ill- or un- or under-served in second language acquisition was the "disabled." Whether it was the rejection of American Sign Language as not "foreign" enough to fulfill "foreign" language requirements, or the exclusion of disability as a topic in language learning, or the (false) assumption that disabled students could not or should not participate in study abroad programs through a misguided notion of *in loco parentis*, "foreign" language departments have tended to see their mission as not extending to the realm of disabled students or Disability Studies. Remember that the so-called No Child Left Behind Law, approved in 2002, built concessions into the law for students who speak languages other than English and for those with severe disabilities. That learning languages and being disabled could be part of the same, positive experience seemed to be beyond comprehension.

There were pioneers who fought these assumptions. Many of them are well represented in this book. What I hope is that the book, which presents a wide swath of work on disability and language study, will encourage teachers in departments of modern and classical languages to see Disability Studies as a space where language learning takes place for self-styled "normal" students as well as for "disabled" students. Tammy Berberi, Elizabeth C. Hamilton, and Ian M. Sutherland should be pleased with this volume, as it will shake up many teachers of languages across North America—indeed, perhaps to the extent of their imaging a new idea of foreign (notice: no scare quotes) language in which difference and strangeness redefine the very notion of "foreignness" as a quality to be explored and taught in a classroom now open to all.

Sander L. Gilman
Emory University

Acknowledgments

We thank Brie Kluytenaar at Yale University Press for guiding us along the path toward publication. We are also grateful to Annie Imbornoni for her careful shepherding of the book through the various stages of production. Otto Bohlmann merits our appreciation for his careful editing of these pages. We thank Carole Poore of Brown University, Ralph James Savarese at Grinnell College, and L. Scott Lissner at the Ohio State University for their insightful reviews of our manuscript. Professor Matt Senior of the University of Minnesota, Morris, provided invaluable insight and encouragement, for which we thank him most sincerely. Warm thanks are also due Dean Harry Hirsch of Oberlin College for generous financial assistance. These colleagues and mentors have lent their expertise as well as their principled support of inclusive education.

We were saddened to learn of the untimely passing of Facundo Montenegro during the completion of this volume. We are especially grateful to his colleagues Pilar Piñar and Donalda Ammons for completing the work they had begun during a time of loss. Their resulting essay honors Professor Montenegro's deep commitment to the deaf community and broadens educational opportunities for all.

—The Editors

I am grateful to the people who have helped me build the bridge between my life and my life's work, among them: Sarah Buchanan, Susan Burch, Kate Droske, Phyllis Franklin, Molly Kloek, Christa Mims, David Parker, Ralph Savarese, and Engin Sungur. I appreciate the support of the Bush Foundation and the Office of the Vice Chancellor and Dean for Academic Affairs at the University of Minnesota, Morris, which have provided time and resources to experiment in my classroom. I would like to recognize the contributions of my own teachers, in particular Memory Schorr. She made me want to be a teacher when people had only begun to believe that a kid like me could—and should—learn. She's the kind of teacher I strive to be. Although the members of my family are happy at home, they encouraged me to study languages unknown to them and understood that I needed to experience other places in order to know myself. Finally, I reserve my deepest gratitude for Viktor and Henry, for making home wherever we may find ourselves together—and making it a place worth rediscovering at every turn.

—T. B.

Teachers are the most important people in my life, and I am nowhere so much at home as in a classroom. This is surely no accident, for I was named after my parents' beloved college professor, Miss Helen V. Cushman. Now retired from public school teaching themselves, my parents instilled in me a love of learning and confidence in formal education that cannot be shaken. My conviction that all students can learn stems in great measure from their guidance and example. Professor Heidi Thomann Tewarson, chair of the German Department at Oberlin College, merits my deepest appreciation. Her wise counsel ranged from the pedagogical to the scholarly, professional, and practical aspects of editing a book. Her personal encouragement perhaps meant the most of all. My colleague Steve Huff offered generous moral support at every stage as well. I thank Jerry Malone for his care and confidence; his sharp mind and insatiable desire to learn inspire me every day. Finally, I thank Elliott Hamilton for his help and thoughtfulness during the final stages of this project.

—E. C. H.

My experience at Gallaudet University has been greatly enriched by many colleagues in various departments who have shared the accrued benefits and insights of their many years of instruction at that unique institution. I am especially indebted to Dr. Donalda Ammons, who for nearly three decades has exemplified effective foreign language teaching for our students. I am also deeply grateful to Dr. Susan Burch, whose insights and understanding of disability are brilliant, and whose constant support is my staff in life.

—I. M. S.

CHAPTER 1

Bridging Worlds Apart: Disability and Foreign Languages Where We Live and Learn

TAMMY BERBERI

You know, it never occurred to me: eight handicapped parking spaces right next to a flight of ten steps to get into the ground floor, where—get this—there's an elevator! My German class was in the same building, so I used to see her working her way up those stairs all the time.

You think that's bad? I saw this guy in a wheelchair one time, just waiting around. He said somebody had parked in that blank aisle next to his van and he couldn't lower the ramp to get back in. Said sometimes all the spots are taken by people without handicap tags and when he can't park his van with space next to it, he can't get to class. I felt really bad for the guy. I didn't even know disabled people could drive.

*

This morning, this student comes to my office hours to tell me that she has Chronic Fatigue Syndrome, and that's why she failed my course. I know: it's the last day of the semester! Who is she kidding? This is the first time she has visited my office, even though I asked her to again and again. Of course, she comes when she fails the final exam. What frustrates me is, at this point, I really can't do anything to help her. She'll have to take second-semester French again next year to graduate. "Why didn't you register for Disabled Student Services?" I asked her. "Why didn't you talk to me sooner?"

*

You want to know what happened today? My French class was in the language lab, right? And we were all getting settled at the computers to do this assignment on-line and my teacher just, like, fell! Nobody knew what to do. I mean, I looked around and I thought you know, somebody do or say something! But no one did, so like, what am I going to do? Then, you won't believe it: she fell again. Her sticks went flying and her shoe came off. It was totally embarrassing. I don't know. I guess she was okay. I mean, she seemed okay.

All these stories circulate in my world, the American academy. I've heard them, I've lived them, and I repeat them. I don't offer them as proof that every university facility is a fun house of inaccessibility, or because I believe any person pressed for time would park in the accessible aisle, or because I think everyone's sense of kindness and companionship toward others short-circuits when physical difference enters the room. Anecdotes are interesting because they represent the exception—we cordon them off as bits of life worth retelling because they offer something idiosyncratic—as well as the rule. Listeners know enough about a shared cultural context for them to be able, without explanation, to supply the backdrop to the story.

For a long time, anecdotes have been letting me off the hook: they have allowed me to participate in a complex social question without making a genuine commitment to change the culture we live in; they've replaced meaningful encounters with colleagues and students who have disabilities. These are isolated incidents, and no one is really to blame. Or better stated, if there were someone to blame, who would it be?

By law, existing public buildings and facilities need not meet minimum specifications for accessibility until they are updated. By law, the student with Chronic Fatigue Syndrome must disclose her disability in advance and register with Disabled Student Services in order to be accommodated in her courses. There are no laws governing incidents like harnessing every muscle in your face and every cell of your consciousness in order *not* to see someone fall, but American custom does dictate norms for such interactions. If I had a quarter for every well-intentioned mother I've seen drag her child in a direction away from where he is looking as she whisper-shouts, "Don't stare!" between clenched teeth, I would buy every one of those kids the lollipop he deserves. Children recognize physical difference, and they want to know more about it.

These incidents that dot my world here and there aren't my fault, but in recent years I've come around to the idea that they are my responsibility. I have been accused of promoting my own political agenda in this regard, but exactly which agenda I get to lay claim to isn't clear. If it's promoting equal access to education, many before me have already taken up that agenda. As a result, schools are no longer officially segregated, and women outnumber men on co-ed college campuses today. If it's the agenda about the norm being constructed and therefore being at least as worthy of analysis as the exception, I wish that one were mine. I am reminded that in college I had the opportunity to read Hélène Cixous (a woman) alongside Tzvetan Todorov and Jacques Derrida, Assia Djébar and Aimé Césaire (Francophone African writers) alongside Victor Hugo and André Breton. I learned that what is absent is as important as what is present in the world around me. Disability isn't my political agenda because I walk with crutches. I learned to see and value underrepresented people, ideas, and ways of life at school.

I loved school so much as a child—and as an adult—that I've opted to live here. For me it has been the gateway to a world that's intimately mine and utterly fulfilling. I have spent three full decades living, learning, falling in love (with languages, writers, protagonists) and moving on. Where would I be if I drove a van with a ramp, or if a chronic illness prevented me from taking a full course load but financial aid eligibility meant that I had to take a full one? I probably wouldn't be here, and I wouldn't be me. My parents bought a house with sixteen steps so I would learn how to climb them. Good thing, because I am the woman who climbed the steps into that university building nearly every day for eight years. I am also the teacher who sent that student packing because she hadn't registered with Disabled Student Services. Even while I support equal rights and access for disabled people (and I suspect most of us do), I contribute daily to an environment that can make success—and life—more difficult than it has to be for many people.

Although this first chapter of this book is, in large measure, about whom we educate, the rest of the chapters address how we educate. While here I strive to describe the problem as I see it—ableism in the American academy—the essays that follow offer solutions. Broadly defined, ableism is the systematic exclusion of people with sensory, emotional, physical, or cognitive impairments, based on deeply held beliefs about health, intelligence, productivity, and beauty. Like other kinds of oppression, ableism shapes interactions between individuals as well as institutions and cultures. Thomas Hehir, former director of the U.S. Department of Education's Office of Special Education, writes of ableism in education, "The devaluation of disability results in societal attitudes that uncritically assert that it is better for a child to walk than roll, speak than sign, read print than read Braille, spell independently than use spell-check. . . . There is an ingrained prejudice against performing activities in ways that might be more efficient for disabled people but that are different from how non-disabled perform them."[1]

We authors share the conviction that we can and should examine how our efforts in the foreign language classroom can contribute to a healthier campus atmosphere surrounding physical difference and, more important, to the success and lifelong learning of students with disabilities. We maintain that all students benefit from these efforts, and that discussions of lives lived fully (with impairments) should not be left to specialists but concern us all.

The number of students with disabilities pursuing postsecondary education has tripled since 1978 as a result of the Disability Rights Movement and legislation that guarantees them access to a college education. Today, one in nine undergraduates report having one or multiple disabilities.[2] Statisticians parse the data in so many different ways that it's difficult to offer a clear picture of this population, but most coincide in the finding that about half of these students report a learning disability. Another 30 percent or so report disabilities that are either "health related" or "other." Surveys tracking enrollment patterns and progress of underrepresented students are a useful and necessary advocacy tool. They interest me for a number of reasons, the least of which is to know how many students disclose a particular impairment. I'm intrigued by how often the diagnosis fails to capture the person. It is quite likely that a young person accustomed to impairment entertains the diagnosis for others, and thinks about it himself only when he comes up against a barrier. To quote an old college buddy of mine who is blind, "I don't wake up every morning and think, 'I'm blind.'" Unfortunately, the same data meant to track and promote inclusion are often cited to undermine it. For example, a skeptic might wonder why one should be aware of techniques to educate blind students when data suggest that blindness is a very low-incidence impairment. Using such data to remove responsibility for teaching the students in our classrooms defies both logic and my sense of vocation. Moreover, it is tantamount to applying a medical diagnosis to a cultural issue.

It may be helpful to examine for a moment where these first-year college students who identify themselves as having a disability come from and where they are headed. The fact that they are able to disclose a disability means that they have a clear sense of a diagnosis and the limitations it may impose on their daily lives. It is likely to mean that they are one of 13 percent of students who received federally funded services in a regular public school day.[3] These may include partial or full-day placement in special education classes; working with a physical or speech therapist, an audiologist or a psychologist; getting intensive help with basic skills, such as reading and writing, or specialized ones, like reading Braille; being assisted for part of the day or all day by a paraprofessional; and taking paratransit services to school. The array of services required to enable the K–12 success of a student with a disability is determined by a team composed of teachers, relevant specialists, and parents who develop an Individual Education Plan, or IEP. In 1990, the Individuals with Disabilities Education Act (IDEA), the law mandating a free and appropriate education for all children with disabilities, was amended to include transition services in the IEP beginning at the age of fourteen. Transition services lay the groundwork for life after high school graduation, including living independently, working, and going to college.

By some measures, this system has proved successful: the number of students with disabilities who completed high school rose from 61 percent in 1986 to 78 percent in 2001.[4] However, nationally, only 57 percent of these students receive standard diplomas. Others drop out or receive an alternative diploma, a document that affords them access neither to the military nor to higher education. In some places in the United States, the numbers are even more disheartening. As I write this chapter, Beth Fertig of National Public Radio reports that only 23 percent of New York City's special education students earn a standard diploma after five years. Another third of them drop out, and the rest are given an alternative diploma.[5] These students are victims of what Thomas Hehir describes as the most damaging result of ableist assumptions in K–12: low expectations. Hehir predicts that standards-based reforms will improve outcomes for young people with disabilities, enabling more and more of them to continue to college.[6] Indeed, by all projections, enrollments will only continue to increase: a four-year degree is considered a necessity these days. In 2004, a man with at least a bachelor's degree averaged 67 percent more in annual income than a man with a high school diploma.[7] (One wonders about the average annual income of a person with an alternative diploma.) Yet while the numbers of students with disabilities entering four-year degree programs continue to rise, the rate of persistence among college students with disabilities is very low: according to the U.S. Department of Education, of those students with disabilities who began college during the 1995–1996 academic year, only 15 percent had obtained a bachelor's degree by 2001, compared to 29.8 percent of nondisabled students; 41.2 percent of students with disabilities had dropped out.[8]

The same patterns—ever higher numbers enrolled and low rates of persistence—intersect for minority students: demographic projections for the next decade predict very high numbers of minority students graduating from high school across the United States. A recent study in Minnesota found that African American students enrolled in a college-prep curriculum received lower American College Test (ACT) scores than white students not enrolled in the college-prep curriculum.[9] The parallel is clear: we must strive to recognize and remove myriad obstacles that contribute to very low rates of persistence among college students with disabilities and other underrepresented groups.[10] To fail to alter the terrain that halts their educational progress is to acknowledge that despite advancements difference remains a spectacle to be found in worlds imagined and has no place where we live. This failure reiterates difference as the object rather than the subject of inquiry. Whether we feel at home here or not, we are at a crossroads in higher education. We can either uncritically accept a growing population of young people who are unprepared to succeed in life, or we can pledge to educate them.

For those disabled students who gain admission to college, the ordinary issues of adjustment confronting all college students are compounded by their disabilities. Inclusion in elementary and secondary education sets a clear precedent for access to higher education, and both IDEA and the Americans with Disabilities Act provide protection against discrimination, but the legal framework for postsecondary education is altogether different. Thomas R. Wolanin and Patricia E. Steele, authors of *Higher Education Opportunities for Students with Disabilities,* describe the many ways that college marks a watershed in the lives of students with disabilities. Their education is no longer free and appropriate. Students must meet the requirements to gain admission to college and maintain academic standards throughout their college career. The IEP and the team of experts are no more. Students with disabilities must learn to be advocates for themselves virtually overnight, and at the same time as they are acquiring other life skills—managing their time without the constraints of a home environment, finding their way around campus, living with a roommate, doing their own laundry, understanding financial aid, finding a part-time job, making friends, passing French and Chemistry. That is, in order to benefit from accommodation, they must register with Disabled Student Services, provide official documentation of their impairment, and work individually with professors they have in all likelihood just met to discuss the details of accommodation. Data suggest that the prescribed process for getting needed services often fails: among students reporting disabilities, 26 percent received the accommodations they needed; 22 percent did not.[11]

Wolanin and Steele emphasize that transition services often do not include self-advocacy skills. Those that a student possesses may be stunted by aspects of special education that foster dependence. An explanation of the ways in which college will be different for a student with a disability is often completely overlooked in transition discussions, and, at least according to anecdotal evidence, the information provided in transition services is sometimes inaccurate. For example, a student in my Disability Studies course came to me at the end of the semester to say goodbye. He had been a stunning student in the course—passionate, thoughtful, creative, helpful toward others—and, he then told me, he also had a learning disability. He was about to graduate and shared some regrets about his college career. Years before, a high school guidance counselor had advised him not to seek accommodations through Disabled Student Services in college. Doing so, he was told, would automatically exclude him from participation in a variety of cocurricular options, including intercollegiate athletics and the Honors Program. So he didn't. Instead, he tolerated repeated admonitions from his professors and mediocre performance. He decided he probably wasn't "honors material," and didn't apply for the Honors Program. In the final semester of his college career, he learned that exclusion based on disability is prohibited by law. Nine days before his graduation, he understood how misinformation and stigma had shaped his own choices in college.

Consider the ways in which this student differs from the one who disclosed that she had Chronic Fatigue Syndrome after she had failed the final exam in French. He was in his final year of college, she in her second. The manifestation of his impairment was reliably stable, and he had benefited from years of working with experts in K–12; the effects of hers were more difficult to anticipate, and she had been coping with them for only a year. Much is understood about learning disabilities, and we are accustomed to accommodating them; far less is known about Chronic Fatigue Syndrome—indeed, some question its validity as a diagnosis. He disclosed his impairment in the context of a course that allowed him to consider disability a social construction, the product of built (physical and ideological) environments and enduring prejudices. He and I had the opportunity to think critically and talk openly about disability. On the other hand, although I did not understand it at the time, her disclosure in the face of failure was a patterned response to ableism. I am neither targeting my course as the culprit nor excusing it, but I am arguing here that our shared failure is the product of ingrained responses to physical difference.

When I asked her why she hadn't registered for services or spoken to me sooner, she answered, "I didn't want the stigma." She and I agree on that point: I don't want it (for her, for me, between us) either. In my estimation, however, she misunderstands the nature of that stigma, which is a product not of impairment but of the meaning our culture attaches to impairment. By culture I mean to refer both to the American academy and to individual institutional cultures. We live and work in an environment that prizes intellectual ability, articulateness, and (hyper)productivity; an environment where commitment is measured by lost sleep and dishevelment; where the mind must thrive at the expense of a body we are not to notice; where we readily nurture the myth that opacity in the delivery of course material indicates a measure of brilliance; where we emphasize outcomes over process; where the sheer pace of the courses we design makes it impossible for students to backtrack and reconsider material; where innovations in methodologies, techniques, and curricula are rarely recognized for the purposes of tenure and promotion; and where slowing down or making course notes, old exams, or sample papers available for study purposes is tantamount to endorsing lower standards.

Each time a student with a registered disability enrolls in my course, I receive a confidential memo detailing the accommodations required. It is only confidential because it is part of a student's official record, but in this context, "confidential" has a rather pregnant ring to it, conjuring an aura of secrecy that compounds typical uneasiness about growing up and making the grade. By virtue of this system, that student must rely on one professor and the staff of a single office to lay the groundwork for meaningful learning. Ideally, the professor represents an early step in a proactive process to imagine and achieve success. Often, however, I am a student's last chance—"Maybe she'll give me a break." It's worth pausing to reflect on this situation. To my mind, such tactics are symptomatic not of a student's laziness but rather of a system that allows for low expectations of some students. By the time she reaches my office, the student may be well conditioned to allow others to do a lot of thinking for her, to believe herself capable of little, to consider her life and experiences to be quite different from those of her peers, and to count as her only options working the system or leaving it. She may lack the skills to advocate on her own behalf (especially because she is still adjusting to impairment), but this what-do-you-have-to-say-for-yourself moment may be quite familiar to her. This pattern, however deleterious, is reversible. Short of a wholesale shift in academic culture, one might consider offering any student with a disability heading to college the book *100 Things Every College Student with a Disability Should Know*.[12] This small volume is an unintimidating, nontechnical, and very portable resource that explains a disabled student's rights and responsibilities and offers tips for communicating needs, connecting with advocacy and service resources, and thriving in college. It helps students navigate the typical college environment.

With our book, however, we as a group are beginning to imagine a different place in which to live. Here, disability is no longer a matter of private struggle or public shame but a matter of diversity in learning and living. To shed disability of its stigma within the academy would be a Herculean achievement, but it is an incremental task—we can accomplish much by making minor adjustments in teaching priorities, methodologies, and course content.

The chapters in this book span the experience of college foreign language study, from acquiring rudimentary skills to pursuing study abroad. Where possible, we have opted to pair expertise with personal perspective, a strategy that keeps the student always in view and reminds us why we teach. In chapter 2, Elizabeth C. Hamilton continues the discussion I've begun here by describing her work with a blind student learning German. Hamilton first teaches us what she learned about the medical complexities of blindness and low vision, then turns to an exploration of blind culture and the ways that it has shaped her perspective on German culture. In chapter 3, Ian M. Sutherland introduces us to daily life at Gallaudet University, America's only four-year liberal arts college for the deaf, and explores the science and culture of deafness as a backdrop to teaching Latin.[13] Sutherland offers teaching strategies that enhance learning for deaf students and hearing students alike. In chapter 5, Brenda Jo Brueggemann discusses the complexities of recognizing American Sign Language (ASL) as a foreign language in the American academy. She demonstrates how, despite burgeoning enrollment, ASL remains burdened by ableist prejudice. In chapter 6, Rasma Lazda-Cazers and Helga Thorson explore the legal, curricular, medical, and pedagogical implications of learning disabilities in the foreign language classroom and describe a range of practices for accommodating them. In chapter 7, a group of authors from the faculty at Gallaudet University present quantitative research suggesting that simultaneous instruction in LESCO (Costa Rican Sign Language) and spoken and written Spanish improves retention, motivation, and performance among deaf students.

Although the book is intentionally organized to decenter the role of medical impairment in thinking about disability issues in education, it is worth pausing to underscore the obvious, that is, that considerable space is given to the consideration of deaf foreign language education. Chapters devoted to the classroom, research, and curricular design describe worlds that are at once largely unknown to the hearing reader, yet the insights of each author compel us to reflect upon assumptions we regularly make about foreign language learning. For example, we ask students to demonstrate proficiency in four modalities: listening, speaking, reading, and writing. How does acknowledging deafness in our classroom fundamentally alter the ways we think about foreign language skills? Would we allow any student the opportunity to demonstrate proficiency in the ways a deaf student can? If not, why not? Or, to paraphrase Brueggemann, what constitutes "real language," and who should be able to study it? Do we, teachers of spoken foreign languages, hold prejudices like the ones Brueggemann describes? Because it prompts us to reflect upon these questions, deafness is relevant to our work as language teachers, whether we teach a deaf student or not.

Chapter 9, by Nicole Strangman, Anne Meyer, Tracey Hall, and C. Patrick Proctor, introduces us to Universal Design in Learning (UDL), an educational paradigm that, rather than isolating a struggling student, offers strategies that enable the learning of all students. The extent to which current foreign language methodologies overlap with principles and strategies of UDL suggests that the journey toward inclusion in our courses will be that much easier. With its emphasis

on providing multiple means of delivery and of demonstrating proficiency, UDL nonetheless challenges us to examine our course materials, priorities, and practices. Implementing UDL is not a matter of
lowering standards. Rather, it is a matter of examining the standards
we hold and how we put them into practice. As Teresa Cabal Krastel
confirmed in her workshop with foreign language teachers in public
schools and describes in chapter 4, when we examine our standards
and practices, our teaching is transformed for the better. When these
questions replace the one I began with—that is, Why should one
learn to teach a blind student when blindness is a low-incidence
impairment?—we begin to dismantle ableism in education.

In philosophy and practice, UDL emphasizes the power of technology to better serve students with impairments. With its capacity
to enlarge and voice texts, technology has vastly improved the lives of
blind people, as Michelle N. Abadia discusses in chapter 8. Moreover,
the associative structure of technology-based learning materials (as
opposed to the linear structure of textbooks) enhances outcomes for
students with learning disabilities and appeals to a broader variety
of learning styles. Materials that invite learners to engage multiple
learning modes (visual, auditory, reading/writing, kinesthetic) simultaneously and that offer immediate opportunities to examine errors
and correct oneself show promise for improving language acquisition and retention. Especially in light of the comparably lower costs
of producing a CD-ROM, one wonders why textbook companies
continue to produce printed texts (with technological ancillaries)
rather than products that offer CD-ROMs, DVD-ROMs, or Web-based
materials as their primary component. Exploring the full potential of
technology in foreign language learning may bring a renewed sense
of purpose to a language learning center.

In these chapters, the authors examine disability and foreign
language learning less with the aim of enabling a student to overcome impairment than to examine how pairing the two enriches our
understanding of both. Because disability is universal and culturally conditioned, the foreign language classroom is an ideal space
for exploring physical difference. New editions of foreign language
textbooks show improvement, yet, on the whole, textbooks routinely
abet the exclusion of people with disabilities, promoting a worldview
that is intrinsically body-normative. While chapters in beginning
foreign language textbooks readily teach students how to discuss
temporary illness and transient difficulties, they have only begun to

incorporate basic information for living with impairment or alongside it in the culture being studied—words like wheelchair, crutches, mobility impaired, deafness, depression, and diabetes, as well as images of and readings about impairment. Joseph P. Shapiro, NPR correspondent and author of *No Pity: People with Disabilities Forging a New Civil Rights Movement,* asserts that there is a "disability angle" to every story.[14] I have found that to be true. For example, in a unit devoted to transportation and travel, teachers of first-year French might address accessibility in the Metro. American students who rarely if ever rely upon public transportation should know that it is prescribed custom for able travelers to give their seat to disabled travelers; the students will appreciate having translated relevant placards and considered their cultural significance in advance. If more time can be devoted to the topic, one should consult the official Web site of the Régie Autonome des Transports Parisiens (RATP) or a newer site, infomobi.com, for materials regarding accessibility in Paris.[15] One might also consider discussing Dans le Noir, a blind restaurant experience for sighted patrons that began in Paris and now exists in Berlin and London as well. As Elizabeth C. Hamilton points out in chapter 2, students can broaden their language skills by describing the world by means of senses other than sight. An activity introducing Dans le Noir is a ready frame for such an exercise. Moreover, the restaurant serves as a gateway to other valuable cultural information. The organization that founded the restaurant is a major advocacy organization for the blind in France and supports many public events to raise awareness of disability. A more advanced course on modern France should address the status of people with disabilities and might include discussion of the Collectif des Democrates Handicapés, the political party founded in 2000 to support disability rights in France. One might also study the emergence of inclusive education (as guaranteed by law in 2005) in France through sweeping educational reforms, or Julia Kristeva's *Lettre au président de la République sur les citoyens en situation d'handicap.*[16]

Resources for teaching about disability in other cultures include chapters 12 and 13. Chapter 12, by Salwa Ali Benzahra, offers a literary study of Rachid Mimouni's *Tombéza,* a novel in which the central protagonist's multiple disabilities propel him to the heart of French-Algerian relations. Benzahra's analysis is rich in discussions of both Algerian and Western customs and traditional gender roles in North Africa, and examines how disability operates within the narrative. Chapter 13, by Katharina Heyer, offers analysis of *No One's Perfect,* a memoir of growing up with impairment in Japan. As a vehicle for pushing past social structures to glimpse how they have shaped the lives of people with disabilities, memoirs are an essential genre. Ototake Hirotada's story, full of wit and good humor, develops primarily at school, where the teachers offer neither accommodation nor comfort. Examining disability within an educational setting that is very different from our own, Heyer's reading of *No One's Perfect* teaches us as much about our own educational system as about Japan's.

More than once, my efforts to examine disability in my French classroom have met with odd looks or a stifled giggle. I don't perceive such reactions to be an indication that I should avoid addressing such topics. On the contrary, I take them to mean that I should discuss them more frequently. When I do, I no longer worry about whether we're discussing disability at the expense of something "more important." Issues of impairment amplify and add nuance to discussions of more general topics, and living with impairment is of general interest to a great many people, whether in France or at home. I have on occasion wondered whether I know enough about disability to talk about it at all: What if I say something inaccurate or unjust? That's stigma talking. I don't have an exhaustive knowledge of any topic. I have learned to resist the temptation to segregate disability from other aspects of life in France that interest me. To recognize in our classroom the range of impairments that shape human experience is to broaden students' understanding of the target culture and to honor the basic tenets of humanistic education by engaging the thoughtful consideration of difference within our own culture and within ourselves.

Actively acknowledging disability in the foreign language classroom prepares students to reflect upon cultural differences that might otherwise go unnoticed when they are in another country. It also ensures that students with a disability will find a place for themselves abroad. Chapters 10 and 11 address the many obstacles facing students with disabilities who, like their peers, wish to enrich their studies with a prolonged experience in the target culture. In chapter 10, Elizabeth Emery describes traveling to France with a student with a mobility impairment, and the trials of planning an accessible study abroad trip in cities that, despite improvements in the past few years, remain rather inaccessible. Emery shows that including a student with a disability on a trip requires no prior expertise; she offers strategies for helping the student understand the barriers she will face and describes the many unanticipated benefits of her efforts for everyone involved. In chapter 11, Michele Scheib and Melissa Mitchell of Mobility International, U.S.A., discuss the many obstacles facing students with disabilities who hope to study abroad, demonstrating that these obstacles are predominantly attitudinal and institutional rather than physical. Scheib and Mitchell discuss the legal issues hampering full access to study abroad, strategies for changing attitudes and planning accessible travel, and offer many examples of successful and rewarding adventures.

These chapters approach the intersection of disability and foreign language from a variety of perspectives, bringing to bear on the discussion the neurosciences, the education sciences, the legal arena, assistive technology, and the humanities. Despite their diversity, the chapters rest on a pair of essential principles. The first of these is to strive to see the person behind the impairment. To do so is not to ignore disability or to decide a person "is normal," or "seems normal," but rather to recognize and value difference as an essential thread in the tapestry of human experience, of life lived in one's home country and in other places. What makes this thread unique—and this is the second principle—is not the impairment itself but the uniqueness of courses taken, lives lived, and worlds experienced *through* impairment. To separate the person from the impairment—"Were it not for that, he would be normal"—is to deny the subjectivity of that person and his experience. Disability represents a dimension of life that, thanks to a variety of physical and ideological impediments, we don't often notice and don't often wonder about in real terms. Moreover, it represents a dimension of human life—whether lived in America or elsewhere—that is far closer to us than we acknowledge in everyday discourse and exchanges with other people. Our American culture is quite adept at picking out this thread when it weaves a story of personal triumph or tragedy, and is capable of exhibiting due sympathy. We are far less able to recognize and value disability as part of every day at school and at work, even while we easily do so at home where someone we care about lives with impairment. Disability remains a private affair.

About three years ago, as part of this project, Elizabeth C. Hamilton and I created DISFL, an Internet listserv devoted to issues of disability in the foreign language classroom. We put the word out, and within a very short period of time, eighty foreign language teachers had subscribed. To us, this represented a groundswell of interest in a topic that remains far from mainstream, even within the field of Disability Studies. Yet over the past three years the list has hosted only a handful of messages (Elizabeth and I call each other each time one appears). Every person who initially subscribed remains on the list, which we take as an indication of enduring commitment to disability in our classrooms. Many of the issues I'm discussing in this chapter may account for silence on the list. Let's start talking.[17]

On our own campuses, we can foster genuine empathy for the efforts of our students by training ourselves in the variety of implements and software programs they may use in order to learn. To do this, we must forge sustained collaborative relationships with offices across our campuses, in particular with Disability Services, Computing Services, and Instructional Technology. Moreover, we can take a cue from Joseph P. Shapiro and assume that there is a "disability angle" to every aspect of campus life. Thomas Hehir discusses the implications and benefits of applying principles of Universal Design in school organization, citing evidence that a broad, bottom-up approach to a range of inclusive issues is transformative.[18] We must actively champion disability as a diversity issue, by sponsoring and attending campuswide events—student panels, brown bag lunches, public speakers, and events in the performing arts—that highlight disability. In efforts to forge alliances across groups, we can engage the office of Student Activities to ensure that a given event intersects with the experiences of another constituency. We can foster learning partnerships among faculty through a reading group, regular formal discussions of classroom issues, and faculty mentorships, and strive to recognize participation in these activities as a worthwhile and challenging aspect of our jobs. Through these efforts, disability becomes part of everyday life where we live and learn.

Despite our principled efforts, it will always be true that not every student possesses the skills or makes the effort to succeed in college, but it is every student's right to try. However committed and talented we may be as teachers, we cannot work miracles. We mustn't strive to cure impairment or ask a student to "overcome" his impairment in order to study foreign language. Our role is to examine critically the learning environment we are asking him to navigate and to remove likely barriers to learning; we must examine our expectations and ensure that course tasks and goals are tied to objectives he will face in real life. If the occasion presents itself we must help him face failure and devise an attitude and strategies for future success. We must respect him and recognize him as a person capable of far more than we alone can measure, and we must foster an environment in which our colleagues are called to do the same.

I have already begun to imagine *Worlds Apart II*, a collection I hope will be ready in about ten years' time. This future volume will include the work of many teachers who have successfully challenged ableist practices in their foreign language classrooms. It will also include a variety of essays written by students and will offer the perspectives of populations that are not acknowledged in these pages. As just one example, I dearly wish we had been able to include here a chapter about college students with Autistic Spectrum Disorders (ASD), likely to be an increasingly large population of students on college campuses over the next ten years. Consider the 2002 book *Aquamarine Blue 5*, a collection of unedited personal narratives by college students with ASD, or *Autism Is a World*, a 2005 Oscar-nominated documentary about Sue. A personal assistant enables Sue to live independently. She uses a simple keyboard to communicate, obsesses about running water and buttons, and does not make direct eye contact. Her ability to hold a focused conversation is limited, and she is easily upset. Sue is also a college student with many friends, a lot to do each day, and a lot to accomplish. *Autism Is a World* is an informative and touching glimpse of a meaningful life lived among college-age peers.[19] Sue's life and many successes point to what we can achieve in terms of meaningful inclusion—as a result not of singularly heroic efforts but of collaboration.

Ten years from now, the preoccupations of the envisaged second book may well be altogether different, given the developments in the summer of 2006. In July, the U.S. Department of Justice signed landmark agreements with two colleges, the University of Chicago and Colorado College, in order to avoid litigation over issues of access and accommodation. These agreements mark a considerable shift in policy and practice: whereas in the past the Department of Justice launched investigations in response to formal complaints of violations, it is now proactively pursuing compliance. These agreements stipulate access to campus facilities, accessible emergency and evacuation procedures, and accessible pathways on university Web sites.[20] The National Instructional Materials Accessibility Standard (NIMAS) picks up where these agreements stop short, guaranteeing access to learning environments. Endorsed by the U.S. Department of Education in July 2006 and signed into the Federal Register on August 14, 2006, NIMAS guarantees that all new textbooks used in K–12 classrooms will be available in XML, a format that is more easily converted to Braille, audio, or digital formats.[21] New York has agreed to adopt NIMAS for the SUNY system, and in my opinion it is only a matter of time before NIMAS applies generally to higher education. The situation in foreign languages seems particularly ironic. Our textbooks are already enriched by elaborate CD-ROMs, interactive DVDs, and on-line resources, yet the central component of the course remains the printed text, a medium that poses a formidable barrier to students with low or no vision, students whose hands are too palsied or weakened to hold a book or turn pages, or students with some learning disabilities. We must exert pressure on foreign language publishers to build upon what they already do very well and to put themselves ahead of this curve, producing texts that are interactive, infinitely adaptable, *and* in compliance with NIMAS. While the door to higher education has long been open to students with disabilities, data and anecdotes suggest that they come up against myriad barriers once past its threshold. I'm genuinely optimistic that NIMAS and the new proactive tactics of the Department of Justice will not only lead to meaningful improvements in access to learning and campus life for students with disabilities but also point the way to further change.

If you will indulge me in just one more story, I'd like to tell you about one of my falls. I was in the campus bookstore on a drab and rainy day. The floors were wet, and my crutches slipped at every turn. I am a seasoned linoleum skater, so I was able to stay on all fours for some time, but eventually I hit the floor pretty hard. My crutches went clatter-smacking, and I banged my funny bone. You know what that's like. It doesn't exactly hurt, but it isn't comfortable, because every muscle between your jaw and your big toe gets tense. You just have to wait for your whole body to relax. Or maybe it's different for you, I don't know. Anyway, I was just lying there waiting for the tension in my leg to dissipate, and six or seven kind and well-meaning people came running, each pulling on a limb to set me upright. I've never understood why people get so flustered about that, as though it's their fault. I've always wanted to ask them, but the moment is never right. I tried to explain that what I really needed to do was just lie there and wait for that funny-bone feeling

to go away. (I was actually kind of amused at the prospect of loung-
ing on the floor. From there, I had a very clear view of the bottom
shelf, and I was trying to remember how long it had been since I had
read any Tolstoy.) I couldn't stand yet because my leg wasn't ready to
straighten up. No one was listening to me, but suddenly they all let
me go. As the small crowd broke apart and I was thinking, "Great,
somebody called the paramedics," a perfect stranger plopped cross-
legged on the floor near my head and put a cup of coffee in front
of me. "I bet you could use this," she said, smiling. I was stunned.
It's been years, so I don't remember whether she sat with me for a
spell or left, but we didn't talk. Somehow, we both knew not to. I'm
glad I finally have the opportunity to thank her here. She gave me a
glimpse of the world I want to live in.

Notes

1. Thomas Hehir, *New Directions in Special Education: Eliminating Ableism in Policy and Practice* (Cambridge, Mass.: Harvard Education Press,
   2005) 15, 18.
2. In the 2003–2004 academic year, 11.3 percent of undergraduates reported a disability, as cited in CNN, "Program prepares disabled youth
   for college life," http://www.cnn.com (accessed July 19, 2006).
3. Thomas R. Wolanin and Patricia E. Steele, *Higher Education Opportunities for Students with Disabilities* (Washington, D.C.: The Institute
   for Higher Education Policy, 2004), vii.
4. Ibid.
5. Beth Fertig, "New York City Accused of Neglecting Students with Disabilities," Weekend Edition Sunday, National Public Radio, June 18,
   2006.
6. Hehir, *New Directions in Special Education.*
7. U.S. Department of Education, National Center for Education Statistics, 2006 (NCES 2006–071). Cited in NCES, "Fast Facts," http://nces
   .ed.gov/fastfacts/display.asp?id=77 (accessed July 2, 2006).
8. As reported in CNN, "Program prepares disabled youth for college life."
9. Minnesota Minority Education Partnership, "State of Students of Color
   Report," 2006 edition, http://www.mmep.org/Report_Information.html
   (accessed May 10, 2007). For data and analysis of similar demographic
   shifts across the United States, see The National Center for Public Policy
   and Higher Education, "Policy Alert: Income of U.S. Workforce Projected
   to Decline *If* Education Doesn't Improve" November 2005, http://www
   .highereducation.org/reports/pa_decline/pa_decline.pdf (accessed June
   22, 2006).

10. National Council on Disability, "People with Disabilities and Postsecondary Education," September 15, 2003, http://www.ncd.gov/newsroom/publications/2003/education.htm (accessed July 1, 2006).

11. U.S. Department of Education, Institute of Education Sciences, *The Condition of Education 2003: Services and Accommodations for Students with Disabilities,* Indicator 34.

12. Kendra D. Johnson and Trudy N. Hines, *100 Things Every College Student with a Disability Should Know* (Williamsville, N.Y.: Cambridge Stratford Study Skills Institute, 2005).

13. Whether one ought to refer to deaf people as "deaf" or "Deaf" is an important debate within deaf culture and disability studies. Simply put, "deaf" is understood by some as connoting a medical impairment, and "Deaf" a linguistic and cultural community. My decision to adopt the term "deaf" in this chapter should not be misunderstood as a refusal to acknowledge that community, but rather an effort to broaden the purview of this book to include those who may not identify with that community. Contributors to this book have made their own decisions in this regard.

14. Joseph P. Shapiro, *No Pity: People with Disabilities Forge a New Civil Rights Movement* (New York: Times Books, 1993), 10.

15. http://www.ratp.fr (accessed July 5, 2006); http://www.infomobi.com (accessed April 22, 2007).

16. Collectif des Démocrates Handicapés, the official site of the French political party dedicated to disability rights in France, http://www.cdh -politique.org (accessed July 5, 2006); Julia Kristeva, *Lettre au président de la République sur les citoyens en situation d'handicap* (Paris: Fayard, 2003).

17. To subscribe to DISFL, contact the list moderator, berberit@morris.umn .edu.

18. Hehir, *New Directions in Special Education,* 99–110.

19. Dawn Prince-Hughes, ed., *Aquamarine Blue 5* (Athens, Ohio: Swallow Press and Ohio University Press, 2002). *Autism Is a World,* directed by Geraldine Wurzburg and produced by State of the Art, Inc., first aired on *CNN Presents* on May 22, 2005.

20. "Colleges Feel Heat to Help Disabled," http://www.chicagotribune.com (accessed September 3, 2006).

21. http://www.nimas.cast.org (accessed December 3, 2006).

Teaching and Curricular Design

Teaching German to Students Who Are Blind: *A Personal Essay on the Process of Inclusion*

ELIZABETH C. HAMILTON

> I have the feeling that I have only now really
> begun to see.
>
> —ANNE SULLIVAN on her earliest days
> with Helen Keller

I am an American teacher of German, and I am not (yet) blind. I find deep purpose and pleasure in teaching German, and I hope never to lose sight of why I chose this path in life. My colleagues will likely share many of my views: we teach and learn foreign language so that we may see more clearly how others live. We show students how to look closely at language and to see it as one of the building blocks of culture. We observe other societies and picture ourselves traveling in other lands. We recognize similarities and reflect upon differences. We clarify, identify, regard, visualize, witness, look at, envision, and watch. Knowledge of a foreign language allows us to gain perspective. When we do not understand, we attempt to remove those barriers that conceal the truth, cloud our vision, or hide the facts. We break down whatever obstructs our view, distorts the picture, disregards the evidence, overlooks the details, or, worse, blinds us to what we need to see.

Vision is a fundamental channel of learning, and not simply because vision provides many of the most frequently used figures of speech to describe the processes of understanding. A substantial portion of the German language is regularly acquired through sight. Traditional structural approaches to German have long relied on charts of article declensions and tables of verb endings. Newer communicative methods of language instruction rely even more heavily on visual aids: learners use pictures as advance organizers, they interpret graphs and data, and they use nonverbal cues to assess a situation and create an appropriate response. Cultural information is routinely conveyed through maps, photographs, videos, or films. How, then, does a student whose vision is limited fare in a foreign language classroom? My discussion here identifies unintentional barriers of contemporary language pedagogy and offers classroom-tested activities for making the classroom not only accessible to students who are blind but also as inclusive as possible.

Attitudes and Approaches to Inclusive Teaching

Knowing why people learn is intrinsically related to knowing how they learn. A teacher's answers to basic questions of purpose will yield a framework for designing instruction: Why should students study German? Why should a teacher work extra hard to teach a student with uncommon needs? Why should classmates without visual impairments be expected to be patient while a teacher works to meet a blind student's needs? My response begins with a counterquestion: What do blindness and Germanness have in common in my classroom? Both describe people I know, people I care about, and, to a great extent, people who are different from me. Their surroundings are not like mine, and their daily routines include activities that are foreign to me. As a sighted North American I rarely close the door to every room in my house, use a brailler, rely exclusively on public transportation, use a white cane with a red tip, hold my fork in my left hand and my knife in my right; I neither decided in fifth grade between an academic or a vocationally oriented school nor ever learned to work with a guide dog. On the other hand, "blind" and "German" also describe people who have much in common with me: we read, are attentive to language, appreciate the arts, work, choose partners, raise children or pets, deal with prejudice, make career choices, achieve success, and sometimes meet with failure. As an American I study the German language and its literature and traditions not only to understand a place and a people who are different from me, I also learn German and about Germany to gain a new vantage point from which to view my own life. As a sighted person I can learn by putting myself in another's position to examine my life and my world. Just as Germany is a place I can visit, I may also "visit" blindness in my life as I age. I have begun to need reading glasses within the past year. Is it not reasonable, even likely, that I will lose substantially more vision during the course of my life? Knowing about blindness, like knowing about Germany, is part of knowing humanity.

In fact, my work is based in the humanities. Thus my pedagogy de-emphasizes the behaviorist, rehabilitative, occupational, and even technological aspects of blindness in favor of the humanistic. I am interested in the perspective, the view, the human being in the blind student. The blind student in my course is not the object but the subject of my work and his.[1] This approach stems very much from Disability Studies as practiced within the humanities. A medical model does not apply in my classroom, nor does my teaching draw from the tired teleology of heroically overcoming disability or normalizing behavior through training. Instead I incorporate into my philosophy and planning new narratives like Georgina Kleege's *Sight Unseen*, Stephen Kuusisto's *Planet of the Blind*, and, in German, Sabriye Tenberken's *Mein Weg führt nach Tibet*, creative nonfiction that honors bodily difference without defining a person in terms of impairment alone.[2] All three authors describe lives lived with blindness and low vision, detailing with frankness, humor, and wisdom the adjustments they routinely make in a world built for the sighted. As they all write extensively about reading, writing, going to college, and teaching, they have much to offer us.

Moreover, each book will change, for the better, what sighted teachers know and can know about blindness. Kuusisto identifies the sighted world's "patterned response to blindness," a phrase that reveals much more about people who can see than about people who cannot.[3] Acknowledging my assumption that I am writing to teachers with usable vision, let me start with our limitations: we as teachers guide students through the learning process but we do not "treat blindness." We are not ophthalmologists, optometrists, or psychologists but German teachers, and therefore not qualified to diagnose a disability. It is our responsibility, however, to know that blindness and visual impairments come in many degrees and emerge as disabling under varying conditions. Elisabeth Salzhauer Axel notes that "estimates indicate that between 10 and 20 percent of persons labeled as legally blind are totally without sight, and only about 20 percent of school-age children labeled as 'visually handicapped' have no usable vision. As many as 80 percent of visually impaired individuals have vision that could be used in daily activities."[4] People lose vision from glaucoma, diabetic retinopathy, cataracts, scotoma, macular degeneration, aging, lachrymal disease (tear-sac infections), trauma, strabismus, and exotropia (a condition where one or both eyes deviate outward), among others. Most pertinent to our planning and teaching are the three major effects of these disorders: a loss of central vision caused by disease; loss of peripheral vision; or an overall blurring or haze. These types of vision loss are experienced in different ways. The person with a loss of central vision may have difficulty reading standard print or his ability to distinguish color may be diminished. For him, increased light and enlargement or magnification of visual material may be effective. For the person with a loss of peripheral vision, more light may be helpful, but large print may exceed her usable field of vision. The person with hazy or blurry vision may respond well to enlarged print but also require a more specifically focused light.

It is not our place as German teachers to recommend or require specific adaptive technologies; however, it is our responsibility to familiarize ourselves with their use, to know whether and how our students are using them, and to consider accepting students' work created or undertaken in appropriate alternate formats. My purpose here is not to promote one type of equipment but to engage students in choosing the best resources available and to find nonvisual alternatives to foster their progress in German. American educators have a legal mandate to make our classes accessible: Section 504 of the Rehabilitation Act of 1973, the Americans with Disabilities Act of 1990, and the Individuals with Disabilities Education Act of 1997 explicitly prohibit discrimination against individuals with disabilities.[5] I believe foreign language teachers have an ethical mandate as well that operates in concert with principled foreign language instruction.

As teachers we must above all hold the same high expectations for the blind student as for the student without visual impairments. We must seek out and incorporate the input of the student before, during, and after class. A personal conversation at the beginning of a semester is essential, yet in this litigious era, teachers may have received mixed messages about what they may and may not address. Similarly, students with disabilities often arrive at college without the vocabulary to act as their own advocates. You may be the very first school employee to approach your students about their needs, and the more specific your questions, the more informative their responses will be. Construct questions that address a learner, not questions that target strife or disability. Find out how your student sees and how he processes visual cues. Have your student describe what is difficult for him to see. Ask the student how he has learned to read and write. Does he know Braille? Not all blind students do. Ask your student with low vision how she takes tests or submits work in other classes. Ask how effective this has been for her. Give the student a tour of the classroom and discuss the seating that will give her the best access. What in the classroom poses a visual barrier? Talk about when she may choose to move closer to or farther away from the blackboard, the bulletin board, or the video screen. What kind of lighting does the student need in the classroom? Should she sit near the window or directly under the light? If your student does not have a ready answer, ask where she sits at home and how you might recreate that setting in the classroom. Will she use optical devices in class, such as handheld or standing magnifiers? And particularly important: ask what else the student would like you to know. The earlier the teacher knows that a blind student will be in her class, the better, for many accommodations that can help that student will require advanced preparation. The teacher will need to provide substantial personal attention, and the accommodations that can help a student learn will often require an additional investment of time.

Removing Stigma and Fostering Self-Awareness

Such early knowledge usually depends upon a student's self-identification as a person with a disability, and at this point it is necessary to acknowledge the unreliability of self-disclosure. Stigma frequently accompanies disability, and students at times choose not to identify themselves as having a disability or requiring accommodation in order to learn. Unfortunately, stigma reproduces itself, sometimes even as policy, unless it is checked. That disability in all its manifestations has joined the cadre of unacceptable personal topics reveals the degree of misinformation that guides our profession: where disability remains a taboo, we act as though it were not present at all. This is the double-edged sword of stigma. It is of course invasive to ask a student about his body or his medical history, but questions about a student's abilities and experiences are appropriate. We must learn to ask the questions that do concern us and allow us to teach effectively.

One former student chose not to disclose his low vision, yet persisted in wearing darkened glasses that appeared to me to be sunglasses. I wondered whether his wearing "sunglasses" to class was a fashion statement or a sign of aloofness; both typified his very confident demeanor. In either case, he distanced himself from me by prohibiting eye contact, a posture that was matched by his actions every time he insisted he did not need to speak to me personally during office hours. When at the end of the semester he acknowledged his low vision, it was too late to salvage his failing grade. Work that he simply did not submit did not warrant an extension of time, because he had not disclosed his need for accommodations in a timely manner. This responsibility rested squarely upon his shoulders. Nonetheless, I was upset about not having known about his vision problems, and I continue to chastise myself for not having guessed as much.

Stephen Kuusisto writes of having passed for sighted well into his thirties. His coming-out story describes parents who did not want him to walk with a white cane or attend a special school for fear of the stigma surrounding blindness, an attitude of shame and disgrace around which Kuusisto patterned his own adult life. He writes that, "so thoroughly has my life been spent in the service of passing, I have almost no blind skills." This is not as unusual as it might seem. At the time I was drafting this chapter, an employee of my institution's Services for Students with Disabilities related that only five people on campus identified themselves as blind or having low vision, but that there are "a lot of others who are blind but don't admit it."[6]

A teacher's awareness of disability can go a long way to dispel potentially harmful stigmas and enable the student to develop the skills and avail himself of the resources that he needs. A statement on a syllabus, for example, can invite students to talk with you about accommodations without singling out any individual or putting a student on the spot. Still, as Kuusisto's example makes clear, students may resist acknowledging their disabilities or turn a cold shoulder to a teacher's attention to their needs. The double bind that results is among the most frustrating that my colleagues and I have ever experienced. How can a disabled student expect his disability to find appropriate acknowledgment and inclusion in the classroom when he will not work cooperatively to identify those barriers to his own learning that most teachers would gladly remove?

The possibility clearly exists that a student with blindness or low vision may never work cooperatively, may not yet have the skills of self-disclosure to do so, may drop classes, or may fail them. At present, this is a troubling reality that teachers must accept until convincing information that might make a positive difference reaches the students themselves. Andrew Leibs's outstanding *Field Guide for the Sight-Impaired Reader* is one such resource that should be read by students and teachers alike.[7] Leibs speaks directly to students and shows them how to take control of their education. He explains from personal experience why it is in their best interest to be forthcoming: "Once you introduce yourself to new teachers and describe your disability in a forthright manner, you will receive more than assistance—you will have a chance to develop relationships that add efficiency and joy to schoolwork. Department meetings or memos flagging your entry into a new grade . . . might leave some teachers not knowing what to expect or how to react. The initiative you take to let them know you as a person will make them eager to help." For its sound advice and detailed information about accessible reading material for blind or sight-impaired readers, the *Field Guide* is a book that should be available on every campus. It reflects the spark of people who love reading and learning. Its chapters encourage students to be self-motivated, to pursue and form strong relationships with people and service providers, and to become lifelong readers.

The *Field Guide* is also the only book-length study of education for the blind to devote a section to foreign language learning. Leibs notes that "foreign language classes present a paradox for sight-impaired students. For the most part, all students enter beginning classes on the same level; there is much vocal participation (listening and repeating) that does not tax the eyes, and, until advanced courses, there is little outside reading. Yet there are conjugation-lined placards, pronunciation charts with tiny accent marks over indecipherable letters, and a teacher writing tense constructions or participles across the blackboard." Although Leibs's estimate of the amount of outside reading is questionable, his book is quite correct to acknowledge that "such courses are, after all, one of the few areas of study with a rich tradition of learning through listening to recordings." Finally, the *Field Guide for the Sight-Impaired Reader* provides viable guidelines for negotiating the thorny territory often perceived to separate rights from responsibilities. Leibs states unequivocally that students have both, and I concur wholeheartedly. Using the specific instance of selecting texts in alternate formats, Leibs tells students that "you have the right to choose which version or combination of versions suits your needs. You also have the responsibility to be sure these works end up in your hands."[8] Noting gently that some teachers' efforts to provide for their students are misguided, Leibs writes, "Too often, such calls are made on behalf of students instead of by them, and so vital connections are never made."[9] The balance between rights and responsibilities can be recalibrated to ensure long-range success. When teachers appeal to their students' (perhaps latent) desire to take control of their education, they enable students to develop their "blind skills" further and to gain critical independence and autonomy.

Guidance is available. Most campuses have an office of Disabled Student Services or similar academic resource center, and I would encourage all faculty members to meet the people who work there and inform their students and themselves about what tutoring, technological, and funding support is offered there. Ask about the actual facility and the equipment housed there. For example: What space is available for a student to take tests? Does the center have a closed-circuit television monitor for enlarging a printed text? A Kurzweil machine for converting text to speech? A program like Dragon Naturally Speaking that converts student speech into printed text? Such programs can often work in foreign languages as well as in English, but it takes time to become proficient in using them, and the work produced by them requires additional editing. Disabled Student Services might also serve as a meeting ground for student and community groups organized around disability. This center should be viewed as a resource and a partner, and you should look upon your work there and your expanded ability to work with disabled students in your classes as a contribution to its services.

Stephen Kuusisto describes his pleasant surprise at the center where he trained to use a guide dog. Still feeling that as a blind person he is less than a whole human being, he writes: "Nothing like this has ever happened to me. I am among sighted people who respect blindness."[10] The bluntness of his statement took me aback. What would he have said about my college or my department? Would he have encountered respect for blindness in my classroom? I am acutely aware of the politically charged chasm between "special help" and regular teaching, yet I stubbornly refuse to accept the antagonistic terms of this debate. I view my work with blind students as less an instance of catering to a political constituency than an opportunity to know my students. There are, after all, obvious parallels between a blind student who needs a text in an alternate format and a sighted student who needs additional work with a particularly difficult concept or grammatical form. For students who struggle with a concept, teachers simply devise suitable materials. Why does disability so often meet with resistance?

Universal Design in Instruction

Lest anyone worry that "respect" is another word for "favoritism" or "unearned privilege," let me emphasize that the respect teachers show for blindness will also enhance the learning of students who are not blind. Consider a simple technique. When writing on the board, repeat frequently what you have written. Underscore capitalization, plural formation, and word order rules, for example, by reading your written sentences aloud more than once. When referring to your sentence, repeat it again. I often introduce a topic by playing a game of hangman on the board, and if a blind student is in my class, I say aloud and repeatedly how many blank spaces remain, and I highlight the location of letters that have been correctly chosen. My goal with this game is to draw all students' attention to aspects of German phonology, the length of German words, and common progressions of letters. My increased repetition for a blind student only enhances the learning of all students in the class.

Instead of only having printed material read aloud and taped for a blind student, a procedure that usually takes place in a setting far removed from the classroom and is carried out by anonymous readers, why not engage all students in your class in recording a reading? This could be a classroom activity or a homework assignment for small groups: three or four students could each read a text, one after the other. They could listen to each other and practice the reading aloud. The recipient would then be able to hear the text in three different voices. Repetition would allow all of the listeners to anticipate the vocabulary that is coming and to become more aware of pronunciation, phrasing, and inflection. The sighted students benefit as much as the blind student who moves from being the sole recipient of assistance to being a participant in a group activity.

Furthermore, students without disabilities are engaged in making class more accessible, thus demystifying the process of adaptation. This cooperative work establishes an attitude and a pattern of responding to very human needs.

Foreign language learning invariably includes giving and receiving directions. Consider expanding conventional terms of distance and direction by incorporating landmarks and referents that a blind person might use. Orientation and mobility are key skill areas for people with low vision. This is a genuine opportunity for sighted students to gain new awareness of their surroundings by learning from their sight-impaired classmates. Georgina Kleege writes: "My directions tend to mystify people because they're too topographical. I may not know street names, but I retain a memory of the contours of land, of architectural features, of landscaping. Peripheral vision is not only the side-to-side view but what's overhead and underfoot."[11] All students could apply that knowledge. Your classroom activity could be to explain how to find the pencil sharpener in the classroom or where to put homework assignments. This might entail singling out the blind student, and this should only be done if the student agrees. Tactfully done, however, this type of activity could heighten awareness of disability as well as provide practice in German. The teacher might say, for example, "John could use very specific instructions for reaching the recycling bin from his seat. Who can describe how to get there, making sure that the front desk and the bookshelf don't get in his way?" This could easily be expanded to include the whole campus, and the visually impaired student could describe to the others his landmarks for finding his way around. Such an activity is well suited to lessons on geography, culture, and of course German two-way prepositions.

Student Assistants as Notetakers and Readers

Universal Design should become a guiding principle of instruction, yet accommodation of disability is nonetheless often necessary. Classmates, student employees, and members of the local community can provide valuable assistance as notetakers (sometimes called scribes) and readers. Leibs's *Field Guide* devotes an entire chapter to hiring and working with readers, a process that might entail preparation and perhaps expense to the institution, although reader's aid money is usually available from each state's Department of Education. According to Leibs, "a student is allotted a specific amount each semester to pay readers. The funds are usually sent to and administered by a liaison at the college's financial aid office, though the student is responsible for hiring readers, setting wages, and submitting monthly time sheets."[12] Assistants can provide a spectrum of services, ranging from reading aloud to transcribing notes to an audio format. At my home institution a blind student taking a course in Chinese has another student trace the Chinese characters into the palm of his hand. Your students with low vision might choose to arrange for a notetaker who is not enrolled in the class, or they might ask classmates to enlarge or record and share their notes on a regular basis. In the latter case, advance contact with the others is again very important, and it is particularly helpful if two or more students submit their notes together to ensure the greatest coverage. Leibs's "good tips for finding readers" encourage students to begin with family members and immediate circles of friends. "Classmates," he notes, "make great potential readers because they have similar goals—they, like you, have to finish all the required reading in a course, and many will relish an opportunity to get paid at the same time."[13] Expanding the circle, Leibs suggests asking for recommendations from teachers, religious leaders, or local librarians. Students could also post announcements in their dorms or libraries, or they could contact the nearest Lion's Club to inquire about its services. A primary goal of Lion's Clubs around the world is to support people who are blind.

Arranging for notetakers and readers creates not only possibilities but also serious challenges. Beyond the critical need to communicate well with the teacher and the disabled student, assistants need to be punctual, responsible, and consistent. It is not easy to find an assistant who also happens to have expertise in the target language, and even under the best of circumstances the notetaker or finger speller might not convey the information accurately. This relationship is fertile ground for conflicts, often requiring extra contact with the student assistant and numerous phone calls and e-mail messages to the offices supporting disabled students and student employees. This is where the work can be the most frustrating, and this is often the place where all involved are likely to throw in the towel. Throwing in the towel, however, is a patterned response to blindness that sighted teachers can anticipate, evaluate, and change.

Using Visual Aids

Conventional wisdom holds that people with low vision cannot learn
from visual aids and that they would logically lack interest in the
visual arts, but the many ways in which blind people can engage
with painting, photography, or sculpture render these notions highly
questionable. Visual aids provide orientation to a topic or specific
examples to illustrate a point, and they should not be avoided just
because of a student's blindness or low vision. Continue to incorporate description of paintings, photographs, or films into the class
as a major activity as you would in a class without blind students.
A photograph of a city, a portrait of an author, an illustration of a
scene from a play, or a drawing of a family at dinner can conjure a
setting or provide contextual information for a dialogue or a story.
Paintings and sculpture of course also figure prominently in the
history and culture of German-speaking Europe and are thus worthy of study in their own right. "People who are blind or visually
impaired," notes Elisabeth Salzhauer Axel, founder of Art Education for the Blind, "should and can be provided with the perceptual
information to have full intellectual access to the history and culture
of our world."[14] *Art Beyond Sight: A Resource Guide to Art, Creativity,
and Visual Impairment* is an extraordinary guide to the visual and
plastic arts that can also enrich the foreign language classroom.
Art Beyond Sight contains essays on art and blindness authored by
people from around the world. It offers vivid examples and instructions for teachers, museums, and blind people, their friends, and
their family members to encounter, examine, and appreciate works
of art by others, and for blind people and people with low vision to
create art of their own. Its five hundred large pages are themselves
models of attractive, accessible text. Printed on heavy paper of pastel
colors, the book has a clear and clean layout and is at the same time
lavishly illustrated with photographs, drawings, and prints. Short
biographies provide telling information about canonical and newer
artists, many of whom have disabilities. Along with its many other
practical resources, *Art Beyond Sight* gives step-by-step information
about creating and teaching with tactile images, as well as particularly helpful guidelines for verbal descriptions of art. By drawing
the viewer's attention to shapes, textures, atmospheres, and contexts
that might otherwise go unacknowledged, the book enables both
the blind and the sighted viewer to enjoy a richer encounter with

works of art. Author Joel Snyder explains that "in order for verbal description to be effective, the individuals providing this service must learn to use the sense of sight fully and develop verbal and vocal capabilities beyond day-to-day usage. They must learn to see again, to notice the visual world with a heightened sense of acuity, and to share those images from theater, media, and museum exhibitions with users."[15]

Are these skills Snyder describes not the skills that we German teachers wish to develop in all of our students? When working with visual arts and aids, engage your students in a different kind of translation: have them translate the visual elements into the language of other senses even as they develop their skills in German. Because even the most rudimentary vocabulary expresses a great deal, it is wise to use the target language for these activities. Have your students name the feeling conveyed in the body language of a person, for example, or ask students to gauge in steps or in time the distance of the photographer or painter from the topic. Ask them to imagine the sounds they would hear if they were standing in the center of a landscape. Let volunteers assume the posture of a figure in a painting and describe the figure's clothing, props, or facial expression. Draw attention to the medium and the style of the work. What can your students say about the quality of paint, the level of detail, or the consistency of lighting? Georgina Kleege affirms the value of an intensive encounter with art in *Sight Unseen*. Describing how closely she observes paintings in an art museum, she writes: "With my face a few inches from the canvas, every painting, even the most representational, becomes an abstraction. Paint is paint. But paint is also the point, isn't it? Looking at a work of art is seldom simply a matter of identifying the objects or the people depicted there."[16]

Film or video requires more extensive verbal description, but this could be done as a substantial class activity or homework assignment. In pairs or in small groups, students can describe specific scenes or settings. You might divide the film into narrative segments or have each group take a particular visual motif and elaborate upon its use in the film. Die Deutsche Hörfilm GMbH (DHG) is an organization in Berlin that produces audio description for major motion pictures. A few titles that German students might view in classes today are advertised for purchase on the DHG Web site, including Volker Schlöndorff's *Die Stille nach dem Schuss*, Wolfgang Becker's *Goodbye Lenin*, and Andreas Dresen's *Halbe Treppe*.[17] To be sure, the costs for such films may exceed the budget of the typical German department, but even films without professional audio description can be used productively in class. Because sound and dialogue from motion pictures convey important contextual information, you might consider reversing the order of a technique widely used in communicative learning environments today: instead of turning off the sound and having your class view a film segment to anticipate dialogue and content, play only the sound and have your students anticipate the setting. Your sighted students will work on par with students with low vision, and again, all will benefit from the extra concentration you ask of them.

These suggested strategies go far beyond simply adapting a lesson to accommodate a blind student. When your students use verbal language to probe the language of visual arts, they are engaged in purposeful, pleasurable, and practical critical analysis. Sighted students will without a doubt also gain new understanding of their blind peers as well as new knowledge of blindness itself. Have your class reflect upon the words of Scott Nelson, a blind artist and curator who has an essay in *Art Beyond Sight:* "I had second thoughts about the 'perspectives' of many of history's greatest artists who were known to have vision impairments. These include Monet, Pissarro, Degas, Daumier, Renoir, Goya, and others. I wondered whether their visual impairments could be said to have enhanced their perspectives."[18] Blindness not as a handicap but as a source of authentic perception? What an extraordinary lesson for teachers and for students! Indeed, those of us with full vision must reappraise human life when we view blind people as having a sense, instead of lacking a sense.

Tactile Graphics and Manipulatives

Multisensory activities are well known to foster learning and help students retain new knowledge. When lessons incorporate German food or music, they usually enliven the class, and students often remember the content well after the unit has ended. Most students also appreciate the opportunity to move around the classroom in role-playing, to take a walk outside, and, once initial inhibitions are overcome, to dance. Activities not based strictly upon reading and writing provide rich opportunities for blind students to take part in class. As a primary channel for acquiring information, the sense of touch is often highly developed in blind students and underdeveloped in sighted students. As all students will clearly benefit from your doing so, look for opportunities to use tactile objects in your lessons. A vocabulary-building activity might begin with recognizable classroom objects hidden from view in a large bag or basket. Students draw one object and, without looking at the item, describe in German its shape or the occasions when it is used. The student who names the object correctly in turn describes the next object. No student requires vision in this simple activity. You can use the activity to review increasingly sophisticated vocabulary by varying the types of unseen objects and including, for example, items symbolizing abstract concepts. Students might also compare and classify objects that they touch but cannot see. Let the class feel difficult-to-recognize items that you place in a dark plastic bag or under a towel. Have them take three items and compare them according to size, texture, likely practicality, or frequency of use. At the end of the lesson, uncover the items and have your students evaluate their impressions.

Objects that students can touch, hold, or use as props allow them to engage multiple senses during your class. There are calendars, clocks, and thermometers that can be read through touch. Disciplines other than foreign language have established relationships with businesses and service or advocacy organizations for the blind, and as a result high-quality, commercially produced Braille materials and kits for making tactile graphics are currently available for math, English, and social studies. Foreign language teachers have no such ready resources, though these resources would be well appreciated and easily incorporated into our teaching. A German Braille or tactile graphic kit could include the following standard items: tactile drawing tools for the German "ß" and umlauted letters, tables for producing grammatical charts of definite articles, indefinite articles, and adjectival endings, and verb conjugation rubrics. Also desirable are brailled flashcards with basic vocabulary words and relief maps of Germany and Europe, including national, state, city, and road maps. In order for such tools to be produced and procured, teachers will have to articulate a need for them. Until that day, teachers will likely have to make their own tactile materials or blind students will have to do without them.

Making our own tactile graphics is not as daunting a task as it might seem, and of course teachers have long improvised when essential materials exceed their institution's budget. Felt on a flannel board can make a simple map, illustrate German letters, and differentiate between a German handwritten numeral one and seven. A blunt pastry wheel or pizza cutter on heavy paper or foil can stand in for a more professionally made stylus. A few guidelines should be kept in mind: above all, make your tactile graphic as clear as possible. Always keep in mind the point of view of the Braille reader. For example, omit unnecessary parts of the diagram, such as irrelevant sections of a map, so that the most important shapes and textures can be presented on a larger and clearer scale. Determine whether the original shapes and textures are necessary to convey the concept, or whether simple geometric shapes or Braille signs may be used to illustrate it. Speak frequently with the students who are using your homemade materials, and ask for their feedback and suggestions. They are likely to teach you a great deal about the materials that best help them to learn.

Accessible Reading Materials

Currently it is most helpful to students with blindness or low vision to have a copy of required texts in digital formatting. Electronic texts are easy to enlarge, and voice synthesizing is done with an electronic text as the base. Several speech synthesizers and software programs will read and speak German on personal computers. Although much available technology is remarkable, by itself it is insufficient. Technology requires people to make it work. Preparing a text for Braille usually involves scanning it (if it is not already in an electronic format) and editing it before sending it to the brailler. The editor will have to proofread the text and in the case of German will have to change umlauted letters into the letter +e and "ß" into "ss." German textbooks are replete with charts and tables that are not easily rendered in Braille. A feasible alternative is to create a set of columns and rows without dividing lines.

While published Braille and large-print materials in foreign languages are not readily available, some do exist. Some German publishers and libraries, such as the Leipzig Bücherei für Blinde, provide materials for native speakers who are blind, but they do not as a rule stock material glossed for a foreign readership. Nonetheless, on your next trip overseas consider shopping for authentic German materials in Braille, called alternately "Punktschrift" or "Blindenschrift." The American Printing House for the Blind (APH) lists more than fifty

German titles on Louis, its national database of accessible reading materials. These range from well-known German textbooks, such as *Kaleidoskop: Kultur, Literatur, und Grammatik, Komm mit!* and *Schaum's Outline of German Vocabulary*, to literary works, such as Johann Wolfgang von Goethe's *Die Leiden des jungen Werther*, Günter Grass's *Ein weites Feld*, Christa Wolf's *Gesammelte Erzählungen*, and Rainer Maria Rilke's *Die Aufzeichnungen des Malte Laurids Brigge*. A few German literary texts appear in English translation, including *Summerhouse, Later: Stories* by Judith Hermann. German-English dictionaries are not likely to be available in the near future, nor are any German newspapers or magazines. Foreign language materials may be transcribed into Braille or recorded by the APH after consulting with its contracting department. This may require significant advance notice, yet it is, in my estimation, of the utmost importance. Our collaboration on behalf of current and future students with low vision would mirror the APH's own historical founding. Its Web site reports that "in the mid-1800s, when schools for the blind were being established in the United States, each school was responsible for embossing the books and manufacturing the appliances necessary for the instruction of its own pupils. School leaders soon recognized this as a great waste of effort and resources and saw the need to consolidate efforts to provide embossed materials for blind students. In 1858, in an act of unprecedented cooperation and foresight, seven states established a centralized national printing house to meet their combined demands, thus founding the American Printing House for the Blind in Louisville, Kentucky."[19]

No organization or network specifically geared toward foreign language pedagogy for the blind yet exists, so on campuses across the country, teachers and students are taking a learn-as-you-go approach to finding and adapting materials. At present, teachers have to contact publishers of their course materials individually and request alternative formats. Many American publishing representatives will express a philosophical willingness to help but consider expanding accessibility to be beyond the scope of their services. A few publishers will provide texts in convertible electronic format that can be brailled or enlarged more easily, and most will also readily provide the Internet address and phone number for Large Print Reproduction or Recordings for the Blind. Yet no standards exist, so we must establish ours by stating our needs clearly and holding publishers accountable to this constituency.

Conclusion

Scholarly writing about pedagogy unfortunately can obscure the clearest and most familiar approaches that already encompass the foundations of inclusive teaching. Effective teachers apply pedagogical innovations judiciously and personally to guide their student through the process of learning, and it is in a spirit of collegiality that I offer my own insights into teaching students with blindness or low vision. The approaches I have outlined here should recall some of the basic principles of teaching and learning that we may forget as we evolve professionally: the sheer pleasure of reading a great book, the frustrations and joys of developing skill in writing, the unexpected insights that emerge from struggle, the relationships that form in a classroom, and the self-confidence that emerges from accomplishment. May these rewards never be lost.

Teaching German to blind students is not an isolated endeavor but relates in equal measure both to broader social movements of disabled people and to the goals of foreign language instruction. Teachers who recognize blindness and low vision as an aspect of their students' identity can foster a sense of self worth by providing opportunities for genuine achievement. Their success can be a source of their pride and ours, for it grows from something language teachers have long understood: we can acknowledge and learn from cultural differences, dispel stereotypes, and remove language barriers.

Notes

1. When referring to students and teachers I shall alternate between masculine, feminine, and plural pronouns throughout this chapter.
2. Georgina Kleege, *Sight Unseen* (New Haven: Yale University Press, 1999); Stephen Kuusisto, *Planet of the Blind: A Memoir* (New York: Delta-Dell, 1998); Sabriye Tenberken, *Mein Weg führt nach Tibet: Die blinden Kinder von Lhasa* (Cologne: Kiepenheuer und Witsch, 2000).
3. Kuusisto, *Planet of the Blind*, 161.
4. Elisabeth Salzhauer Axel and Nina Sobol Levent, eds., *Art Beyond Sight: A Resource Guide to Art, Creativity, and Visual Impairment* (New York: Art Education for the Blind, Inc., and AFB Press of the American Foundation for the Blind, 2003), 52; G. T. Scholl, "What Does It Mean to Be Blind? Definitions, Terminology, and Prevalence," in *Foundations of Education for Blind and Visually Handicapped Children and Youth:*

Theory and Practice, ed. G. T. Scholl (New York: American Foundation for the Blind, 1986), 23–33; A. Best and A. Corn, "The Management of Low Vision in Children: Report of the 1992 World Health Organization Consultation," *Journal of Visual Impairment and Blindness* 87 (1983): 307–309.

5. *Rehabilitation Act* (Section 504), *U.S. Code* 29 (1973) Section 791 et seq.; *Americans with Disabilities Act, U.S. Code* 42 (1990), Section 12001 et seq.; *Individuals with Disabilities Education Act, U.S. Code* 20 (1997), Section 1400 et seq.

6. Kuusisto, *Planet of the Blind,* 131; Jane Boomer, e-mail message to author, September 4, 2001.

7. Andres Leibs, *Field Guide for the Sight-Impaired Student: A Comprehensive Resource for Students, Teachers, and Librarians* (Westport, Conn.: Greenwood Press, 1999).

8. Leibs, *Field Guide,* 86–90.

9. Ibid., xvii.

10. Kuusisto, *Planet of the Blind,* 171.

11. Kleege, *Sight Unseen,* 105.

12. Leibs, *Field Guide,* 67.

13. Ibid., 68.

14. Salzhauer Axel, *Art Beyond Sight,* 3.

15. Joel Snyder, "Verbal Description: The Visual Made Verbal," in *Art Beyond Sight: A Resource Guide to Art, Creativity, and Visual Impairment,* ed. Elisabeth Salzhauer Axel and Nina Sobol Levent (New York: Art Education for the Blind, Inc., and AFB Press of the American Foundation for the Blind, 2003), 224.

16. Kleege, *Sight Unseen,* 64.

17. German audio description service for major motion pictures, http://www.hoerfilm.de (accessed October 25, 2003).

18. Scott Nelson, "A Professional Artist and Curator Who Is Blind," in *Art Beyond Sight: A Resource Guide to Art, Creativity, and Visual Impairment,* ed. Elisabeth Salzhauer Axel and Nina Sobol Levent (New York: Art Education for the Blind, Inc., and AFB Press of the American Foundation for the Blind, 2003), 28.

19. American Printing House for the Blind, http://www.aph.org (accessed November 6, 2003).

CHAPTER 3

Everybody Wins: Teaching Deaf and Hearing Students Together

IAN M. SUTHERLAND

Introduction

Teaching disabled students is an opportunity that most American professors have not yet had, but the chance that they will in the future is increasing. This chapter addresses the professor of foreign language who has a deaf student in her course for the first time, and who seeks help in teaching that student effectively. The tableau envisages a single deaf student in a first-year Latin class, but the didactic principles described here can apply to situations of more than one student, to different languages, and to courses beyond the first year. The student may or may not have studied foreign language before, but this is his first exposure to Latin. The discussion assumes that the student is profoundly deaf, not hard of hearing, and that he employs sign language, not oral speech, as his preferred means of communication. A sign language interpreter will accompany the student to class. It also assumes that the student, having either limited or no capacity for oral communication, will concentrate on learning to read and write the target language.

This chapter has three goals. The first is to give the professor background information about deafness in general, as a context for a more informed relationship with the deaf student. I describe characteristics of hearing loss in humans, and how it is manifested, and I examine education of the deaf in America, including how deafness affects the learning process in young people, and methods of primary and secondary education. The second goal is to provide the professor with tools and approaches that can enrich the academic experience for the deaf student. I offer perspectives on the academic experience at Gallaudet University as a point of comparison for a subsequent examination of services for disabled students that are provided by other institutions. I describe working with sign language interpreters and arranging the physical environment of the classroom, and I offer a number of instructional techniques that have proved effective in teaching foreign language to deaf students at Gallaudet.

The third goal of my discussion is that professors will take the broad view of a new pedagogical approach. The instructional techniques offered here can be highly beneficial for all students. A class that incorporates them will emphasize the visual mode of learning more than is typical in a college language class in which all students are hearing. In an environment that employs the auditory and visual modes more equally, a professor who exploits both will promote higher levels of activity, engagement, and response in the class. In addition, the experience of the hearing students will be leavened by exposure to the deaf student's mode of communication as the new approach integrates the group. The title of this chapter reflects the ultimate result: while the students learn the same target language, everybody wins through an approach that enhances understanding of communication in general.

In considering a new approach, the professor who is hearing and whose expertise is foreign language need not be concerned that teaching a deaf student effectively is a task only for specialists in disability education. Let my own experience serve to illustrate this. By education I am a classicist, trained in archaeology and Latin, and my path to deaf education was serendipitous. At a part-time job during graduate school I had a co-worker who was deaf. No one in the work environment knew sign language, so I enrolled in a sign course to improve our communication. Eventually I completed four courses and signed regularly for two years at that job. Meanwhile I finished my doctoral studies, and a few years later joined the foreign language faculty at Gallaudet. As a result, I am a Latinist who just happens to teach the deaf.

The reader is encouraged to view the presence of the deaf student in class as an opportunity to present her subject in a way that she has not presented it before. The teacher should feel confident, and even creative, in including the deaf student fully in the interaction of the class, and in devising an academic environment that stimulates the hearing and the deaf alike.

Manifestation and Variation of Hearing Impairment

Diversity among Deaf and Hard-of-Hearing Individuals

The characteristics of hearing loss among humans are complex, and its manifestation varies widely. Hearing loss ranges from a mild impairment, which still permits understanding of normal speech, to profound deafness. A person may be born with the impairment, or it may occur at any point later in life. Hearing may be lost relatively quickly from illness or trauma, or gradually, from a progressive, degenerative condition. Hearing loss may diminish the full range of audible frequencies, or affect only specific tones. Many profoundly deaf individuals can, in fact, detect certain sounds. Some conditions can be ameliorated by electronic assistive devices, such as hearing aids or cochlear implants, and some cannot. Hearing loss may be genetic, and this is manifested in diverse ways. Hearing parents and deaf parents alike may produce either hearing or deaf offspring, or both. Deafness in consecutive deaf generations, referred to as congenital deafness, appears in some families. Genetic combinations cause some individuals to be born deaf, while others are born hearing and lose that sense later.[1]

The complexities of hearing loss even make it difficult to assign a single definition to terms such as deaf and hard of hearing, and therefore some clarification is in order. The term *hearing impairment* will refer to the entire range of hearing loss, whether mild or total, and this range includes both the deaf and the hard of hearing. The term *deaf* applies to a hearing loss sufficient to prevent the understanding of speech through the ear alone. *Hard of hearing* describes a reduced capacity to hear that still permits the understanding of speech through the ear alone. *Prelingual deafness* refers to deafness at birth or an onset of deafness before an individual acquires oral speech; *postlingual deafness* describes a condition of onset after the individual has acquired oral speech.[2] The transition between prelingual and postlingual states is imprecise, yet researchers have somewhat arbitrarily established the age of two to distinguish prelingual from postlingual deafness.[3]

Size and Distribution of the Hearing-Impaired Population

It is important to recognize that the segment of the population that is both young and deaf, and from which your student is likely to come, is very small. According to the National Center for Health Statistics, in 1991 the total number of persons in the United States three years of age and older with *any* type of hearing impairment measured about 20.3 million people (8.6 percent of the population).[4] Of this number, approximately 1.15 million (0.5 percent of the population) had severe hearing loss or were deaf. Distribution analysis shows that the preponderance of severe hearing loss is a consequence of age (table 3.1). In the younger age ranges, most hearing loss is genetic. The two youngest age groups are also the most germane to our discussion, as they were likely to have been the contemporary and future students in tertiary education. Thus the student I profiled in my Introduction may represent a demographic segment of at most 180,000 people, or 0.08 percent of the population.

Table 3.1

Age	Number of persons with severe or total hearing loss	Percentage of total
65 years and over	744,000	64.6%
45–64 years	228,000	19.8%
18–44 years	128,000	11.1%
3–17 years	52,000	4.5%
Total	1,152,000	100.0%

For some insight as to who may enroll in your class, some other characteristics of the age groups 3–17 and 18–44 are of interest. In the former range 52 percent were male, but in the latter 52 percent were female. Both groups were roughly 85 percent Caucasian and 11 percent African American, and about 12 percent of each group were of Hispanic origin. Geographic distribution of this population segment is not even. The deaf student in your class will most likely come from the South (33 percent), followed by the Midwest (29 percent), the West (20 percent), and the Northeast (18 percent).

One of the reasons why we should be concerned about teaching our deaf students as well as possible is the significant socio-economic impact that deafness has on an individual's life. From the beginning, a deaf person will on average receive less education than a hearing person, and then will continue to lag behind in important aspects of employment and career. The numbers in table 3.2 apply to all persons eighteen years and older, and are age-adjusted to the distribution of persons with no trouble hearing. The final figures show that deaf persons are overrepresented in families that earn less than $10,000 per year and underrepresented in families that earn more than $50,000 per year, compared to hearing persons.[5]

Table 3.2

| | Years of Education | | |
	Less than 12 years	12 years	More than 12 years
No trouble hearing	19.7%	38.8%	41.5%
Cannot hear and understand normal speech	29.7%	38.0%	32.2%

| | Employment Status | | |
	Employed	Not in the labor force	Unemployed
No trouble hearing	67.2%	29.4%	3.4%
Cannot hear and understand normal speech	58.4%	38.2%	3.4%

| | Type of Occupation | | |
	Professional/ managerial	Sales, service, administrative support	Other
No trouble hearing	29.6%	43.4%	27.1%
Cannot hear and understand normal speech	25.7%	32.9%	41.4%

| | Family Income | | | |
	Less than $10,000	$10,000 to $24,999	$25,000 to $49,999	$50,000 or more
No trouble hearing	11.1%	27.3%	36.7%	24.9%
Cannot hear and understand normal speech	18.6%	32.9%	32.5%	16.0%

Finally, age of onset of hearing loss is of especial interest to us. Of all conditions related to deafness, this may be the most critical one from the perspective of the individual's first acquisition of language, and then subsequent education. The 1.15 million people with severe hearing loss or deafness reported their onset as in table 3.3. For more than 83 percent of this population segment, the onset of hearing loss was postlingual, greatly increasing for those individuals the potential effectiveness of primary and secondary education. For the nearly 15 percent of this segment whose onset was prelingual, the issue of when and in what form they acquire their first means of communication will determine to a large extent the effectiveness of their entire course of education. In the next section we will see why this is the case.

Table 3.3

Age at onset	Number of persons with severe or total hearing loss	Percentage of total
19 years and after	830,000	72.0%
Between 3 and 18 years	129,000	11.2%
Before 3 years	168,000	14.6%
Unknown	25,000	2.2%
Total	1,152,000	100.0%

Education of Deaf Individuals

Development of the System of Deaf Education in America

The nineteenth century was the active period of the establishment of schools for deaf students in America. Prior to 1817, educational efforts for deaf children were inconsistent and often unsuccessful. In that year, the establishment of the American School for the Deaf in Hartford, Connecticut, initiated a new era of deaf education with a model for state-funded residential schools. During the next twenty-five years, six more schools were founded in the eastern part of the country, and by 1912, forty-seven states had established permanent schools of primary and secondary instruction for hearing-impaired children. One college was also founded, the Columbia Institution for the Deaf and Dumb and the Blind in Washington, D.C., in 1864. Now known as Gallaudet University, it remains the only four-year liberal arts college in the world primarily serving deaf and hard-of-hearing students.[6]

Broadly speaking, there are two methods of communication used in America to teach deaf individuals: manual and oral. In essence, a manual method employs the use of signs and signed language as the means for communication and instruction. Oral methods concentrate on the development of oral speech, the mastery of English, and lip-reading.

During the nineteenth century diverse educational approaches developed, based on whether a manual or an oral method, or a combination of the two, was used in the classroom. By the turn of the twentieth century, schools commonly emphasized oral over manual communication, on the theory that oral training would most effectively integrate deaf people into a hearing society. Until the 1970s virtually all state schools for the deaf employed some form of oral training for preschool and primary education. Some schools maintained a strict oral approach throughout all grades, while others introduced a combined method at the secondary level.[7] Also, during the twentieth century the reduction in prelingual deafness by the near elimination of childhood illnesses, along with improved technology for hearing aids, audiological testing, and speech therapy, contributed to the popularity of oral programs.[8]

By the 1960s, research had confirmed that the effectiveness of developing oral communication is proportional to the student's residual hearing. Children with moderate hearing loss, and/or conditions that are ameliorated by hearing aids, may successfully acquire usable oral speech. As there are many more hard-of-hearing children than deaf children, an oral program of education is thus potentially effective for the majority of hearing-impaired primary and secondary students.

For deaf children, age of onset is a critical factor, that is, whether the child is prelingually or postlingually deafened. Postlingually deafened children establish the use of oral language and auditory cognition prior to onset and this can facilitate their entry into mainstream education. After their loss of hearing they may retain the use of speech and of phonic relationships between oral and written language, which can continue to assist their academic progress. Because of these conditions, oral programs are most effective among the postlingually deafened.

In contrast, prelingual deafness prevents an infant from developing oral language and auditory cognition. In these cases, the use of a manual, instead of an oral, program is the key to developing communication at a very young age, and initiating an effective early education. Among the prelingually deaf, the use of sign language consistently develops higher skills in reading, writing, English grammar, and social adjustment than does use of an oral method.[9]

The complexity of these developmental conditions—degree of hearing loss, pre- or postlingual onset, and differing methods of communication—means that deaf college students today represent diverse backgrounds and identities. In addition, some may be fully competent in written English and American Sign Language (ASL), while others may struggle with one or both of the languages. Becoming familiar with your individual student's background, abilities, and preferences will help you to plan your class.

Deaf Students at Gallaudet University

For many deaf students in America and around the world, Gallaudet University seems like the shining city on the hill. In contrast to a hearing society, in which access to many services and institutions is usually limited, the environment at the school is liberating and empowering. For those who came from small programs, or who had few deaf acquaintances, the sheer number of other deaf people is astonishing. Communication is open and expedited by pagers, instant messaging, and on-line video conversation. There are videophone booths on campus. The experience is a revelation.

Everyone signs! Classes emphasize visual media, both textual and pictorial. The classrooms have overhead projectors, Internet links, and digital projection systems; they are lined with chalkboards for written work and have variable lighting. Presentations by speakers are interpreted and have simultaneous captioned video. This too is a revelation.

If in a previous school the students had felt marginalized, or were not even expected to grasp fully what was transpiring, this is no longer the case. Academic expectations are high. Students must learn subject matter thoroughly; they must participate in substantive discourse and express reasoned opinion. They learn methods of research and academic writing, and are responsible for quantities of reading that some may never have experienced before. While teachers in secondary school may have shown little interest in a student's future, professors at Gallaudet want to know about his plans for graduate school, career objectives, and professional goals. This is a revelation.

The social world expands considerably, and shows its variety.

Some students are profoundly deaf, others hard of hearing. They come from deaf families and hearing families, they have signed all their lives, or they are learning to sign now. They use hearing aids, cochlear implants, or no assistive device. They may or may not use their voices. Some enjoy listening to music, others sense only vibrations. Some are strongly rooted in deaf culture, while others are more at home in the hearing world; some may seem to bridge both of these easily, while others may not relate well to either. In this diverse community, they will experience strong, and sometimes conflicting, expressions of deaf identity. This too is a revelation.

Foreign Language Instruction at Gallaudet

Gallaudet has a long history of including foreign language in its curriculum, dating back to the nineteenth century. The Department of Foreign Languages, Literatures, and Cultures currently offers Spanish, French, German, Latin, and Italian, with majors in Spanish and French, and a minor in German. Emphasis is on learning to read and write the target language, not to speak it. Nevertheless, a student with voicing capability who wishes to work on speaking the language may arrange to do so. In class, the target language is translated into sign language or written in English. The department provides all levels of undergraduate language instruction, as well as courses in literature in translation and advanced special topics.

Almost all of our undergraduates study foreign language for the first time at Gallaudet. The two-semester, first-year sequence in each language includes a weekly period in a computerized language lab, where diverse visual activities complement the work in class. Colleagues usually employ standard introductory textbooks for these courses, but because the textbooks are not designed for our environment, teachers may make significant adjustments in their use.

It is a challenge at times to explain certain aspects of language that are specifically related to speech, such as the effect of diacritical marks, or spellings that seem irregular but have vocalic rationale. For example, one problematic element of Latin is the vocative case. In spoken languages, it is common to address someone by name or title in direct conversation or greeting; such situations require the vocative case in Latin. But sign language does not use this means of direct address, and so the vocative can be confusing.

Our department sponsors foreign language clubs both to promote interest in the languages and as a vehicle for Americans to meet some of the many deaf international students who come to Gallaudet every year. Colleagues often take advantage of the international presence in Washington by including in their syllabi international speakers and events sponsored by foreign cultural missions. Our department strongly promotes international experiences among the students. Annually it offers faculty-led study abroad courses that emphasize the humanities, including courses in foreign sign language, and it supports a growing program of international internships.

At Gallaudet we see that deaf students reap the same benefits from foreign language study that other students do. The improvement of English, the expansion of vocabulary through shared etymology, and the benefit of studying comparative syntax (including that of ASL) are all abundantly in evidence. Deaf students show that skills developed in language study are applicable to other disciplines. When one is abroad, even if one does not speak the local language, knowing its written form is highly advantageous. In addition, the cultural awareness and international experience that accompanies language study is increasingly valuable to everyone in the current climate of globalization.

Institutional Support and Resources for Deaf Students

Most universities have established the equivalent of an Office of Services for Students with Disabilities (OSSD), directed by a disability coordinator (DC). This office assists a wide range of students, ideally in the mode of communication best suited to them. Its functions may include assisting students with institutional procedures (e.g., admissions, financial aid, and registration), coordination of interpreters, Braille services, providing special environments for exams, and faculty support. Make an appointment to meet with the DC, and get to know her and the OSSD staff. Learn about the services that the OSSD provides, especially those that will pertain to your students, and how to request and schedule these services. For example, for the creation of Braille texts, the OSSD may need copies of the textbooks and syllabi well in advance. Review syllabi and class plans with OSSD staff to integrate their services with your curriculum. Discuss with OSSD staff how to implement other useful provisions, such as captioning or audio description on videos and universal access features on computers.

If a deaf student in your class requires interpreters, it is the responsibility of the OSSD to provide them. With information from the registrar, interpreters will likely be booked for the student's regular weekly class meetings with little or no effort required from the professor. However, if you schedule a special activity outside regular hours, such as an evening class or a field trip, either you or the student should contact the OSSD well in advance to schedule an interpreter for that occasion.

Become acquainted with your deaf student in the same way that you would with any other: in an informal office-hour meeting. Include an interpreter to facilitate communication. Try to meet with the student and interpreter before the semester begins, so that each of you feels prepared for the first day of class.

The student and interpreter will need clear visual access to one another, and it is helpful to ask them how you might assist in this arrangement in the office. Address yourself to the student, not the interpreter. To inquire about her major, for example, ask directly, "What is your major?" In contrast, it would be considered rude to say to the interpreter, "Ask her what her major is." While you speak to her, however, it is likely that the student will be watching the interpreter. This is not intended as disrespectful to you, of course, because the student relies on a visual mode of communication. When the interpreter finishes translating, the student will shift her gaze and respond to you directly. Continue to direct your attention to the student while she signs, as you simultaneously listen to the translation from the interpreter. Interpreters are trained to work at the speed of any normal conversation, so feel free to maintain your natural rate of speech.

For purposes of getting acquainted, the sort of information typical to all students will be of interest: educational background, prior academic experience in fields related to your own, plans for the major, and goals for higher degrees and profession. In this context the student may describe whether in the past she attended a deaf institute or was mainstreamed, was part of a manual or an oral program, and so on. The student may appreciate some questions from you about herself, if they are in the context of arranging the best possible communication: Can voicing clearly in class be of benefit to you? Or, do you employ only signed communication?

Review the syllabus of your course. Describe the course's general characteristics, such as lectures, translating from text, PowerPoint presentations, group work, writing on the board, and so forth. Describe or show the layout of the classroom to the student and interpreter and ask them how they will be best positioned in the space during the various activities and relative to the other students. Discuss with them the lighting options in the classroom, especially how to create subdued lighting for showing videos, and the like, while still allowing them to communicate in sign. Draw attention to classes or activities that will take place outside regular class time and/or at different locations; knowing these well in advance will help them plan the schedule of the interpreter.

Working with Interpreters

As interpreters may play a significant part in your work with deaf students, I will discuss the role of the interpreter in the academic environment. The disability coordinator of your institution may also provide you with additional information.

An interpreter translates one language into another, and this applies to signed languages just as it does to spoken and written ones. Interpreters of signed languages work in a wide variety of circumstances. Most commonly, interpreters for the deaf work with both oral and signed modes of communication, translating voice-to-sign and sign-to-voice between deaf and hearing individuals. Interpreters might translate one form of a signed language into another form (such as Signed English into ASL), or, because signed languages differ widely from country to country around the world, and even between areas within a single country, interpreters may translate one language into another language (such as Signed French into Signed Italian). Tactile interpreters communicate with those who are both deaf and blind by signing into their hands.

Until the 1960s interpreting services in America were often provided by amateurs, many of whom were children of deaf adults, and for whom there were no formal standards of practice, training, proficiency, or confidentiality. In 1964 the Registry of Interpreters for the Deaf (RID) was established with the goal of improving the quality and availability of interpreting services to all deaf people. The RID developed a Code of Professional Conduct, which guides the behavior of interpreters in areas of confidentiality, professional skills and knowledge, conduct and ethics, and their relationships with consumers and colleagues. In the ensuing decades, interpreting developed into a formal profession. Today there are diverse ways to enter the field of interpreting, including academic courses, and in addition to the RID with its national reach there are state-level agencies that establish their own standards for certification and levels of proficiency.[10]

Interpreting well is a complex process. The interpreter must perceive and understand the speaker's vocabulary and nuances of emphasis, idiom, phrasing, and even emotion. The interpreter should also understand the speaker's intention, as well as nonverbal cues, such as gestures and pauses. The interpreter then reformulates all of these accurately in a manner intelligible to the addressee. Ideally, all of this happens in a matter of moments.

Accuracy does not require—in fact, it usually avoids—a word-for-word substitution of synonymous vocabulary. A skilled interpreter often will pause to gather and assimilate a full phrase, and only then translate it for the listener/viewer. This pause by the interpreter will create a short lag time between when the speaker finishes an expression and when the interpreter finishes translating it. Because the deaf student will receive information slightly behind his peers, this will affect classroom dynamics. In order to ensure that the deaf student has full opportunity to share in the class, be attentive to such situations as how quickly you field answers to questions and how quickly you move on to new subjects.

Strictly speaking, the interpreter's role is solely to facilitate communication. Interpreters are trained to transmit the communication between parties, including its intent, as completely as possible, and to do this impartially, without favoring or influencing one side or the other. In your class, be mindful that the interpreter cannot play an advisory role for either you or the student. Also, the interpreter should not be considered an assistant teacher or be asked to perform any didactic function.

Although it is not necessary that an interpreter have expertise in the actual subject matter of a course, she will be able to do her job more thoroughly and confidently when she has an overview of the structure of the course and has foreknowledge of technical vocabulary that will arise. Provide the interpreter with copies of documents for the course, such as the syllabus, study guides, descriptions of projects, and a list of vocabulary. For a Latin course, the vocabulary list might include the names of the cases and such terms as "passive periphrastic."

Classroom Arrangements

Sight Line

Whenever sign communication is used, visual contact is of the utmost importance. Signers must be able to see one another in order to communicate; when visual contact is interrupted, communication ceases. The hearing can converse without actually looking at one another; thus it is common that oral interlocutors look about, watch other things, and so forth, while they continue speaking. With visual communication this is impossible. Among signers, simple actions such as glancing away or turning the head interrupt visual contact and break communication. Thus the vital common theme in the following discussion is the establishment of good visibility for the deaf student. Ideally, he will be able to see the teacher, the interpreter, his classmates, and any focus of work (such as the chalkboard) simultaneously, or with minimal movement or change of position. The student and interpreter should also be free to adjust their positions as needed during a class in order to maintain good visibility.

Seating

In a class consisting only of hearing students, the ability to hear transcends the importance of a seating arrangement, and it will be of little account if each person cannot see every other classmate face-to-face. Unless the teacher specifies otherwise, hearing students customarily find their own seats, and the deaf student in the hearing environment is usually left to do the same. He and his interpreter will position themselves relative to the teacher, and the rest of the class will give little thought to the fact that the deaf student does not know which of the students beside or behind him is actually speaking. This situation emphasizes to the deaf student that access to his environment is limited, and that others are not seriously concerned about his level of engagement.

Simply by placing the seats in a single arc, however, the teacher can create an arrangement in which the deaf student sees everyone, and everyone sees him. This allows him direct communication with the whole group and integrates him much more into the class. Such a disposition also makes a strong statement about his respected status in the group. It may not always be possible to arrange the seats in an arc, but every effort should be made to do so, including requesting a classroom in which doing so will be possible.

Certain situations, such as testing, may require a different seating plan, but the arc will complement most classes, and it is also an asset to the hearing students. Especially in discussions, each person can follow the other speakers more easily and benefit from eye contact and gestures. The arc will also allow the deaf student to gain the attention of others when he participates in the conversation.

Lighting

Adequate lighting in the classroom is essential to the deaf student; inadequate light can be as effective an impediment to visual communication as a blocked view. Lighting should be ample enough to allow the deaf student to see the interpreter clearly, as well as the teacher, other students, and any other point of focus.

In situations that call for reduced light, as when you are using an overhead projector or showing a video, it is important to maintain sufficient light for the deaf student to see the interpreter. If group discussion accompanies the visual presentation, at least partial lighting is necessary for the deaf student to participate in the class. Ideally, adjustable controls will allow variable conditions in the classroom, with moderate lighting in the seating area and greater darkness near the screen. Seek a classroom with flexible lighting and avoid one in which the only lighting option is either full on or full off. This is important, because darkness will isolate the deaf student from the interpreter and the rest of the group, and make it impossible for him to participate.

Chalkboard

Because of the importance of the visual mode, considerable work on the chalkboard will be an asset both to the deaf and to the hearing students. (See "Instructional Techniques" below.) Thus, use a classroom with as much chalkboard space as possible.

Instructional Techniques

Class Interaction

Some aspects of interaction are so common as to be taken for granted, but in the context of access for a deaf student they warrant emphasis. They include speaking clearly and audibly, and speaking one at a time so as not to talk over one another. These are beneficial to all in any case, but speaking one at a time is particularly helpful to the interpreter. An interpreter can translate only one person at a time, so if people speak simultaneously, the deaf student will likely miss much of what transpires.

Visual Access to Information and Applications of Technology

The senses of hearing and sight in combination are a powerful vehicle of cognition because they enable a person to gather visual and auditory information simultaneously. For example, a student can listen to the teacher speak while examining a textbook at the same time, or can watch a movie while also listening to its sound track. The two modes of communication reinforce one another, increasing the efficiency of understanding and memory. The combination of senses even permits learning from two directions at once, when visual and auditory stimuli emanate from remote sources.

Activities that require the use of both visual and auditory senses at the same time place the deaf student at a marked disadvantage; she gathers information only visually, and can do so from only one direction at a time. In class, when her attention is on the textbook she cannot also follow the interpreter; if the teacher continues to speak while she looks at the book, she loses what is being said and gains only part of what the hearing students will learn. Thus we need to employ techniques that allow multisensory participation by the fully abled but also emphasize the visual component, thereby enhancing access to content and interaction by the deaf student.

An overhead projector is well suited to such a situation and is particularly effective for classes that rely heavily on printed material. Photocopy the textbook onto transparencies and project the pertinent page(s) in class with the overhead. Stand right next to the screen so that all students can see both you and the image of the page easily at the same time. While discussing the lesson, refer to the text by frequently pointing to the appropriate place on the projected image. This works well for didactic material, such as lessons and exercises, but it is particularly effective for translating passages from the target language. With a Latin text projected on the screen (enlarged for good visibility), I can point out word order and analyze the syntax very clearly.

The interpreter positions himself to be in the student's field of vision along with the teacher and the screen, so the student can see the image of the textbook and follow the interpreter at nearly the same time. In this way the student need not repeatedly break visual contact with the interpreter by looking down at and up from the textbook. The beauty here is that the same benefit applies to the hearing students as well; they likewise can follow the teacher and text simultaneously at the front of the room, rather than only listening to the teacher while they look down at the book. The process of frequently switching between looking at a textbook on the desk and at the teacher at the front of the room is quite fatiguing for the deaf student and quickly leads to confusion and misunderstanding. Pause periodically in your presentation to allow the deaf student to shift his attention from the interpreter and to study the text.

This technique works equally well when the students translate. When students translate aloud from their desks, it can be difficult for classmates to follow the translator in their own books, especially in the case of poetry, whose word order may be convoluted. Instead, have each student translate from the front of the class while standing next to the projected text, where he can clearly point out the word order and explain the syntax. You may find it helpful to stand on the side of the screen opposite to the translating student, ready to comment or render assistance. Include the deaf student in this exercise in the same way as the others; as he signs, the interpreter will voice the translation, and the student can field questions from the class in the usual manner.

PowerPoint

PowerPoint is another visual medium that can be employed in a manner similar to the way one uses an overhead projector. PowerPoint creates a slide show on the computer, which is then shown via a digital projector and used didactically like the overhead projector. The application creates custom images, with text and/or pictures.

It is particularly effective for reviewing the syllabus, as well as for showing practice sentences. The latter can be changed quickly without taking the time to write each out on the board. Color too can easily be applied to texts (see "Color Coding" below). If you use PowerPoint to show pictures, and comment on the images while you show them in class, caption the pictures with the most important information contained in your oral remarks.

Captioning

When recorded media, such as videotapes or DVDs, are used without captioning, the deaf student is at a distinct disadvantage. The interpreter may position herself near the screen, so as to be in the student's field of view along with the image, yet even with this arrangement the student does not benefit fully from the film, since he must constantly glance back and forth between the interpreter and the image. In addition, the light must be maintained sufficiently for the interpreter to be visible, but this may compromise the quality of the projected image. Captioning enables the deaf student to watch the screen directly, allows the lighting to be reduced in the area of the screen, and permits the students to share the experience more equally without a facilitator. New DVDs produced in the United States normally include captioning. Optional settings specifically for the deaf supplement the text of the dialogue with descriptions of the sound effects and music. Audio description for the visually impaired may also be available.

Chalkboard

To practice or translate only orally in class would considerably limit the deaf student's capacity to participate. The chalkboard, however, is an excellent vehicle for equalizing access to a variety of textual work. Have students write exercises on the board; then have them stand next to the board while analyzing the sentences and pointing out their germane characteristics. Reading aloud can still be practiced in this context by the hearing students, and the deaf student will sign her translation to the group while the interpreter voices for her. But in addition, everyone will benefit from seeing the work displayed, and putting the work on the board creates a multisensory experience for all the students.

Recall that the interpreter may adjust his position in the room, depending on where the focus of attention is.

Color Coding

Let us now examine how a very simple technique, the use of color, can elucidate the explanation of a great variety of morphological and syntactical elements of the language. Color can be employed easily on a whiteboard, on overhead transparencies, and in PowerPoint images. For written exercises, students find it handy to use a specialized ballpoint pen with four barrels, containing four colors of ink.

In introductory Latin, inflections and their significance are commonly taught by using simple sentences that introduce syntactic variants. For instance, the italicized words in the following sentences illustrate case inflections in English.

1. *He* is Julius Caesar. (subjective case)
2. Caesar leads *his* troops. (possessive case)
3. The troops support *him*. (objective case)

Similarly, simple Latin sentences are used to introduce case inflections and to illustrate the flexible word order permitted by such inflections. The following is a typical example. All three sentences translate in English as "The farmer calls the girl."

1. Agricola puellam vocat.
2. Agricola vocat puellam.
3. Puellam agricola vocat.

By encouraging students to figure out what allows a word to change its position without changing its function, this exercise leads them to recognize that inflection is the essential syntactic feature of the language. They gradually learn the morphology of individual words and recognize consistency or variation in spelling as words change position.

This type of exercise is common in introductory curricula, and it works fairly well for many students. But because it relies on orthography, it may not work so well for someone who is a weak speller. That person will recognize that the words have changed position, but may have difficulty tracking the precise spelling from beginning to end of each word, and appreciating that specific spellings correspond to specific functions. Another element makes the words less discrete and the differences in the sentences harder to distinguish: the monochrome appearance of the text.

In the examples above, the mind reads each sentence in full, then examines the three sentences in sequence, and finally tries to figure out the similarities and differences between the sentences together. Using a single color makes it more difficult for the inexperienced eye first to perceive, and then to systematize, both the similarities and the differences.

A simple change—the use of color—can be highly effective in addressing this problem. In each of the sentences above, imagine that the word *agricola* is in red. The reader will conclude that all red words are red precisely because they are spelled the same. If *puellam* and *vocat* were each in a different, contrasting color, the same process would occur with them. Color adds to the text a visual code that helps the mind to track the words and to organize information in a new way. Similarities and differences are more distinct and easier to recognize than in the monochrome version, and the mind more readily deduces that the color represents a system inherent in the words that are spelled the same.

The next step in this exercise is the same that traditionally follows the monochrome examples: the students learn that all three Latin sentences share a single essential translation in English. Nevertheless, the addition of contrasting colors does not diminish the syntactical challenge of the exercise; the student still must analyze the spelling and position changes on his own.

The use of color in Latin texts can be helpful in many situations. When writing sentences on the board, for example, mark each component in a different color: subject, verb, direct object, indirect object, prepositional phrase. When writing out more than one sentence, color the components consistently in each.

Color can be particularly helpful as syntax becomes more complex. For example, the following two sentences are designed to emphasize the difference in case between a subjective complement used with the verb *to be,* and a direct object used with an action verb:

1. Vergilius poeta est.
2. Vergilius poetam salutat.

If both sentences are monochrome, the student may extract that

Vergilius and *poeta* are both in the nominative, and therefore *poeta* is a predicate nominative. In the second sentence, he will figure out that *Vergilius* and *poetam* are in different cases, with *poetam*, in the accusative, being the direct object. Now imagine that in the first sentence *Vergilius* and *poeta* are both written in the same color, and that in the second sentence *Vergilius* and *poetam* are in different colors. The sentence structures have not changed, only their appearance has. But in the colored versions the eye quickly grasps that some syntactic similarity exists between *Vergilius* and *poeta* (in the same color) that does not exist between *Vergilius* and *poetam* (in different colors). The colors do not give the student the "answer"; he must still figure out the cases and syntax on his own. But they create visual cues that prompt him, as he analyzes the sentences, to look for a condition of similarity in the first sentence and a condition of difference in the second. Then, after the analysis, the color also *reinforces* the two conditions in the mind. This kind of visual cue will certainly enhance the comprehension of a deaf student and will be similarly beneficial to hearing students.

Color can also enhance the understanding of prepositional phrases. Consider these examples:

1. Caesar in regiam ambulavit.
2. Caesar in regiam cum legato ambulavit.
3. Caesar in bonae reginae regiam ambulavit.

In the first sentence, imagine *in regiam* written in a color different from *Caesar* and *ambulavit*. In the second, imagine *in regiam* in one color, and *cum legato* in a contrasting color. In the third, visualize *in . . . regiam* in one color, and *bonae reginae* in a different color. The preceding series efficiently emphasizes (1) the two basic elements of any prepositional phrase (preposition and object of preposition), (2) that prepositional phrases can appear in sequence, and (3) that words placed between a preposition and its object are part of the phrase.

As sentences become more complex, color is very helpful in teaching clauses. Experiment with writing Latin sentences of more than one clause with the conjunctions written in color and/or with the verbs in color, to emphasize that the number of clauses is equal to the number of verbs. Imagine that the italicized and the underlined portions of the following sentences are written in colors contrasting with the rest of the sentence:

1. *Ubi dona sacra portaverant,* deos laudavimus.
2. Agricolae *ubi agros arabant* ab amicis iuti sunt.
3. Dolor *ut ripam* <u>ubi umbrae hominum stabant</u> *adspiciebat* pectus Aeneae cepit.

Contrasting colors can show effectively how clauses can nest inside one another. The same technique works equally well with participial phrases and the ablative absolute.

Color can enhance an English translation to great advantage, especially when the word order of the Latin and English are very different. Consider the following:

1. Avis volantes rusticus spectat.
2. The farmer watches the birds as they fly.

Even if the sentences are monochromatic, the beginning student will eventually grasp the analysis of the Latin and get the point about flexibility of word order. But if *rusticus* and *The farmer* are written in the same color and *Avis volantes* and *the birds as they fly* are in another color, the student grasps the lesson more completely and retains it longer in his mind. This may seem like a lot of work, but with practice the teacher, knowing the structure of the sentence, can easily manipulate the colors and compose a sentence in little more time than it takes to do so in a single color.

Similarly, have the students themselves write in contrasting colors. Assign a color to each important element of a sentence (for example, subject, verb, direct object, indirect object, and prepositional phrase), and then have the students put those elements in the corresponding color as they write sentences in Latin. This is an excellent exercise to encourage first-year students to think carefully about case selection, and it will have the added benefit of enhancing the visual impact of the work.

Signs

While it may be unrealistic that a teacher would become fluent in sign language in order to teach the occasional deaf student, a few basic signs, intuitive and simple to learn, can nevertheless easily be employed for the benefit of all students. To introduce these, let us first look at hand shape. If you are working with an interpreter, she may already be familiar with Latin or other foreign languages and use the hand shapes described here. If not, share with her the information included below. She will grasp the situation quickly, and is likely to model the hand shapes and assist you in becoming adept at using them.

Hold one hand in front of your body about chest high, all fingers spread apart, palm facing toward the chest, and thumb at twelve o'clock. This is called the "5-hand," because all five fingers are extended and visible. Fold the thumb of the 5-hand down onto the palm, keeping the other fingers splayed. This is the "4-hand." Beginning again with the 5-hand, curl the small and ring fingers into the palm, leaving the other three fingers extended, with the thumb at twelve o'clock. As you might expect, this is the "3-hand." These are the hand shapes in ASL for the numbers 5, 4, and 3, respectively, and they are illustrated here from the perspective of the viewer (figure 3.1).

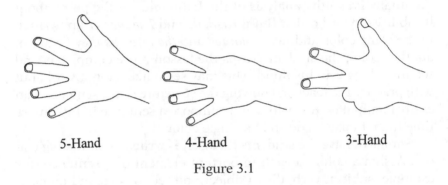

5-Hand   4-Hand   3-Hand

Figure 3.1

Use the 5-hand (figure 3.2) to symbolize the Latin case system. Beginning with the thumb and descending, each digit represents a case, in the order in which the cases are traditionally listed in textbooks: thumb = nominative, forefinger = genitive, middle finger = dative, ring finger = accusative, and little finger = ablative. The sixth case, the vocative, is omitted because there is no finger for it. This is excused on account of the vocative's rarity, and it can easily be described separately when it does appear. Encourage your students to learn the names of the cases in association with their hands; it is easy to do and a helpful technique.

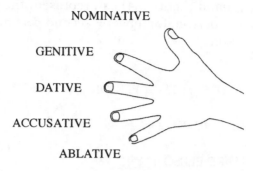

NOMINATIVE

GENITIVE

DATIVE

ACCUSATIVE

ABLATIVE

Figure 3.2

Similarly, use the 4-hand (figure 3.3) to symbolize the four principal parts of a Latin verb. From the top downward, the forefinger, middle finger, ring finger, and little finger represent the first, second, third, and fourth principal parts, respectively. Most American editions of Latin textbooks arrange the principal parts of verbs in the following order: (1) first person singular, present active; (2) present active infinitive; (3) first person singular, perfect active; (4) perfect passive participle. Rarely (as in dictionary listings), the present infinitive is moved from second position to fourth, with the others maintaining the same relative sequence. The 4-hand can easily be applied to either system.

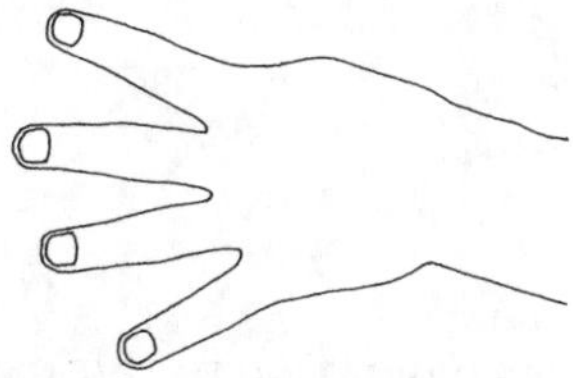

FIRST PRINCIPAL PART

SECOND PRINCIPAL PART

THIRD PRINCIPAL PART

FOURTH PRINCIPAL PART

Figure 3.3

Finally, the 3-hand (figure 3.4) can represent the persons of a verb: thumb = first person, forefinger = second person, and middle finger = third person.

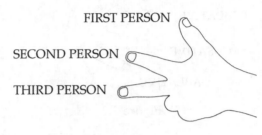

FIRST PERSON

SECOND PERSON

THIRD PERSON

Figure 3.4

To indicate or refer to a specific case, touch the end of the appropriate finger on the 5-hand with the forefinger of the other hand. In the same manner, touching a fingertip on the 4-hand refers to one of the principal parts of a Latin verb, and a fingertip on the 3-hand identifies the person of the verb (figure 3.5).

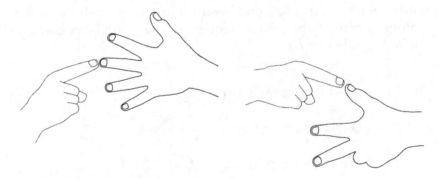

GESTURE INDICATING DATIVE CASE   GESTURE INDICATING FIRST PERSON

Figure 3.5

Once the students associate the fingers of the 5-hand with the case names, they can learn the declensions in the same way, relating each Latin case ending to its appropriate digit. Figure 3.6 shows the endings of the First Declension.

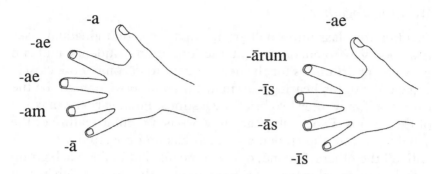

Figure 3.6

Employ these hand shapes from the beginning, when you first introduce the concepts they represent. The students will quickly pick up the technique and find it an excellent mnemonic device. When you quiz the students on these characteristics, simultaneously display the related hand shape. When answering, touch the fingertip corresponding to the appropriate case, principal part, or person, while also naming it aloud. This gesture provides the answer to the hearing and deaf students at the same time. When necessary, also identify the number (singular or plural) by voice as well. Have the students follow suit when they participate.

Use of these signs can also elegantly streamline communication between your deaf student and interpreter. Simply touching a fingertip of the 5-hand will relieve them of the tedious process of repeatedly fingerspelling the case names. Simply touching the small finger of the 4-hand substitutes for the entire expression "perfect passive participle."

These signs quickly become a fluid part of normal usage; in short order, as soon as you raise a hand shape, the students will know immediately the context of your next remark. But even more than this, it will be an element of the deaf student's language used as a means of shared communication for the class. It will send a strong message that he is a class member whose presence is important and valued.

Working Together

Dividing the class into small groups that focus on individual tasks is a good way to encourage interaction among students, and can provide opportunities for the deaf student to become more closely engaged with his hearing classmates than otherwise might be the case. I will only offer two brief suggestions. First, vary the makeup of the groups. Especially if group work is a regular feature of the syllabus, rotate the students so each has an opportunity to work with all the others. Second, devise a means that makes each group member responsible for a certain amount of the work, which is then shared by all to complete the group assignment. This will encourage the accomplishment of both individual practice and communal interaction.

By incorporating the knowledge and instructional strategies I have discussed here, teachers may feel confident and even creative in including the deaf student fully in foreign language learning. But even more than this, teachers will find that having the deaf student in class can be enriching to the whole group. The deaf student's participation will broaden everyone's appreciation of what it means to learn a foreign language and to communicate in general. Creating a more accessible atmosphere for the deaf student benefits hearing students as well. Thus everybody wins.

Notes

1. Donald F. Moores, *Educating the Deaf: Psychology, Principles, and Practices*, 3rd ed. (Boston: Houghton Mifflin, 1987), 81–92.
2. Ibid., 7–10; Stephen P. Quigley and Robert E. Kretschmer, *The Education of Deaf Children: Issues, Theory, and Practice* (Baltimore: University Park Press, 1982), 1–4; John V. Van Cleve, ed., *Gallaudet Encyclopedia of Deaf People and Deafness* (New York: McGraw-Hill, 1987), 1:251–52.
3. Kathryn P. Meadow, *Deafness and Child Development* (Berkeley: University of California Press, 1980), 7.
4. U.S. Department of Health and Human Services, *Vital and Health Statistics: Prevalence and Characteristics of Persons with Hearing Trouble: United States, 1990–91*, 10, no. 188 (1994): 7–9.
5. Ibid., 11–12.
6. Jack R. Gannon, *Deaf Heritage: A Narrative History of Deaf America* (Silver Spring, Md.: National Association of the Deaf, 1981), 1–58; John V. Van Cleve and Barry A. Crouch, *A Place of Their Own: Creating a Deaf*

Community in America (Washington, D.C.: Gallaudet University Press, 1989).

7. Moores, *Educating the Deaf,* 10–13.

8. Hallowell Davis and S. Richard Silverman, *Hearing and Deafness,* 4th ed. (New York: Holt, Rinehart, and Winston, 1978), 293–336, 358–73.

9. Meadow, *Deafness and Child Development,* 17–43; Moores, *Educating the Deaf,* 195–205, 238–39; E. Ross Stuckless and Jack W. Birch, "The Influence of Early Manual Communication on the Linguistic Development of Deaf Children," *American Annals of the Deaf* 111 (1966): 425–60, 499–504.

10. David A. Stewart, Jerome D. Schein, and Brenda E. Cartwright, *Sign Language Interpreting: Exploring Its Art and Science* (Needham Heights, Mass.: Allyn and Bacon, 1998).

CHAPTER 4

Making a Difference: *Evaluating, Modifying, and Creating Inclusive Foreign Language Activities*

TERESA CABAL KRASTEL

> Some people think that learning disabled is a blanket
> term that can be applied to everyone. But I think that I
> have learned that being learning disabled is more than
> not being good at something. It's more like when you
> have an itch in the middle of your back where you can't
> reach it and you really want to scratch it, so you contort
> yourself in every way possible and you still can't get it;
> it's just out of reach for you.
>
> —Journal entry by ALEXANDRA,
> Italian instructor

Alexandra's metaphor of the backscratcher as a tool to help reach
an itch is a powerful reminder that we as foreign language teachers
must provide learning tools for students with learning disabilities
to enable them to process material that would otherwise remain
inaccessible to them. Alexandra's journal entry allowed her to reflect upon the ways in which her knowledge, techniques, and philosophy of teaching facilitate successful experiences for students
with learning disabilities. This chapter describes the outcome of
a teaching methods program entitled "Technology for the Twenty-
first Century," held at Springfield Technical Community College in
Springfield, Massachusetts, in 2002. During the course, participants
(foreign language teachers) used journals to reflect upon and transform their teaching to better meet the needs of diverse learners in
their classes. Participants explored various activities that aim to
accommodate the diverse needs of students in an inclusive foreign
language classroom and are also especially effective for students
with learning disabilities.

In general, a learning disability is defined as "a disorder in one or more of the basic psychological processes involved in understanding or in using language, spoken or written, that may manifest itself in an imperfect ability to listen, think, speak, read, write, spell, or to do mathematical calculations, including conditions such as perceptual disabilities, brain injury, minimal brain dysfunction, dyslexia, and developmental aphasia."[1]

In the language classroom, difficulties tend to arise in comprehension and production, depending on the nature of the student's disability. Richard Sparks recognizes the influence that native language difficulties have on foreign language learning; those who have native language difficulties and learning disabilities are likely to experience difficulty in learning a foreign language as well.[2] However, not all learning disabilities are the same, and individuals may experience combinations of learning disabilities that affect learning in different ways.[3] This diversity has led some educators to implement a Universal Design approach to teaching, which offers the kinds of accommodations that students with learning disabilities typically request. However, Universal Design builds accommodation into course design, reducing time spent working to accommodate students individually while benefiting other students in the class as well.[4]

Let us imagine a typical activity in a beginning foreign language course in which three students have been diagnosed with learning disabilities. One student has a disorder that affects auditory processing, the second has one that affects the comprehension and production of written language, and the third has one that affects spoken language. A listening activity involves a conversation between two French students on the first day of school. After listening to the conversation, students are to read a series of statements about the conversation and decide whether they are true or false. Providing the first student with photographs or illustrations of the speakers, the school setting, and other contextual information while listening to the conversation may help the student anticipate the conversation's content. The second student may need to hear the statements in addition to reading them, and be permitted to respond orally. This student may find the photos helpful as well. The third student may be able to complete the activity without additional modification. A Universal Design approach offers all of these modifications. The inclusion of modifications within a standard lesson plan gives students several options for accessing content and meaning.

Research on learning disabilities suggests that direct instruction of grammar and sound-symbol correspondence through multisensory approaches, such as the Orton-Gillingham Method and the Audio-Lingual Method of foreign language instruction, is very effective in enabling the success of students with learning disabilities.[5] However, Universal Design strategies, based on the principles of experiential and communicative learning, are already built into many communicative and proficiency-oriented language activities.[6] I wish to emphasize in this chapter how the modification of communicative, interactive foreign language activities can accommodate learners with learning disabilities, an approach that is typically easier to implement and support in college foreign language programs.[7]

In a compelling discussion about teaching students with learning disabilities, Richard Lavoie stated that a combination of knowledge, technique, and philosophy influences teachers' decision-making processes, to the benefit of students.[8] He confirmed that, as teachers, we constantly reflect on our own knowledge, techniques, and philosophies about teaching and learning, and our belief systems change based on these reflections as well as our experiences. We may not consciously monitor how classroom activities and outcomes shape our development as effective teachers, but a teaching journal enables reflection about how we teach, how our attitudes change as we know more about learning disabilities, what can be learned from both successful and unsuccessful activities, and how beliefs and techniques evolve, often spontaneously, as we learn more about the individual needs of students in a given class. All of this information enables us to make choices about language teaching tools, methods, and resources.

The five-week course "Methods for Teaching Foreign Language to Students with Learning Difficulties" offered as part of the Springfield program was held via videoconferencing in January and February 2002. It involved elementary, middle, and high school foreign language teachers in the Springfield public school system. Seven are instructors of Spanish, one teaches Italian, one teaches French, and one teaches both Spanish and French. Three are itinerant resource teachers, one each for elementary, middle, and high school. All the teachers involved in this project teach in inclusive classrooms in which the teachers provide accommodations according to the Individual Education Plan (IEP) of each student with learning disabilities. Throughout the duration of the course the teachers monitored their own development through journals in which they reflected on teaching and learning disabilities with questions generated by the content of the methods course. (See Appendix 4.1.) Although the journals are not the central focus of my discussion here, they provide powerful insights into the development of each teacher.

The journals encouraged teachers to express their attitudes and beliefs as they learned more about learning disabilities, their own students' needs, and the types of modifications that worked best in their classes. Through their reflections, they evaluated their decisions and made changes according to the results of their decisions, a process that further shaped their beliefs about learning disabilities. The ensuing excerpts from the journals highlight the complex relationship between knowledge, technique, and philosophy. These reflections, in combination with the activities presented later in the chapter, also reveal the influence of the teachers' belief systems on their classroom decisions and actions.

In her journal, Susan, a Spanish instructor, describes the role that knowledge acquired through workshops on learning disabilities has played in her teaching. This knowledge has offered her insight into how students with learning disabilities learn, and it has had a direct bearing on how she structures lesson plans, chooses activities and modifies course materials. "When teachers and students share their thinking, they become more aware of how learning/understanding takes place. . . . [This] has helped me tremendously in developing and organizing my lessons to address the needs of all students. I add my own ingredients to the modeled strategies presented at the various workshops that I have attended and change them to fit the needs and abilities of my students. . . . My acquired knowledge from the many workshops that I have attended has given me a certain insight on the learning process of the learning disabled student."

Katherine, a Spanish instructor, reflects on how her techniques and activities are always open for revision; no single technique is the solution, but through collaboration and communication with her students, she chooses and adjusts her teaching techniques to meet their needs. "I have asked [my students with learning disabilities] what they'd like me to do differently and how I can make the classroom an environment that allows them to learn better. . . . I also let them know that I was going to be trying a series of different activities in the classroom on a day to day basis and that I wanted their feedback. I wanted to know why they liked or disliked each day's activity and wanted to know what I could do to make it better to learn."

Carla, an instructor of Spanish, states her philosophy about foreign language learning; her beliefs will undoubtedly influence the types of activities and techniques she chooses. "Among the essential elements of how best to teach learning disabled students is found in the basic tenet of not accepting from them the 'I don't know' response. In fact, this goes in tandem with the premise we need all embrace which is a firm belief that ALL students can learn."

These three teachers (whose activities also appear below) all engaged in reflection and took action in their classes. Whether or not we maintain a teaching journal, we all regularly engage in similar cycles of reflection and action, and can gain greater understanding of how our beliefs about teaching and learning combine with our knowledge in implementing a repertoire of teaching techniques that we believe works best for our students.[9] The relationship between knowledge, technique, and philosophy changes constantly and can ultimately have a direct bearing on whether we meet the needs of our students with learning disabilities. In addition to keeping journals, the teachers created activities that they found to be effective for their students with learning disabilities. This chapter will showcase their work, the result of many hours of reflection, changes in attitude, and evolution of a philosophy aimed at a greater understanding of the needs of students with learning disabilities. Although they were originally created for elementary, middle, and high school students, the activities can be adapted for use in college and university classes as well; they are presented in such a way that teachers may use and adapt them directly to any foreign language.

Each activity presented here focuses on one particular language skill. Many of the activities may be familiar to you, and you may have even used these activities in your own classes. They are included here because they have proven effective in meeting the needs of students with learning disabilities. Yet, without exception, teachers reported that they genuinely believe these activities to be effective for all students.

In all examples, I have provided English equivalents so that the activities can be tailored to any language. Suggestions for varying a particular activity will be included in procedures; following each activity, I offer analysis of how the activity accommodates students with learning disabilities, based on my experience in working with students with learning disabilities and their teachers, and supported by the research done in this area.[10] I will also include variations that can emphasize different skills and maximize each activity's potential to strengthen foreign language skills. Modification of activities need not be a daunting and complicated process.

I Say, You Say: A Pronunciation Activity (Katherine, Spanish Instructor)

Level: Beginning
Language: Spanish
Task objective: Pronunciation practice with sound-letter correspondence
Specific difficulties addressed: Pronunciation, sound-symbol recognition, spelling, auditory discrimination
Materials needed: chalkboard or overhead transparencies, poster board for variation
Steps:

1. Write the Spanish alphabet on the chalkboard. Students copy the alphabet into their notebooks.
2. Pronounce each letter slowly and then pronounce a word that begins with that letter. Students repeat the pronunciations individually or as a group.
3. Students work in pairs to find one other word for each letter.

Analysis

Research on learning disabilities and foreign language learning suggests that students with learning disabilities may have difficulties recognizing the correspondence between letters or symbols and sounds in the foreign language.[11] Katherine's pronunciation activity may seem elementary at first glance, but such base-level activities can enhance skills for future listening and reading. Several aspects of Katherine's activity are beneficial to students with learning disabilities. Research suggests that early exposure to sounds and letters improves pronunciation, making rote skills automatic, and may even help sound and letter recognition in the student's native language. Richard Sparks, Leonore Ganschow, Silvia Kenneweg, and Karen Miller have identified these types of pronunciation activities as beneficial to students with learning disabilities.[12]

There are many ways to expand upon this activity: the instructor might pronounce a word, to which students react by holding up a card bearing the first letter of the word. Follow-up work might include creating posters or nametags with objects beginning with a particular letter. Using the letters of their name, students come up with adjectives, likes or dislikes, favorite activities, or anything related to the vocabulary they are studying at the moment. The example in figure 4.1 is based on a lesson on hobbies.

Actividades favoritas

> **T**omar el sol (to sunbathe)
> **E**scribir (to write)
> **R**eirme (to laugh)
> **E**nseñar (to teach)
> **S**alir con amigos (to go out with friends)
> **A**prender el español (to learn Spanish)

Figure 4.1. I say, you say: my sample poster for Katherine's pronunciation activity (English equivalents in parentheses)

A student might interview a partner to create his or her activities poster, or make the poster about a favorite movie or sports star, and so forth. A student might also draw pictures of activities for each letter for a partner to identify using new vocabulary. Whether presenting new material, practicing a given lesson, or reviewing for a quiz, this type of activity can help build vocabulary and enforce pronunciation skills in a structured, interactive, and engaging manner.

Guess Who? A Speaking Activity (Gloria, Spanish and French Instructor)

Level: Beginning
Language: Spanish
Task objective: To gather information to try to guess a classmate's identity
Specific difficulties addressed: Organization and attention, auditory and visual processing, oral production, social skills

Materials needed: A baby picture of each student; construction paper; 8 × 11 cards, numbered; colored pen, markers or pencils; glue
Steps:

1. Students trace both of their hands on construction paper and cut them out. Then students place their paper hands on an 8 × 11 inch card, side by side, thumbs touching each other. The students then place the baby picture between the two hands, temporarily obscuring the other students' view of the photo.

2. Ask students to answer five questions that do not directly reveal their identity. Students use the personal card grid (figure 4.2a) to write their questions and answers. This will be a rough draft for the next step.

Nombre _____

Preguntas (Questions)	Respuestas (Answers)
¿Cuándo es tu cumpleaños? (When is your birthday?)	
¿Qué te gusta hacer? (What do you like to do?)	
¿Qué materia te gusta más? (What class do you like best?)	
¿Cuántos/as hermanos/as tienes? (How many brothers/sisters do you have?)	
¿Cuál es tu comida favorita? (What is your favorite food?)	

Figure 4.2a. Guess who? Personal Card Worksheet
provided by Gloria (English equivalents in parentheses)

3. Before gluing the paper hands to the 8 × 11 card, students write one of the five questions on each of the fingers of the left paper hand. They will also write their personal answers to those five questions on the five fingers of their right paper hand. It is important that students do not see their classmates' responses. Students' hand cards might look something like mine in figure 4.2b.

¿Cuándo es tu cumpleaños?

¿Qué te gusta hacer?

¿Qué materia te gusta más?

¿Cuántos hermanos tienes?

¿Cuál es tu comida favorita?

Mi comida favorita es pescado.

Tengo dos h ermanos.

Me gusta el español

Me gusta jugar al tenis

Mi cumpleaños es el 18 de agosto.

Figure 4.2b. My model of Gloria's paper hands

4. After students have completed step 3, post each student's personal card with the paper hands on the class walls. Next to each card, place a blank piece of paper with a heading YO SOY _____ _____ (I AM _____).

5. Students then roam the room and ask each other the five questions. Each student will interview other students and fill in a survey grid to collect the answers (figure 4.2c). Once they have collected the information they need to guess which hands belong to each classmate, they write the name of the student on the paper marked "Yo soy." Afterward, the teacher calls out the numbers and asks "¿Quién es? (Who is it?)," and either the appropriate student will respond or class members can identify their classmate. The whole class can compare their guesses with the correct answer.

	¿Cuándo es tu cumpleaños? (When is your birthday?)	¿Que te gusta hacer? (What do you like to do?)	¿Qué material te gusta más? (What is your favorite class?)	¿Cuántos/as hermanos/as tienes? (How many brothers and sisters do you have?)	¿Cuál es tu comida favorita? (What is your favorite food?)	¿Quién soy?
1	El 18 de agosto	Jugar al tenis	El español	Tengo 2 hermanos	El pescado	¡Teresa!
2						
3						
4						
5						
6						
7						
8						
9						
10						
...						

Figure 4.2c. Guess who? Personal Card Worksheet
provided by Gloria (English equivalents in parentheses)

Analysis

Gloria's activity integrates speaking with listening, reading, and writing through a review of target vocabulary and communication for real-life purposes. This integrated approach focuses primarily on interaction to gather information, yet students practice skills in a structured manner. You have broken down the information into smaller, more manageable steps in which the students build new information onto previous knowledge in every step of the activity. This framework, otherwise known as scaffolding, structures the foreign language input and students' output in a meaningful and personal way and helps students construct new knowledge from previously existing knowledge.[13] For students with learning disabilities, the structure provides the main organization of the activity in a predictable yet flexible format that allows them the freedom to interact with each other but keeps the focus on the grammatical point and vocabulary through completion of the grid and subsequent drawings. This activity engages several modalities—kinesthetic, visual, and verbal interaction, as well as writing—and includes opportunities for review and repetition.[14]

Variations

When the students reveal their identity, ask the class how they know who the person is, thereby reviewing the answers to the questions. For more advanced students, the activity might incorporate the baby pictures to practice different verb tenses (e.g., "When John was a baby, he had no hair. Now he has hair."). This activity can also be adjusted to other thematic content areas: physical attributes, hobbies, classes, and family, to name just a few.

The Story of My Life: A Writing Activity (Karen, French Instructor)

Level: Intermediate
Language: French
Task objective: Writing with a focus on grammar in context
Specific difficulties addressed: Organization and attention, meta-cognitive awareness, written production, structure and morphology of language

Steps:

1. As homework, ask students to create a time line on which they include a minimum of ten sentences. The time line does not have to start at birth or end with death, but it must include the following:

   Two sentences using the passé composé;

   two sentences using the imperfect tense;

   no more than three sentences in the present tense;

   two sentences using the simple future tense; and

   two sentences using the conditional tense.

2. Students peer-edit in the following session, ensuring that the requirements for the assignment have been met and checking for accuracy.

3. Students then pass the work to you for further editing.

4. Students go to the computer and record their answers into a time-line software program that can display their work in several formats.

5. Time permitting, students can incorporate graphics or scan photos into their time line and print it.

6. Students present their lives to classmates, in small groups or as a whole class.

Analysis

Karen's writing activity is flexible enough to allow for variety and creativity in learners' self-expression, but she has scaffolded the task, breaking the exercise into a series of discrete tasks to provide structure throughout the writing process. One important feature of this particular activity is its structure: step-by-step instructions, with a checklist of obligatory items and variations to allow for creativity. In addition, each step builds upon the information produced in the previous step, yet permits flexibility in outcome. Organizing an activity into a series of steps and providing simple instructions for each step (rather than a complicated overview of the whole activity) has been shown to help students with learning disabilities.[15]

Perhaps the most salient feature of this activity is that it is motivated by details of the students' lives. Furthermore, the optional multimedia component enables students to express themselves through visual as well as written modalities and, furthermore, to build upon their learning and artistic strengths. The way in which the software encourages them to personalize their work may well improve motivation. Throughout the activity, form is never disassociated from meaning. This integration of networks of meaning and grammatical content through multiple steps of reinforcement in the writing process automatically incorporates into the activity the repetition and review of information that is so critical to students with learning disabilities. Finally, Karen's activity encourages development of metacognitive strategies through a checklist that the teacher provides. Regular use of checklists encourages students to strategize on paper and chart their progress, a skill that will serve them in other arenas. Indeed, direct instruction in study skills and strategies for monitoring one's own learning clearly foster successful foreign language experiences for students with learning disabilities.[16]

Three Square Meals and a Snack: A Vocabulary-Building Activity (Carla, Spanish Instructor)

Level: Beginning, low intermediate
Language: Spanish
Task objective: Vocabulary building and categorization
Specific difficulties addressed: memory, organization and attention, auditory and visual discrimination
Materials: Four large sheets of paper, different colored markers (one for each group)
Steps:

1. Initiate a warm-up by asking students to name three daily meals, what time they generally eat them and what foods they prefer. They can use *Me gusta/No me gusta* (I like/don't like . . .) and *Prefiero* . . . (I prefer . . .).

2. On the wall, prepare four large sheets of paper that are divided in two. The top half of the paper has the name of one of the three daily meals (breakfast, lunch, and dinner), and the fourth piece of paper has the word "merienda" (snack) written on it. The bottom half of each paper has questions related to that specific meal. For example, at what time do you eat breakfast? What do you like to eat for lunch? What do you like to drink with dinner? At what time do you usually eat a snack? Figure 4.3 illustrates this step.

EL DESAYUNO
(BREAKFAST)

---

1. ¿A qué hora desayunas? (What time do you eat breakfast?)

2. ¿Qué sueles comer para el desayuno?
(What do you usually eat for breakfast?)

3. ¿Qué bebes con el desayuno? (What do you drink for breakfast?)

4. ¿Qué comida nunca comes para el desayuno?
(What food do you never eat for breakfast?)

Figure 4.3. Three square meals and a snack:
my version of one meal in Ann Carla's vocabulary building activity
(English equivalents in parentheses)

3. Divide the class into different groups and give each group a different colored marker.
   Groups will rotate from chart to chart and answer the questions. At the end, each group's answers will be written in different colors, so that the class can see how each group's answers compared with those of the other groups.
4. The class decides which group has given the most information, and that group decides which snack you will bring for the next class period.

Analysis

Carla's activity is a good example of using semantic associations to enhance memory. Vocabulary sets embedded in meaningful, culture-bound contexts are among the best practices in communicative language teaching.[17] With context-rich vocabulary, students begin to categorize the target language input to build networks of meaning from the active vocabulary. In this case, when a learner recalls one word, she or he is likely to recall a whole set of semantic associations, or schemata, as well. These schemata are all part of stored knowledge embedded into contexts and meanings with which most learners are already familiar, simply by virtue of previous experience.[18] Often learners are not aware of these schemata stored away in their memories, but you can take full advantage of them to help students access target language meaning.

Carla uses different colored markers to help her students visually discriminate among each group's answers. Research and practice in Special Education often cite visual cues for organization as an essential tool to help students with learning disabilities discriminate discrete units of information.[19]

Variations

Food vocabulary picture/word flashcards can be used to enhance recall. Allow students to draw the foods on extra chart paper. Have each group make a chart of all the foods they ate the day before and compare and contrast their preferences. This activity can be tailored to any vocabulary or adapted to cultural content. For example, for the same unit on food, the posters might be used to compare meal times and types of foods in the home and target cultures.

How's the Weather? A Listening Activity (Gary, Spanish Instructor)

Level: Beginning
Language: Spanish
Task objectives: Practice and refine listening skills and practice numbers
Materials: Video or audio weather forecast
Specific difficulties addressed: Auditory perception
Steps:

1. Prior to this class, introduce students to the basic weather and seasonal expressions in the target language.
2. Initiate a discussion of weather and temperatures, and review numbers 1–100 by showing a transparency of a regional or na-

tional weather map. Review basic math calculations to help prepare students for the forecast.

3. The class then views the videotape of a genuine weather forecast, twice. The second time, pause the tape when the reporter
announces the temperature. Students volunteer to state the temperature for the class.

4. For homework students are asked to watch and listen to the
weather forecast and complete a table containing the temperature
highs and lows for the next two days in your city (figure 4.4).

LAS TEMPERATURAS (TEMPERATURES)

HOY (today)	Fecha (date):	MAÑANA (tomorrow)	Fecha (date):
	Día (day):		Día (day):
Temperatura	Alta (high): _____° Baja (low): _____°	Temperatura	Alta (high): _____° Baja (low): _____°

Figure 4.4. How's the weather? My version of Gary's
temperature grid (English equivalents in parentheses)

5. On the second day, distribute blank temperature tables for the
students to complete while listening to an audio weather forecast
with the highs and lows that are forecast for the next few days.

An accommodation for students with auditory processing problems
may be the use of a personal headset for each student or a two-
level assessment in which students listen to short segments of the
broadcast, in order for them to focus on the number given in each
segment.

Analysis

We have no doubt all done this type of listening activity with the
weather. However, a few subtleties of Gary's version of the activity
deserve mention. First, the exercise activates students' prior experiences with the language: review of the prior day's work, work with
numbers and calculations, introduction of new material embedded in

the context of previous material, and practice in class and at home to reinforce the new material. This activity relies upon students' background knowledge to access meaning, while its structure provides a cohesive, communicative, real-life listening task with authentic video or audio material. Second, this activity does not require complete comprehension of the clip. Instead, students listen for specific information (in this case, numbers) to demonstrate comprehension. Targeted listening activities such as this provide access to meaning, but they also enable the learner to filter out irrelevant information, making the task more manageable while enhancing auditory discrimination skills.[20] Both of these traits, combined with visual information if you are using a videotape, provide multiple inputs to the learner with learning disabilities within the meaningful context, a schema that almost all of us encounter in our daily experiences. This type of listening activity is tried and true for the general foreign language classroom, and Gary's version of the activity illustrates how communicative techniques and accommodations combine to reach learners with learning disabilities. Once again, breaking the task into smaller steps and providing structured input facilitate target language comprehension and will result in successful language production. One might follow up this activity with a reading (using the Internet or other print media) and then role playing in which students act as weather broadcasters in different countries in which the target language is spoken.

See It, Organize It, and Learn It! (Susan, Spanish Instructor)

Level: All
Language: Spanish
Task objectives: Building metacognitive strategies
Specific difficulties addressed: Organization and attention, metacognitive awareness, memory, oral and written production
Steps: Use a verb map to assist students in transforming information from one form to another. Each step is differentiated with a geometric shape to help students organize syntactic structures, as in figure 4.5.

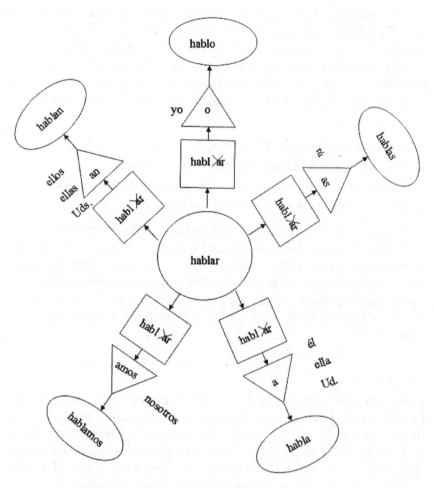

Figure 4.5. See it, organize it, and learn it!
Visual verb conjugation diagram provided by Susan

The circle represents the infinitive form of the verb (*hablar*, to speak).

The square represents the stem of the verb (*habl-*) minus the infinitive ending (*-ar*).

The triangle shape represents the subject pronoun and its equivalent verb ending (*yo-o*).

The oval shape is the result of the combination of steps 2 and 3 (*habl + o*).

This graphic organizer helps students expand their knowledge, organize and understand different units of language to create a whole, and learn how the combinations of the steps provided are necessary as a base to develop a complete sentence. In addition to using the graphic organizers for verb morphology and sentence construction, students can also use them to produce sentences with themes.

Topic: seasons

The first step in each arm represents subject pronouns.

The second step in each arm represents actions.

The third step of each arm represents location, destination.

The fourth step of each arm represents the time of day.

Susan's use of graphic organizers helps students develop metacognition because the students are active participants monitoring their own progress and controlling their own learning development. This step-by-step process provides help not only to the student who has a learning disability; it applies to students at all ability levels. Students know exactly what is expected of them at every step of the way.

Analysis

This particular activity's focus on rote skills and strategies highlights the step-by-step integration of visual, reading, and written modalities. What is perhaps most exciting about this activity is its versatility and applicability to multiple areas in foreign language learning. As Susan has pointed out, it can be used for rote work with verb conjugations as well as for sentence structure through picture prompts.

The diagrams in this activity can be used in a variety of ways both in class and at home. Their main function is to organize information in a visual manner, and if students are accustomed to them, they will come to rely on predictable structures to help them produce language (whether in conjugating verbs or sequencing a story). The verb paradigm version of the diagram can be used for studying and memorization, or can even be a visual reminder for students on tests. The picture building and story building diagram can be used as a template to organize written work and oral story building.

In her reflections on these activities, Susan credits Project CRISS (Creating Independence through Student-Owned Strategies) as fundamental to her foreign language modifications. This program enhances learning through reading and writing, and Susan has adapted its guiding principles for foreign language teaching. This approach encourages all of the strategies that I have discussed here, activating learners' background knowledge, involving students actively in the tasks and discussion, and helping learners develop metacognitive skills through reading, writing, and active discussion.[21]

Conclusion

These different activities suggest a variety of ways to modify your teaching methods and priorities in order to facilitate learning for students with learning disabilities. In the videoconference course, I was most inspired to learn that much of what I already do as a foreign language teacher appeals to diverse learning styles and meets the needs of students with learning disabilities.

Rather than limiting content delivery and outcome to a single option that may coincide with students' weaknesses and impede their learning, the activities in this chapter address specific difficulties by appealing to a variety of learning strengths. By maximizing multiple learning modalities, accessing meaning through students' background knowledge, and organizing tasks as a series of manageable steps, these activities provide predictable structures that ultimately train students to anticipate activities, content, and expected outcome. These activities emphasize both the structure and the meaning of language, and the integration of language skills facilitates communication in meaningful contexts. This lends strong support to the notion that evaluating your foreign language materials in light of your students' particular needs is vital. Much as your students' experience informs your instructional choices, the choices you make about materials and instruction become part of your students' foreign language learning experience. When you allow students to pursue a variety of paths to success, you not only enable their learning of a foreign language and very likely strengthen their skills in their native language, you also teach them to seek the alternative paths to success that may be necessary throughout their lives.

Acknowledgments

I would like to acknowledge Rita Oleksak and Kathleen Riordan of Springfield Public Schools for conceptualizing and creating the methods course via videoconference. Thanks especially to Rita for facilitating each class session on-site in Springfield. Thanks also to Vincent Yacovone of Springfield Technical Community College and Nuray Pearson at the University of Maryland for their technical support. Finally, many thanks to the teachers who participated in the course and offered us their insights and creative activities.

Appendix 4.1: Questions for Foreign Language Teacher Reflection

1. Describe the range of student abilities in your classes. Think about how you teach and describe how your teaching accommodates this range.

2. Think about the activities that you did in class this week. In what ways did they accommodate the needs of different students (visual learners, tactile learners, auditory learners, learners with disabilities)? What do you think was successful about these activities? How would you have changed them and why?

3. Leaf through your textbook. Are there elements of the textbook that you do or do not like, in light of what you are learning about students with learning disabilities? Explain.

4. Look at the last test that you gave (or the next that you will be giving) your class. Critically evaluate the test as a whole and by section in terms of what you are learning about students with learning disabilities. Is each section effective in accommodating students with learning disabilities? How will you change these sections of the test and why?

5. What kinds of study strategies do your students with learning disabilities need in order to succeed in your class? If you teach your students study skills and metacognitive strategies, describe them and comment on how you feel students with learning disabilities can benefit from them.

Notes

1. *Learning Disabilities Fact Sheet (FS7) January 2004* (Washington, D.C.: National Dissemination Center for Children with Disabilities, 2004), http://www.nichcy.org/pubs/factshe/fs7txt.htm (accessed 21 April 2007).
2. Richard Sparks, "Foreign Language and the At-Risk Learner," *Research and Training in Developmental Education* 12, no. 1 (1995): 39–53.
3. Joan Harwell, *Complete Learning Disabilities Handbook* (West Nyack, N.Y.: Center for Applied Research in Education, 1989), 5.
4. Patricia Silver, Andrew Bourke, and Kregg C. Strehorn, "Universal Instruction Design in Higher Education: An Approach for Inclusion," *Equity and Excellence in Education* (1998): 47–51.
5. For more on the Orton-Gillingham Method, see Leonore Ganschow, Richard Sparks, James Javorsky, and Jon Patton, "Factors Relating to Learning a Foreign Language among High- and Low-Risk High School Students and Students with Learning Disabilities," *Applied Language Learning* 3, nos. 1–2 (1992): 37–63, and Richard Sparks, Leonore Ganschow, James Javorsky, Jane Pohlman, and Jon Patton, "Test Comparisons among Students Identified as High-Risk, Low-Risk, and Learning Disabled in High School Foreign Language Courses," *Modern Language Journal* 76, no. 2 (1992): 142–159. For more on the Audio-Lingual Method of foreign language instruction, see E. E. Bilyeu, *Practice Makes Closer to Perfect: Alternative Techniques for Teaching Foreign Languages to Learning Disabled Students in the University* (Ellensburg, Wash.: Central Washington University, Fund for the Improvement of Postsecondary Education, 1982). *Eric Document Reproduction Service* no. ED234558.
6. Teresa Cabal Krastel, "Accommodating the Needs of Students with Learning Difficulties in the Foreign Language Classroom," unpublished diss., University of Massachusetts—Amherst, 1999, 13.
7. See *Landmark College Foreign Language Project*, 1998, http://www.landmarkcollege.org/flp/index.htm (accessed 15 February 2000); Ann Mabbott, "An Exploration of Reading Comprehension, Oral Reading Errors, and Written Errors by Subjects Labeled Learning Disabled," *Foreign Language Annals* 27, no. 3 (1994): 293–324; Judith Shrum and Eileen Glisan, *Teacher's Handbook*, 2nd ed. (Boston: Heinle and Heinle, 2000), 266–70.
8. Richard Lavoie, *When the Chips Are Down . . .*, The Learning Disabilities Project (Washington, D.C.: WETA; videocassette, PBS Video, 1997).
9. Jack Richards and Charles Lockhart. *Reflective Teaching in Second Language Classrooms* (Cambridge: Cambridge University Press, 1996), 29; Devon Woods, *Teacher Cognition in Language Teaching* (Cambridge: Cambridge University Press, 1996), 204–12.

10. For more on accommodating students with learning disabilities see Cabal Krastel, "Accommodating."

11. See Richard Sparks and Leonore Ganschow, "Foreign Language Learning Difference: Affective or Native Language Aptitude Differences?" *Modern Language Journal* 75, no. 1 (1991): 3–16; Sparks, Ganschow, Javorsky, Pohlman, and Patton, "Test Comparisons among Students," 150.

12. Richard Sparks, Leonore Ganschow, Silvia Kenneweg, and Karen Miller, "Use of an Orton-Gillingham Approach to Teach a Foreign Language to Dyslexic/Learning-Disabled Students: Explicit Teaching of Phonology in a Second Language," *Annals of Dyslexia* 41 (1991): 96–118.

13. See Shrum and Glisan, *Teacher's Handbook*, 10; James Lee and Bill Van Patten, *Making Communicative Language Teaching Happen*, 2nd ed. (New York: McGraw Hill, 2003), 142–43, 168; Gerald Duffy and Laura Roehler, "The Subtleties of Instructional Mediation," *Educational Leadership* 43 (1986): 23–27.

14. *Landmark College*, 7.

15. Harriet Barnett, "Foreign Languages for the Learning Disabled: A Reading Teacher's Perspective," *New York State Association of Foreign Language Teachers Bulletin* 36 (1985): 7–9.

16. *Landmark College*, 8.

17. H. Douglas Brown, *Teaching by Principles: An Interactive Approach to Language Pedagogy*, 2nd ed. (New York: Longman, 2001), 377; Lee and Van Patten, *Making Communicative Language Teaching Happen*, 35; Alice Omaggio Hadley, *Teaching Language in Context*, 3rd ed. (Boston: Heinle and Heinle, 2000), 376.

18. Lee and Van Patten, *Making Communicative Language Teaching Happen*, 218.

19. See Sandra Rief and Julie Heimburge, *How to Reach and Teach All Students in the Inclusive Classroom* (West Nyack, N.Y.: Center for Applied Research in Education, 1996).

20. Omaggio Hadley, *Teaching Language*, 185–87.

21. *Project CRISS*, 2002, http://www.projectcriss.com (accessed 5 October 2003).

CHAPTER 5

ASL: *The Little Language That Could*

BRENDA JO BRUEGGEMANN

Once upon a time, and not so very long ago, American Sign Language (ASL) was barely known to the Modern Language Association (MLA), an organization of more than three hundred thousand members in one hundred countries whose "members have worked to strengthen the study and teaching of language and literature."[1] Until 1997, in fact, ASL was listed in the definitive *MLA International Bibliography* only under "invented" languages—followed directly by the Klingon language of *Star Trek* fame. In 1997, the MLA formed the Committee on Disability Issues in the Profession (CDI). Spurred on by some members of the MLA's newly formed CDI and by the linguistic scholarship over the previous two decades documenting the unique but also common language features of ASL, a formal request was made to the MLA that ASL be included among the "natural" languages, alongside Spanish, German, French, and the like. The MLA bibliographers, staff, and executive director, then Phyllis Franklin, listened intently to our argument. We gathered a substantial record of linguistic scholarship not only about ASL but also about sign languages around the globe, demonstrating the foundational nature of sign languages *as languages* and illustrating their unique contributions to both the study and the expression of language as we had come to know it in oral/aural and print-dominated cultures.

Yet, interestingly enough, some forty years after William Stokoe's groundbreaking dictionary on ASL and despite considerable linguistic research pouring in from all around the globe that could easily prove that ASL is indeed a natural language, a real language, even a wondrous language (as indeed all languages are), we are still trying to "invent" ASL as an entity within such key academic organizations as the MLA and within the academy generally.[2] Scholars of

ASL literature, literacy, and linguistics continue to struggle to find a comfortable place within the MLA—especially deaf scholars whose access is still limited at the MLA conferences and ASL teachers who might belong to the national American Sign Language Teachers Association (ASLTA) but who generally do not hold terminal degrees and often only teach part time, at most, in colleges and universities around the country.[3]

I think, however, that it is time to move on. It is time to move away from the defensive outsider and approval-seeking positions that ASL has typically occupied in the academy, especially in relation to other foreign/modern languages. It is time to move our discussions, perspectives, and placements of ASL into a position of potential, promise, and linguistic-cultural power. In the spirit of that move, I will ground all the points I make in this chapter by invoking ASL as the little language that could: the little language that could in fact turn out to be anything but little for those students who get the chance to learn it during their college years; the little language that could make us think hard about what language *is* and *can do,* challenging and yet also affirming our ideas and beliefs about languages and culture; and the little language that could rumble and steam right through the established stations of language and literature programs in the academy, potentially overtaking some of the bigger trains.

An Academic Home for ASL?

Take but one brief and bold example of the challenges offered by the little language that could: ASL offered to American college students and confirmed as credits on their transcripts—as a *foreign* language. In the United States, how can an *American* language also be a *foreign* language? What nation declares its own language to be foreign?[4] Perhaps, then, what ASL helps illuminate is the very nature of terms like "foreign" (as opposed to "modern") used in describing languages during an era of fluid and frequent global interactions.

Just as ASL questions the place of adjectives like "foreign" and its own place within a construct of "foreign," it also articulates—and complicates—questions of disciplinary and departmental boundaries in the academy at large. We might think of ASL as the engine with no house—the gypsy language, as it were. Sheryl Cooper's 1997 dissertation on the academic status of sign language programs in institutions of higher education in the United States demonstrates ASL's wanderlust. Although 36.8 percent of the programs and administrators that Cooper surveyed recommended placing ASL among the modern or foreign languages, this percentage obviously did not constitute a majority, let alone a strong one. Interestingly enough, 12.6 percent recommended that sign language should be a department of its own, a situation that rarely exists for any language. Meanwhile, 10.5 percent placed it in speech pathology/audiology departments, and a nearly equal number suggested its placement in any one of five different places: Deaf Education, Deaf Studies, Interpreting, Linguistics, or Special Education.[5]

Such variation in views regarding ASL's academic affiliation highlights the challenge of administrative structure for ASL in the academy. And this challenge, I would argue, illustrates how much the ASL has gathered steam in challenging the university overall and our ideas about language departments more specifically. Consider for a moment what it means when a language can stand on par with other modern languages in the university structure—even occupy a space all its own—but can also be placed in domains alongside the professional instruction of those who "help" or "service" deaf and hard-of-hearing people. Imagine for a moment if we taught so-called third world languages only within departments that might send professionals to relevant third world countries to "help" their people, or if religion (through missionary work) or medicine (through general health care or even AIDS research or care programs) became the predominant home for such languages. What a "foreign" idea that would be![6]

At my own university, Ohio State, we have built an ASL program that gives students general education credit (GEC) in a "foreign" language, in a unique answer to the "placement" question posed by Cooper's dissertation.[7] The program is now in its fourth year, and we are also building a new master's program specializing in ASL teaching within our College of Education. Our ASL program for undergraduate foreign language credits spans and involves three different colleges. The two introductory courses, ASL I and II, are taught in the College of Humanities, under the wing of the English department. And while "under the wing" does have significant metaphorical potential, both positive and negative, we argued that we could place part of the ASL program there because at Ohio State we have nothing like an American Studies program. English Studies, where American language and literature is typically taught, is the closest fit. We could also argue that ASL would best be housed in the English department because the department is widely familiar and has a long track record of running a significant number of the university's required "general education" and basic-level courses—courses like the first- and second-year required writing courses and Introduction to Fiction, Introduction to Poetry, and so forth. The English department knew well how to handle the "business" of all those students in introductory, skills-based courses. (And this argument has, I would add, proven to be all the more important as we have worked to iron out policies and procedures for hiring qualified teachers, for continuing the professional development of our teachers, and for addressing student concerns and complaints.)

After a student has completed ASL II, he or she can then move to the third- and fourth-level courses in the sequence (four courses in a language are required for the completion of the general education "foreign language" requirements at Ohio State); these last two courses can be taken either in the College of Education (in the Department of Teaching and Learning) or in the College of Social and Behavioral Sciences (in the Speech and Hearing department). What we have tried to set in motion, then, is a triangulated program in which students will get at least two (and possibly even three) different disciplinary entries into and intersections with the language. The content of each course—the actual skills taught—is supposed to remain the same in each level of the course, no matter where it is taught. The teachers and coordinators have worked out a kind of standard curriculum and syllabus for each course; while variation is allowed in an individual teacher's approaches and activities, the key objectives and elements for the courses remains the same, no matter where it is being taught. In theory, at least.

We are still not sure how all this is playing out in practice. The ASL program is currently undergoing an extensive "outcomes" assessment as well as engaging in its own study of itself via focus group discussions of students, teachers, and program administrators across the three colleges/units. ASL at Ohio State is new, and we are in fact still driving it without a dashboard of standardized assessment measures in place. In some ways this reminds me of how I learned to drive growing up in western Kansas: my parents and grandparents turned me loose behind the wheel of grandpa's old blue Ford pickup in the big open cow pasture behind their farm house, gave me some basic instructions on gears, clutches, brakes, accelerator—and then let me go. It was exhilarating, fun, and wild to just get the feel of the thing, bumping along over gopher holes with dried cow patties flying behind me, creating a little dust cloud to mark the path I had taken, and not worrying over which way I should turn or go next. And I learned well the basics of the machine and its movement by driving this way. But soon I wanted more: a road to travel, a radio that actually worked, a destination and goal, a more finely tuned knowledge of navigation involving blinkers, lights, different driving conditions, and—most important of all—the ability to travel and negotiate with others also on the road.

In thinking about ASL's attempts and abilities to navigate and negotiate with other languages currently on the road, let me dwell for a moment on our own enrollment numbers and issues. With approximately 130 new students enrolled each quarter in our ASL I classes and up to 300 students on the waiting lists for that first-level course every quarter (some students wait up to four quarters), ASL is obviously a language that is very popular with our students these days. And that popularity on my own campus has been borne out by a recent survey completed by the Association of Departments of Foreign Languages (ADFL) and published in the *ADFL Bulletin* in 2004.[8] Whatever the reasons for ASL's considerable popularity—and we do have some sense of those various reasons from our survey of students in the ASL I course—the evidence does seem to indicate that ASL has the potential to *threaten* other languages being offered on college campuses.[9]

I use that verb *threaten* quite deliberately. For in a university fiscal environment where budgets are now built on enrollments generated—the "butts in seats" budget, as I have heard it called at my own university—ASL constitutes a potential "cash cow." When one adds to its revenue-generating status the fact that foreign/modern language enrollments on college campuses overall have been noticeably lower over the past decade or so (although they are now showing a slight increase again), the threat of one language "stealing" seats from another becomes very real. At Ohio State University, in fact, our Foreign Language Center (FLC)—which houses virtually all the other languages taught at our huge university—would not touch ASL with the proverbial ten-foot pole when we began trying to build the program five years ago. It was explained to me that while the FLC faculty were not at all "philosophically opposed" to the language, they also did not want to take on the sizeable faculty resistance that would likely be encountered from colleagues in German, Italian, French, and so forth when ASL might begin to siphon off their already dwindling enrollments. Only Spanish, it seems, remains unaffected by ASL enrollments.

What's more, when our FLC proposed and received significant funds from the SBC-Ameritech communications company to establish research and innovation in instruction using various technologies as part of its presence in Ohio State's new World Media and Culture Center, ASL was not included in that funding proposal. On this matter, I cannot help but ponder the irony of Alexander Graham Bell's legacy in relationship to deafness and deaf people: his early role as an oral-focused teacher of the deaf (including his future wife); his place as the son and husband of deaf women (his wife, Mabel Hubbard Bell was, of course, the original "Ma Bell"); his niche in the American eugenics movement, carved out predominantly because of his work on charting and graphing the "marriages and progeny" of deaf people in order to prove that when deaf people married deaf people they tended to produce deaf children, and that therefore their marriage should be discouraged and even forbidden; his invention of the telephone resulting from his search to find an oral/aural mechanism to help teach his method of oral instruction, called "Visible Speech," to deaf students. Thus, when SBC-Ameritech, the offshoot of the once powerful Bell phone company, provides significant funding for the study of "foreign" languages at my university that conveniently does not include ASL, Bell's legacy seems to continue to haunt us.

The Association of Departments of Foreign Languages Survey

But perhaps we should not look backward, yet again, to "Bell's toll" on ASL and the American deaf community. Perhaps we should instead cast our gaze forward to the 2002 ADFL survey and study the face that ASL is showing us, at present and for the future. The report published in the Winter–Spring 2004 issue of the *ADFL Bulletin*, written by Elizabeth B. Welles, presents not one but actually many interesting faces for ASL. What I want to do here is outline a few of the faces that I find most interesting and prominent. Let me confess before I go any further that, much like a witness profile, my sketch here will be, at its best, probably only sketchy. I also want to clarify that the ADFL survey covers "foreign" language enrollments up to 2002 in institutions of higher education. This is important even to me because the program at Ohio State, as but one significant example, has been built *since* 2002.

Among undergraduates and graduates at four-year (or plus) colleges, ASL ranked fifth in language course enrollments, with Spanish, French, German, and Italian placing ahead of it. This constitutes a shocking 432 percent increase in ASL enrollments at four-year colleges since 1998. When the ADFL began its survey in 1986, ASL did not even exist in numbers on the survey. This ADFL report also tells us that ASL has only been recorded in the ADFL survey of foreign language enrollments since 1990 and that it "has shown a tremendous increase for each survey since then as more institutions begin to report it." As the report tries to analyze this trend, however, my own analysis finds the report's analysis considerably lacking. That is, I want to suggest that there is much left unidentified as to the impact and place of ASL within the ADFL and its official surveying. As Welles begins to work through the massive data now piling up for college enrollments in ASL, she indicates: "The comparison of the 1998 and 2002 institutional figures is particularly useful for explaining the enormous growth of ASL [because] the bulk of the increase occurred through the reporting of institutions that had not responded previously."[10]

But why, we should ask, did these institutions previously not respond? Were they perhaps not asked the right questions to begin with? If the right kinds of questions weren't being asked in order to elicit responses about ASL offerings and enrollments in the past, would it be surprising that the ADFL was not really receiving any responses? We know that ASL was not even listed in the *MLA International Bibliography* as a "natural" language until 1998; this is the place and point at which I began this chapter. It would probably be hard for an institution's response regarding its ASL offerings even to be "heard" if the language itself had not yet been placed in the *MLA International Bibliography*. It seems possible that at this point even the ADFL and MLA do not yet know exactly what questions they could, should, or would ask regarding ASL's entrance and growth in colleges and universities across the United States. It is only through some solid affiliation with such organizations as the American Sign

Language Teachers Association or with the full participation of ASL and Deaf Studies scholars in the MLA and the ADFL that we are likely to get the right questions—followed by some meaningful answers—about ASL in the academy.

I do not presume to have all the questions (much less the answers) that should be offered, since, as I suggest, framing them would require the knowledge of a body of ASL and deaf scholars and teachers. However, I might quickly outline a few key questions: Are there any patterns in the *kinds* of colleges offering ASL? Where is ASL located within the structures of these colleges in relation to the other languages offered there? Is it included among the modern languages or located elsewhere in the college's disciplinary structure? What are the reasons students give for their interest in taking ASL classes? What do students say they gain from taking ASL as a language? How do overall enrollment patterns (entry level, retention, completion of a sequence of courses) compare between ASL and other languages taught in U.S. colleges? How does the teaching pool (faculty, part-time teachers, and graduate students) in ASL offerings on college campuses compare to the teaching pools in the other languages offered? How many "native" users of ASL teach it in comparison to "native" users teaching other languages? How does the professional development and research base in ASL linguistics, teaching, and literature compare to that in other languages?

The 2002 survey report published by Welles in 2004 does in fact suggest some food for further thought while leaving a lot unchewed. In puzzling over the formidable increase in ASL enrollments, Welles offers the following explanation:

> Besides student interest, the increase recorded in 2002 also has to do with a change in the nature of our survey. For over thirty years we have elicited enrollment data on less commonly taught languages by requesting information about "other languages" rather than listing them individually on the survey form. Through the 1998 survey, ASL was in this category, but with the enrollments reported in that survey it joined the list of the more commonly taught languages, then numbering fifteen. As a result, in 2002 ASL was among the fifteen languages about which we explicitly requested information. Many institutions that had not reported their existing ASL programs in 1998 did so in this survey. If these institutions had previously reported their existing ASL enrollments, the remarkable growth in ASL in the current survey might have been more evenly spread out

across the three surveys from the 1990s. But it is also notable that 187 new programs were created between 1998 and 2002 to meet growing demand.[11]

There are several things I find interesting in this explanation for the skyrocketing percentages in ASL enrollments between 1998 and 2002. First, it is almost as if institutions are being scolded for not reporting their ASL enrollments and for somehow creating a false sense of "remarkable growth." Shame on us for hiding our ASL programs! But we might look at the explanation another way—in 1998 the re-placement of ASL in the MLA bibliography was only just under way. How, then, would one report and register a language not yet even sanctioned as a language by the very authorities conducting the survey? (I think here of the way that the 2000 U.S. census finally allowed citizens to check more than one identity box—and people did so in astonishing numbers.)

Why, then, was there no mention in this report of the exclusion of ASL as a recognized "body" within the politics of the ADFL and the MLA in the years before 1998? Why is there not a more careful and thorough attempt to explain the growth in a language that enrolled students in numbers somewhere between Ancient Greek and Biblical Hebrew in 1998 but then rose 432 percent in its numbers to take fifth place behind Spanish, French, German, and Italian (all languages that did not increase enrollments by more than 30 percent in those same years)? Why is this remarkable increase brushed off in a single paragraph that ends really before it even begins any real discussion or consideration, simply saying that "it is also notable that 187 new programs were created between 1998 and 2002 to meet growing demand." Notable indeed. Yet somehow even the more phenomenal weight of ASL offerings in two-year colleges—where it now places second in numbers, behind only Spanish, and has seen a 457 percent growth in the past six years—goes utterly unnoted in this report. What are we to make of these omissions?

I do not have the answers to this seemingly rhetorical question, and I realize that an organization such as the ADFL may not often focus exclusively on one language. I do not intend to point fingers only at the ADFL or MLA but, in fact, to beckon us all to the table to discuss this together. That is, I believe that the question of ASL's clear presence in current college language offerings but its absence in overall discussions about language (and culture) learning within higher education is a question that we—meaning not only academic organizations such as the MLA and the ADFL but also scholars of Deaf Studies and ASL (and organizations such as the ASLTA)—ought to be taking up. And taking up together.

Pointing: Toward Politics, Power, and Philosophy

Let me first turn back to my title, "ASL: The Little Language That Could," and gesture toward at least some of the important and interesting things we can learn through the study and use of ASL, and contact with it. I want to point to what I hope is a significant amount of promise and potential for the future of ASL in universities like my own, and then take us back to what I believe are some of the biggest challenges and potential crises we still have ahead of us for ASL instruction in higher education.

First, the potential. The unique nature of ASL—its performance and passage as a nonprint, nonwritten, visual, and embodied language—is, of course, one of the most significant things that students of the language learn about, through, and with ASL. Consider, for example, the role of new technologies in relation to ASL. What happens to a language like ASL in the wake of digital and video technologies that can now enable sign language literature to be "published" and shared across distance, time, and space? These are the kinds of questions students, and future scholars and teachers of ASL, can explore about the little language that could. At my own university, for example, we had some of our ASL students consider these very questions as they participated in a project funded by Battelle Foundation awards for "technology and human affairs."[12]

"The ASL Literature and Digital Media Project," further funded by a local central Ohio organization called the DEAFund, involved three groups of people: local, national, and international sign language storytellers and poets; a troupe of digital media people, including students learning about digital media technologies alongside people using these technologies as part of their daily work in various studios around our large campus; and students in contact with ASL from at least three groups: deaf and hard-of-hearing students in central Ohio, grades 9–12, participating in CHIPS, the Columbus Hearing Impaired Program; students in grades 7–12 at the Ohio School for the Deaf in Columbus; and college students (mostly hearing) enrolled in ASL courses at Ohio State. These three groups met for three primary events over the course of two days in May 2005: a three-hour dialogue between scholars and critics who had written about ASL literature and some of the ASL authors/performers who created that literature; a public evening performance of ASL literature; and all-day workshops where participants learned some of the fundamentals and techniques for creating their own ASL literature. All of these events were recorded with multiple video cameras (in order to capture the language itself in more of its 3-D dimensions), and then the summer of 2005 was spent editing and creating a master DVD of the three events for further public distribution.[13]

To date, ASL poetry and storytelling exists in some degree and quantity on videotape and DVD/CD-ROM. But the movement of ASL literature into the digital realm—on-line and thus potentially shared globally and for free anywhere a person can get to a networked computer—is a fairly new phenomenon. And the potential is vast for the further development of sign language literatures.

Yet we also still have some advancement to do in the teaching and learning of ASL. And while I am buoyed by the potential of endeavors and events like the ASL Digital Media Project, I am also admittedly a bit deflated by the daily teacher shortage we face as we ride on the crest of that 432 percent enrollment increase wave. We have a crisis already near at hand in the adequate instruction of ASL in both higher and public education: we simply do not have enough qualified teachers to meet the demand for these courses. Sometimes we have very qualified interpreters who love the language and also like the idea of teaching ASL; sometimes we have native signers from the deaf community who have taught community service courses in ASL; and sometimes we actually do have a few truly skilled and qualified language instructors. But it is not easy at this point in the history of ASL instruction, particularly at the college level, to find someone who knows the language well; who knows how to teach a skills-based and skills-level language program course at the college level where a student's ability to attain skills at one level can seriously affect the student's ability to succeed at the next level; who knows what it means to teach the average college student between eighteen and twenty-two years old; who knows what it means to teach in a freshman-sophomore-level General Education required course; and who is willing to teach only part time (and with no real benefits) at our university while also trying to earn a living elsewhere.

As I keep having to remind administrator after administrator in meetings too numerous to remember, just because someone is able to "speak" and "use" the English language, or even write it, does not necessarily mean that he or she is equipped to teach those skills to young college students. The same principle applies to ASL use and to ASL instruction, specifically to college-level instruction of ASL. We simply do not yet have the programs to train the needed teachers or even to establish the qualifications we would want those teachers to have. The American Sign Language Teachers Association (ASLTA) has been working on the training, qualification, professional development, and ethical issues for ASL teachers for almost two decades now, although, by its own admission, it is still an organization largely focused on secondary (9–12) instruction of ASL.[14]

In addition to the valuable work of the ASLTA, we also need the MLA and its ADFL—and they need us. We need to work together, in affiliation, to establish teacher hiring, professional development, promotion standards for ASL teachers, and the programs that train such teachers—in a way that will allow ASL to continue as a unique language among the others so often offered at our colleges and high schools while also permitting ASL to function equally on the language-learning playing field. American Sign Language—its scholarly research, its literature, and its pedagogical theories and practices—needs a place at the ADFL executive committee table and also in the MLA delegate assembly. From our place at the MLA and ADFL tables we can watch and learn, among other things, how to negotiate for standards and employment with benefits, dignity, decent pay, and advancement for all those ASL teachers now joining the academic ranks, largely without a Ph.D. in hand and with only part-time employment.

And as we find our place at those existing tables of language power, we will also need to borrow and adapt knowledge from them to inform the ways we create our own new responses to and knowledge about issues that are important and unique to ASL. There are at least four major considerations we need to hold before us when we place ASL within the academy. First, we need to consider how a college ASL program can help provide access and equity at that institution to deaf and hard-of-hearing members in the community it serves and surrounds. Second, we need to ensure that we develop ASL responsibly—with caution and careful deliberation—in the academy so that we maintain its linguistic and cultural integrity in the face of the cash cow role it potentially plays. Third, we need to consider how an ASL program within higher education can best work to "give back" to the deaf community, finding ways to invite, involve, and invest in the skills and presence of local deaf people. Finally, we cannot ignore the fact that it surely means something for the shape and change of ASL when so many hearing students in American higher education are eager to learn it, while deaf or hard-of-hearing kids all across the country are still all too often kept away from learning ASL. These are four of the most significant issues we will need to continue to address as ASL grows in the academy. I want to end by emphasizing as strongly as I can our need to organize our political and intellectual forces to advance the promise of ASL literature and language instruction with dignity and grace, with quality and care, and with all the *could* that we can muster.

Notes

1. See the Modern Language Association's Web site at http://www.mla.org/about.
2. William C. Stokoe Jr., Dorothy C. Casterline, and Carl G. Croneberg, *A Dictionary of American Sign Language on Linguistic Principles* (Washington, D.C.: Gallaudet College Press, 1965).
3. See the American Sign Language Teachers Association's Web site at http://www.aslta.org/index.html.
4. See Christopher Krentz on the "foreign" and "familiar" nature of ASL, especially within American universities, in "Proposal for ASL to Satisfy Foreign Language Requirements," at http://artsandsciences.virginia.edu/asl/t8.html.
5. Sheryl B. Cooper, "The Academic Status of Sign Language Program in Institutions of Higher Education in the United States." Ph.D. diss., Gallaudet University, 1997.
6. Yet even though this idea might be somewhat "foreign" to many people, as someone who grew up deaf/hard-of-hearing in the years right before "mainstreaming" became a popular form of deaf education, I could (and would) just as easily argue that I, for one, would like nothing more than if every speech pathology/audiology professional, every physician in training, and every special education teacher (indeed, every teacher, "special" or not) learned some basic ASL!
7. See Ohio State University's American Sign Language Program Web site at http://asl.osu.edu/.
8. Elizabeth B. Welles, "Foreign Language Enrollments in United States

Institutions of Higher Education, Fall 2002," *ADFL Bulletin* 35, nos. 2–3 (Winter–Spring 2004): 7–26.

9. Some of the data we have collected from students who are enrolled in ASL 101 (the first-level course) over a three-year period show us that undergraduates enrolled in the ASL I class are students from the following colleges: (1) 56 percent from Arts and Sciences, including the Colleges of Arts, Biological Sciences, Humanities, Math and Physical Sciences, and Social and Behavioral Sciences; (2) 15 percent from Health, Medical, and Biological Sciences; (3) 14 percent from Journalism and Communication; (4) 3 percent from Human Ecology; (5) 3 percent from Education; (6) and 6 percent other colleges. The student survey also indicates that while 44 percent of the students enrolled in ASL 101 claim they are taking it primarily to fulfill their General Education language requirements, 56 percent of the students are taking it for other reasons and do not need it for their General Education requirements. Of those 56 percent who are taking it for reasons other than just to meet the language requirements, 39 percent claim they are taking it because of some "affinity" for the language due to an ongoing or previous personal interest in ASL and/or deaf culture; having a deaf friend/neighbor; having a deaf family member; just to learn more about deaf people and communicate with them; or because of their own current or partial deafness. In addition, 28 percent of the students taking ASL 101 say they have chosen it as an "alternative" to learning other languages because it is "interesting," "new/different," "nontraditional," or "unique," or because the student is a "visual learner."

10. Welles, "Enrollments," 8–15.

11. Ibid., 15.

12. See http://english.osu.edu/asldmp//default.htm.

13. See the American Sign Language (ASL) Literature and Digital Media Project, Ohio State University, at http://english.osu.edu/asldmp/default.htm.

14. See http://www.aslta.org/index.html.

CHAPTER 6

Teaching Foreign Languages to Students with Disabilities: *Initiatives to Educate Faculty*

RASMA LAZDA-CAZERS AND HELGA THORSON

Introduction

According to Section 504 of the Rehabilitation Act and the Americans with Disabilities Act, U.S. colleges and universities receiving public funding are legally bound to provide reasonable accommodations for students with disabilities. Foreign language faculty members at institutions of higher education across the United States are often at a loss about how to accommodate the various needs of these students—and sometimes question whether it is even possible for some students to learn a foreign language.

Are there discipline-specific issues involved when teaching a foreign language to students with disabilities? Is teaching a foreign language different from teaching a subject like biology or literature? Does the fact that students must learn to read, write, speak, and listen in a new and different language affect the classroom environment in ways that are distinct from what applies in other disciplines? To what extent do physical and learning disabilities play a role in the acquisition and learning of a foreign language? What if a student has a physical disability that makes it difficult to hear or speak? What if a student has a learning disability that interferes with comprehension or spelling?

Listening, speaking, reading, and writing are key modalities in a foreign language classroom. Since a learning disability may interfere with the study of language, instructors must be aware of how various learning disabilities may affect students' classroom performance. The National Joint Committee on Learning Disabilities has defined learning disabilities as follows:

Learning disabilities is a general term that refers to a heterogeneous group of disorders manifested by significant difficulties in the acquisition and use of listening, speaking, reading, writing, reasoning, or mathematical abilities. These disorders are intrinsic to the individual, presumed to be due to central nervous system dysfunction, and may occur across the life span. Problems in self-regulatory behaviors, social perception, and social interaction may exist with learning disabilities but do not by themselves constitute a learning disability. Although learning disabilities may occur concomitantly with other handicapping conditions (for example, sensory impairment, mental retardation, serious emotional disturbance) or with extrinsic influences (such as cultural differences, insufficient or inappropriate instruction), they are not the result of those conditions or influences.[1]

Many students are diagnosed with a learning disability as children or teenagers—either in primary or secondary school—yet countless others are not diagnosed until after they have entered college or university. Reports have shown that it is often students' inability to complete the foreign language requirement that leads to the testing and diagnosis of a learning disability. Often students with a learning disability have learned strategies to compensate for their disability in their native language but have trouble when faced with a language system that is new and abstract to them. The first accounts of students with learning disabilities in foreign language classes were anecdotal. In 1971, for example, Kenneth Dinklage, a counselor at Harvard University, described students who exhibited signs of dyslexia and were unable to meet the foreign language requirement.[2] These students, all of whom were highly intelligent individuals, could handle the rigorous academic pressures of their regular academic course load at Harvard, yet were unable to pass their foreign language courses.

How can faculty members educate themselves about both the legal and pedagogical issues of teaching foreign languages to students with disabilities—both learning disabilities and physical disabilities? Faculty handbooks may include a section on university policies, and on-campus disability service offices usually provide much-needed information—yet most of the existing materials are not specific to academic disciplines. Disability service providers on most campuses know little about the nature of foreign language learning and effective foreign language teaching pedagogy. Similarly, foreign language educators are often knowledgeable in their own field of expertise but not familiar with the complex issues involved in teaching students with disabilities. It is therefore important that foreign language faculty and disability service providers work closely together and educate each other about strategies for the effective inclusion of students with disabilities. As a result of the 1990 Americans with Disabilities Act (ADA), more and more students with disabilities are entering colleges and universities. The need to educate faculty becomes even more urgent when considering that in large universities most of the beginning language courses are taught by teaching assistants who are in the process of learning how to teach. They not only rely on the information provided by the language faculty but also constitute the next generation of secondary and postsecondary teachers.

Language instructors may ask: To what extent do students' first-language ability and foreign language aptitude affect their success in foreign language learning, and to what extent do teaching methodologies, in-class accommodations, and program goals and curriculum play a role in that success? Is it possible, given the right methodological approach, that learning a new language—with its unique phonological, morphological, syntactic, and semantic features—may actually lead to improvements in the native language coding and decoding abilities of all learners? Have the chances of success increased or decreased with the move toward proficiency and a standards-based curriculum? What is the best way to accommodate and teach students with learning disabilities in the foreign language classroom in the twenty-first century?

In this chapter we discuss issues involved in accommodating and teaching students with learning disabilities in the foreign language classroom. We address four questions that may help faculty to make decisions about departmental priorities, mission, curricular goals, and teaching methodologies that would address the needs and challenges of today's increasingly diverse student body:

1. Is there a unique foreign language learning disability?
2. In what ways is the teaching of a foreign language to students with disabilities different from teaching other academic disciplines in a student's first language?
3. What is meant by "reasonable accommodations" in terms of teaching foreign languages and cultures to students with learning disabilities?

4. Are there specific teaching methodologies or techniques that facilitate the foreign language learning process of students who have
a learning disability?

In order to address issues that are unique to foreign language learning, we also discuss campus initiatives that attempt to educate foreign language faculty about teaching students with disabilities.

Is There a Unique Foreign Language Learning Disability?

Over the past several decades there has been an ongoing debate
on many American college and university campuses as to whether
it is even possible for some students to learn a foreign language.
Are students who consistently fail foreign language courses merely
underachievers, or do they possess an innate cognitive deficit that
makes it extremely difficult for them to process the complexities of
foreign language learning? In other words, do affective and social
factors (e.g., classroom atmosphere, student anxiety levels, motivation, the use of effective language learning strategies, and so forth)
play a decisive role in a student's ability to learn a foreign language,
or are there individual cognitive or genetic factors that determine
whether a student can or cannot learn a foreign language? Do some
students possess a natural ability to learn a foreign language with
ease while others do not?

Much research has been conducted on the issue of foreign language anxiety. Just as there is a well-documented "math anxiety,"
many foreign language students have said that they experience great
anxiety when learning a foreign language. In fact, Elaine Horwitz
claims that approximately "one third of American college learners
have been found consistently to have moderate to severe levels of
foreign language anxiety."[3] Other researchers have maintained that
anxiety may not be the cause of foreign language learning problems
but rather be the result of some deeper underlying factor. The actual
cause of foreign language learning difficulties, they suggest, may
stem from students' difficulties in their first-language abilities.[4] According to Richard Sparks, Leonore Ganschow, and their coauthors,
students who struggle to learn a second language have been shown to
have native language difficulties—particularly in the areas of phonological and syntactic coding—and this weakness in language ability,
in turn, may create foreign language anxiety.

These authors have developed the Linguistic Coding Differences Hypothesis to explain the connections between native language and foreign language learning.[5] This hypothesis suggests that "(1) language learning occurs along a continuum from very strong to very weak performance in a FL [foreign language]; and (2) some learners have stronger skills in the components of language (i.e., phonological/orthographic, syntactic, semantic) than do other learners."[6] The studies of Sparks, Ganschow, et al. compare the native language skills, foreign language aptitude, and foreign language proficiency of students diagnosed as having a learning disability with high-risk and low-risk foreign language learners who do not have learning disabilities. Students who experience difficulty learning a foreign language (both students with and students without a learning disability) have significantly weaker native language skills, lower foreign language aptitude scores on the Modern Language Aptitude Test, and lower levels of written and oral foreign language proficiency after two years of foreign language study than do students identified as highly successful language learners.[7]

As to whether there is a unique language learning disability, the answer is by no means simple and straightforward. While both students with and students without a learning disability can struggle in foreign language classes, there is no statistical difference between them in native language skills, foreign language aptitude, and foreign language proficiency.[8] Viewing language learning as a continuum— with poor language learners at one end and successful language learners at the other end—can be useful because it highlights the fact that not all poor language learners have learning disabilities and not all students with learning disabilities manifest their disability in the same way when learning a foreign language. However, viewing language learning as a continuum bears the danger of automatically grouping students with learning disabilities into the lower end of this continuum.

Is it possible for students with learning disabilities to succeed in the study of a foreign language? Although many students with learning disabilities do indeed perform at the lower end of the language learning continuum, there is ample evidence that students with learning and other cognitive disabilities do succeed in learning a foreign language. For example, Ann Sax Mabbott has provided case studies of several research subjects who were thought to have a learning disability but became successful language learners and, in a few instances, even foreign language teachers.[9] Similarly, testimony from language teachers also dispels the myth that individuals with learning and other cognitive disabilities cannot learn a foreign language.[10]

What can we learn from the cognitive sciences about the origin and processing of language? How are language and the complex workings of the mind connected? The publication of Noam Chomsky's *Syntactic Structures* in 1957 had an immense impact on the way we think about language and the human mind.[11] Chomsky claims that a Universal Grammar underlies all utterances, and that children need no formal instruction for mastering the complexity of the vast amount of syntactic patterns of speech. The existence of a Universal Grammar leads to the conclusion that language must be innate and not shaped by evolution. However, if a child is not exposed to language in the critical period for language acquisition during childhood, the child will never learn how to speak grammatically correctly. An example of the inability to acquire full language beyond this critical phase is the documented case of the modern "wild child" Genie, who grew up without language until she was thirteen. Genie had intensive language instruction for years afterward and later learned how to speak, but she never mastered the syntax of English, even though her IQ was in the normal range.[12] The same observations have been made in similar cases. The discussion on the origin of language gained popularity during the 1990s through the publication of Steven Pinker's *Language Instinct*.[13] Building on Chomsky, Pinker argues for the innateness of a language faculty, the existence of a language instinct that recedes around the time of the onset of puberty. Pinker also refers to the importance of human interaction in the "here and now" for a child learning to speak. Meaningful communication with the child is essential.[14]

Cognitive sciences have brought researchers from various disciplines together in order to begin to map out the inner workings of the human brain. With advances in the neurosciences, we might at some point be able to pinpoint exactly how, when, and where language works in the brain. The collaboration of researchers from different disciplines and seemingly opposing points of departure has led to new explorations of how language works. An example is the collaborative work of the theoretical neurophysiologist William H. Calvin and the linguist Derek Bickerton, an expert in protolanguages. These researchers cowrote a book in which they attempted to reconcile

Darwin and Chomsky. Their close analysis and combination of what at first appear to be seemingly opposing positions has led to a new understanding of the emergence of language. Calvin and Bickerton were looking for invention following Darwinian conversions of function, rather than simple step-by-step linear and gradual improvements. They analyzed the transition from simple word association as a protolanguage to longer and thus more structured sentences requiring syntax. The emergence of a complex syntax over millions of years may thus be supported from both ends of the nurture/nature debate. Calvin and Bickerton explain that their collaboration is "an attempt to bring peace to a conflict" and to show that both approaches are "fully reconcilable," while underscoring that science is not a "coldly objective, squeaky clean process."[15]

Advances in the cognitive sciences confirm that every human being can learn a language, whether it be native or foreign. The only condition concerns age: the exposure to language must happen early in life. This does not mean that it is impossible to master a foreign language beyond that window of opportunity. If a child has mastered the syntax of a first/native language, all languages can be learned, even if entirely different from the native language. A child can also master more than one language at a time, the true definition of bilingualism. However, after the onset of puberty, language learning requires more effort.

It is not yet possible to say conclusively whether a unique "foreign language disability" exists. Ongoing research in the cognitive sciences shows the complexity of language itself. Furthermore, as Elena Grigorenko has pointed out, languages differ in many ways. Difficulties in learning a language may vary depending on the language learned—learning Spanish, for example, may involve quite different processes from learning Russian, English, or Chinese—on the level of proficiency a learner wants to achieve, and on the learner's own native language. In addition, students with learning disabilities are a heterogeneous group. While some may have difficulties with phonology, others struggle with morphology or syntax. Some may have difficulties with visual memory, others with verbal memory, short-term memory, or long-term memory.[16] Until we gain more knowledge from brain research, we need to draw conclusions based on observations stemming from both quantitative and qualitative research. In any event, one cannot discount the effects of first-language ability as well as affective and social factors inherent in foreign language classroom learning. Both play a key role in the ease with which a student studies a foreign language.

In What Ways Is Teaching a Foreign Language to Students with Disabilities Different from Teaching Them Other Academic Disciplines in Their First Language?

Because foreign language learning involves both a concerted focus on various language modalities—listening, reading, speaking, and writing—and an attempt to build fluency in a language that is relatively new to students, the subject matter of a foreign language is inherently different from the subject matter of most other academic disciplines. Language teaching methodologies also differ from those of other disciplines, in that they provide students with opportunities to use the foreign language in various contexts and to practice communicating about a wide range of topics. Further, languages introduce students to different language functions (asking questions, narrating, hypothesizing) and text genres (from lists to extended discourse). Finally, language teaching strives to build both fluency and accuracy, and to recognize culturally appropriate responses. Whereas other disciplines may focus on one instructional format (lecture, individual or group lab activities, class discussion), foreign language instructors often employ a multitude of approaches and formats in order to meet their curricular goals.

It is also important to note that foreign language courses today are quite different from courses of fifty, thirty, or even ten years ago. When many people think of foreign language learning, they think of conjugating verbs, memorizing vocabulary, and learning rules of grammar and pronunciation. This might still hold true for students studying languages that are no longer spoken, like Latin and classical Greek. However, most foreign language professionals today are convinced that language learning involves much more than dealing with the intricacies of a linguistic system. Proficiency also involves gaining cross-cultural awareness and understanding, developing communication and learning strategies, improving critical thinking skills, and learning ways to connect with target cultures within the community by traveling or by exploring the Internet. In fact, the *Standards for Foreign Language Learning in the 21st Century,* published in 1999, help define performance standards for what have become known as the "five Cs" of language learning: communication, cultures, connections, comparisons, and communities. The *Standards* imply that students should not only learn to communicate in a foreign language but also gain knowledge and understanding of other cultures, connect with other academic disciplines as they acquire information, develop insight into the nature of language and culture through comparisons, and participate in multilingual communities at home and around the world.[17]

Given the differences in foreign language learning as compared to other academic disciplines, along with current changes within the field itself, it is clear that foreign language faculty members face a unique set of issues related to disability. Given the importance of all four language modalities, how should foreign language departments accommodate a student whose disability severely impedes speaking, listening, reading, or writing? For example, how should foreign language departments teach and assess students who are deaf, blind, or have a speech impairment? For the most part, foreign language departments have clearly defined curricular goals and objectives that outline the extent to which students must demonstrate proficiency. When working with students with disabilities, however, it becomes clear that what foreign language professionals usually refer to as four distinct modalities become blurred. If a deaf student is watching a closed-captioned DVD or video, for example, is that a listening activity or a reading activity? If a student has a speech impairment that makes it difficult to be understood and types the appropriate responses in an oral interview, would that be a speaking activity or a writing activity? Moreover, issues of accommodation are often more complex in foreign language classes than in classes conducted in English, because tutors, notetakers, and interpreters must possess a certain degree of fluency in the foreign language. Finally, DVDs, videos, films, and software devices must be captioned or programmed in the foreign language.

The need for modifying one's teaching practices to accommodate a student with a physical disability appears self-evident. One would provide without question an accessible workstation for a student in a wheelchair. Less is understood about provisions for learning or other cognitive disabilities. Misinformation and stereotypes prevail because these disabilities are less noticeable and often invisible. A good example is the debate that surrounded the 1996 lawsuit against Boston University by several students who had previously been diagnosed with a learning disability. The president of Boston University at that time publicly referred to students with learning disabilities as "draft dodgers" who could overcome possible academic difficulties "with concentrated effort" but instead chose to take advantage of the disability rights movement in order to avoid difficult courses. The judge in the case concluded that comments referring to students with learning disabilities as "lazy" or "fakers" definitely "reflect misinformed stereotypes."[18]

The prejudice and ignorance inherent in this example ring clear, yet identifying an appropriate pedagogical response to a learning disability is difficult for a variety of reasons. Faculty may have students in the class who have a learning disability that has never been diagnosed—either because the disability is not severe or because the student has learned coping strategies that seem to compensate for the disability in the native language. What should foreign language instructors do if they notice that a student has difficulty spelling in the foreign language or exhibits other signs of a learning disability? Should they advise the student to get tested for a disability? When talking to the student, instructors need to be careful not to use any labels in advance and should rather point out specific observations regarding the performance of the student. The instructor should make suggestions for improving the student's study habits and refer her or him to the on-campus disability services office if problems continue. First talking to the student in a private meeting instead of immediately referring the student to disability service providers may mitigate self-stigmatization, that is to say, students' internalized feelings of inadequacy. The Office of Faculty Resources for Disability at Emory University, for example, favors such an approach.[19] It is a good idea for foreign language faculty to consult with the disability service providers on their campus to discuss whether intervention is appropriate.

What Is Meant by a "Reasonable Accommodation" in Terms of Teaching Foreign Languages and Cultures to Students with Learning Disabilities?

Colleges and universities in the United States receiving public funding are legally bound to provide reasonable accommodation to students classified as learning disabled. Typical accommodations include using alternative assessment techniques, allowing the students extra time during a test, tolerating poor spelling and/or pronunciation, allowing the use of a spell checker for written work, providing supplemental tutoring, offering modified classes for students with learning disabilities, providing course substitutions, or waiving the foreign language requirement altogether for these students. Do foreign language departments have to provide all of these accommodations, or can they choose which ones they deem to be most reasonable and appropriate? This debate was the focus of the lawsuit at Boston University that centered on how a university with a foreign language requirement should accommodate students with learning disabilities. We will discuss the implications of this lawsuit for foreign language departments and provide examples of what some universities are doing to provide reasonable accommodation to eligible students.

As mentioned above, several students diagnosed as having a learning disability filed a lawsuit against Boston University in 1996, after the president of the university had mandated a new policy that would no longer allow course substitutions for the foreign language requirement. The judge in the case ruled that although a course substitution can be seen as a reasonable accommodation, it is not the only possible accommodation. The laws, as mandated by the ADA and the Rehabilitation Act, do not "require a university to provide course Substitutions [*sic*] that the university rationally concludes would alter an essential part of its academic program."[20] The judge further ruled that the university must provide a procedure for determining whether foreign language course substitutions would greatly change the nature of its liberal arts program. After undertaking a "deliberative procedure" that supported the case that foreign language learning is an essential part of students' educational experience at Boston University, the judge ruled that the university did not violate the law by refusing to provide course substitutions.

Two of the expert witnesses in the case have conducted extensive research on students with learning disabilities in the foreign language classroom. Robert Shaw, associate dean and Learning Disabilities administrator at Brown University, served as an expert witness for the plaintiffs, and Richard Sparks, associate professor in the Department of Education at the College of Mount St. Joseph in Cincinnati, Ohio, was a witness for the defendants. In a later interview, both shed light on the debate over the appropriate response for postsecondary institutions at which foreign language learning is deemed a necessary part of the undergraduate curriculum:

Shaw: There are many sound educational reasons why FL instruc-
            tion should be part of a student's education, and students
            should not be deprived of these benefits simply because
            they have a learning disability. However, I believe, based
            on fifteen years of experience, that a small number of stu-
            dents cannot learn a FL in a university classroom environ-
            ment, even with extraordinary assistance. These students
            should be allowed to substitute related courses for the
            school's FL requirement. . . . The diversity of curricula
            among colleges and universities in the United States dem-
            onstrates that there are many ways to achieve the goals of
            a liberal education; allowing a small number of students
            with severe FL learning difficulties to meet these goals in
            courses other than a foreign language simply makes good
            educational sense.[21]

Sparks: In several of our articles, we have recommended that the
            LD label not be used as the *sine qua non* for receiving a
            course substitution for or waiver from the FL requirement.
            We also have suggested that grades of W [withdraw] are not
            synonymous with course failure. These research findings
            suggest that the university has two empirically defensible
            positions it could adopt regarding course substitutions for
            and waivers from the FL requirement: either all students
            experiencing FL learning problems are eligible for course
            substitutions and waivers or no student experiencing FL
            learning problems should be eligible for course substitu-
            tions and waivers.[22]

Both expert witnesses maintain that it is essential for each university to develop clear policies regarding procedures for accommodating students with learning disabilities, especially whether these
students should be allowed course substitutions or waivers. Both
also agree that a diagnosis of a learning disability does not necessarily suggest that a student automatically requires accommodation in order to learn a foreign language. According to Shaw, for
example, "The documentation should present evidence of specific
language-processing disabilities that impair performance in a language class."[23] Where the two scholars differ, however, is in their
definition of reasonable accommodation. Shaw maintains that there
is a small number of students with severe learning disabilities who
simply cannot pass a foreign language class and therefore should be
allowed a course substitution or waiver, whereas Sparks maintains

that because the classification of students with learning disabilities is inconsistent and often fraught with error, and because his research findings have suggested that there are no statistical differences in the performance of students diagnosed with learning disabilities and that of other "at-risk"[24] students not found to have a learning disability, there should be a clear policy pertaining to course substitutions and waivers that is available to all students.

It is therefore crucial for foreign language departments to work closely with the disability services office on their campus in order to come up with clear policies regarding how students suspected of having a learning disability are to be evaluated and diagnosed; if and what kind of courses are offered for students with a learning disability; and the extent to which course substitutions and waivers are granted. At most colleges and universities, students suspected of having a learning disability are interviewed and referred to a testing specialist. Some provide in-house testing by a psychologist or educational consultant who follows the appropriate guidelines for documentation of a learning disability as stated by the Association on Higher Education and Disability.[25]

Disability service offices at colleges and universities across the United States vary in their requests for documentation of a learning disability. For this chapter we conducted a brief review of Web sites for disability support services in colleges and universities, ranging from public to private and large to small. The Web pages we analyzed were among the most updated ones, and thus we believe the information can be deemed reliable. We found that in the wake of the 1996 Boston University lawsuit many colleges and universities now specify the documentation that the institution deems adequate and necessary before registering a student for disability services and thus granting access to accommodations. The following specifications are typical:

1. Documentation must include a diagnosis of a learning disability by a qualified expert in the field. Colleges and universities vary in their qualifications for an "expert." Some require a minimum number of years of experience, whereas others call for the highest degree in the field.[26]

2. The testing must be up to date, most commonly not older than three years.

3. Documentation must list the tests used as the basis for the diagnosis.

4. More than one test battery is required. Many institutions list the required test batteries they accept and/or require.

5. Institutions differentiate between LD and ADHD/ADD as a specific subgroup and accordingly differ in their requirements for diagnosis.

6. Disability service offices reserve the right to review the documentation and make appropriate suggestions for accommodation based on the documentation provided.

Typically, the diagnostician carries out a complete intellectual assessment as well as academic achievement tests, among other tests. One way to reach a diagnosis is to evaluate the discrepancy between the individual's standardized intelligence test (IQ test) and academic achievement test scores. The exact measure of the discrepancy, however, may vary from state to state and even from one school district to another. For example, the measure of discrepancy between a student's performance on an IQ test and on standardized academic achievement tests is two standard deviations in Ohio, 1.75 in Arkansas, 1.5 in Kentucky, and 1.25 in Indiana.[27]

The following practices are the most common ways in which postsecondary institutions reasonably accommodate the needs of their students with regard to language requirements and/or advanced foreign language study:

1. Some institutions specifically request a diagnosis of a language-related learning disability.

2. Whereas some colleges and universities see course substitutions as a last resort, and do not mention this possibility explicitly, others offer a list of courses pertaining to another culture that may substitute for the foreign language requirement.

3. Course substitution hours must be equivalent to those for fulfilling the foreign language requirement.

4. Most popular among courses listed for a possible substitution are literature in translation courses and culture courses, such as "Roman Civilization," "Russian History," "Religions of East Asia," and the like.

5. Request for foreign language substitution often requires a petition addressed to the dean of the college.

6. Many institutions allow for course substitutions only after a student has made a serious effort to pass a standard foreign language class, and the institutions will ask for feedback from the instructor.

An assigned grade of "W" (withdraw) does not attest to a serious effort by the student.

7. A smaller number of institutions offer modified courses where either the same material is covered at a slower pace, or the foreign language is taught not communicatively but rather with a focus on phonology and structure. Most common are slower-paced Latin classes without the speaking and listening components. Waivers for a foreign language requirement have become the exception.[28]

As more and more students with learning disabilities enter colleges and universities, some institutions have started offering modified foreign language classes.[29] The University of Colorado at Boulder has a Foreign Language Modification Program for students with a learning disability and a recorded history of language learning difficulty. Other students may also be admitted to the program based on a history of failure in foreign language classes despite recognized effort. These "at-risk" students must take a number of standardized tests in order to verify their eligibility and then may enroll in the program after being advised and admitted by the disability services office. The languages offered within this program are Latin, Spanish, and Italian, and a disability service provider works closely with master teachers who teach in this program. Foreign language faculty at the university are aware of this special program, and they may advise students suspected of having an undocumented learning disability or those perceived as "at risk" to seek the assistance of the disability services office in order to be admitted to the program.[30] The size of the classes themselves is limited to fifteen students.

Such modified classes might be a good idea, but they also raise some questions that institutions contemplating such an option need to consider. Who can take the modified classes—only students with a learning disability or also others who have tried a standard class but find it too difficult? Given the fact that research indicates there is no statistical difference between students with a learning disability and those "at risk" in terms of success in foreign language courses, then should not all "at-risk" students have the right to attend such a class? The University of Colorado at Boulder has decided to open its modified classes to this group of students as well.

The main challenge in implementing a modified foreign language track is funding. Modified classes are usually smaller than regular classes, and they can be set up to cover the same amount of material at a slower pace: for example, the material of two semesters may be covered in three semesters. This requires hiring extra instructors or providing extra compensation. A second major issue is that students may only have a limited choice of languages offered in a modified format, most likely Latin and/or Spanish. Is it fair to offer the student who wishes to take French or German only the choice of a modified Spanish class? One could argue that not all colleges are able to offer all world languages, anyway. If a student wishes to study Swedish but the college does not offer Swedish, the student must take a different language. In the modified track, the student must choose either language or format. What about the business student who wants to work for an international company and needs French? What about the major in chemistry who has been advised that German is the most important language because most of the research in chemistry has been published in German? The ADA requires only "reasonable accommodation." Nevertheless, the question remains: Do such students have an unfair disadvantage?

Language departments find themselves increasingly caught between possible legal ramifications and educational considerations. It is up to the legal counsel at each institution to interpret the legal framework and advise its faculty accordingly. In turn, faculty must pursue the ideal educational setting for all students and ensure that educational goals and objectives are being met.

A third issue with regard to modified classes concerns mainstreaming. Does it really benefit students at the lower end of the language learning continuum to attend class only with other such students? Would they not benefit from working together with more "successful" language learners? And if these "at-risk" students do benefit from modified classes, would all students benefit from them? It is essential to consider what makes a modified class a better course.

Are There Specific Teaching Methodologies or Techniques That Help Facilitate the Foreign Language Learning Process of Students Who Have a Learning Disability?

More research needs to be conducted on teaching methodologies that best aid the language learning process. One method that Sparks, Ganschow, and their colleagues maintain positively affects the language learning process is Multisensory Structured Language (some-times referred to as the Orton-Gillingham method), which was first developed for native language learning problems. This approach demands the explicit teaching of phonology, orthography, and gram-mar in a highly structured fashion. Students learn to read, hear, and write the various sounds and symbols of a language in a step-by-step manner. In several studies, Sparks, Ganschow, et al. claim that significant gains were made by groups of "at-risk" high school students who learned Spanish through Multisensory Structured Lan-guage conducted in both English and Spanish. Their progress was compared to that of groups who learned Spanish using the same ap-proach and were taught solely in Spanish, as well as to the progress of groups who learned Spanish using a more traditional approach. Their research findings suggest that "at-risk" students who were taught using Multisensory Structured Language in both Spanish and English made gains in their native language skills, foreign language aptitude, and levels of oral and written foreign language proficiency after both one and two years of language study. Their gains were on par with those of their peers not deemed "at risk."[31]

These research findings, however, should be interpreted with cau-tion. First, this method has only been tested against groups learning through traditional, textbook-based instruction—a one-size-fits-all approach to a diverse community of learners. Second, language learning in these studies is narrowly defined as an analytical sys-tem that depends upon coding and decoding sounds and symbols. Furthermore, study of this system is limited to a focus on phonology and syntax, which ignores sociolinguistic aspects of communication, cultural components of language learning, classroom dynamics, and the ever-changing personal relationships that one has to one's own language and culture. As Peter McIntyre writes, "Language learning is more than acquiring the technical skill necessary to encode and reproduce sounds. It is the act of learning a new communication system, of opening doors to new experiences through travel and interaction with other groups of people. It is the act of inheriting someone else's language and culture with the corresponding threats to one's ethnic identity and self-concept."[32]

McIntyre's view predominates in today's *Standards*-driven cur-riculum. Foreign language learning in the twenty-first century is not so much about learning the rules of language as it is an exciting avenue to find out more about the world as well as one's own position in the world. We do not deny that learning grammar rules is integral to the study of world languages. However, we believe grammar is just one of many tools needed to communicate effectively in a foreign language and interact with target cultures.

The Multisensory Structured Language approach includes many elements that benefit all students regardless of whether they have a disability.[33] The multisensory nature of the method allows students to come into contact with the language visually, aurally, orally, tactually, and kinesthetically so that students with various learning styles can fully benefit. For a student with a physical or cognitive disability, a multisensory method is often the key to success. Another positive aspect of Multisensory Structured Language is that it lends itself to comparisons between the foreign and the native language. Students frequently comment that learning a foreign language has actually helped them better understand their native language. In fact, the structure of a foreign language invites comparisons—one of the "five Cs" associated with the standards movement and an important element of language study. It is, however, only one subset of one of the "five Cs" that the foreign language profession considers essential to foreign language study today and, therefore, should not be the sole focus of the course curriculum.

In her interviews with five successful students with perceived learning disabilities, Ann Sax Mabbott discovered that many of them achieved their high level of proficiency in foreign language in an immersion setting rather than in a traditional classroom setting.[34] Mabbott stresses that foreign language instructors need to focus on Krashen's distinction between learning versus acquisition when dealing with students with a learning disability. Second-language acquisition theory distinguishes in general between language acquisition as a more natural and less conscious act of acquiring versus language learning as more conscious learning of rules. Applied to the teaching of a world language, language acquisition theory will attempt to teach the language in a meaningful and communicative classroom environment. Mabbott writes: "Students who may have trouble with language learning (that is, learning the rules about language) or with reading may be able to acquire a second language orally if it is presented in a context that allows ample negotiated interaction. It is often the requirement to display 'learning,' as Krashen defines it, which presents obstacles for such students."[35] Mabbott maintains that it is primarily the way foreign languages are taught and tested in the classroom that leads to difficulties for many students with learning disabilities. She calls for the creation of contexts that are meaningful to students, the implementation of alternative assessment techniques, and increased opportunities for students to study abroad in immersion settings.

Although many textbooks as well as foreign language professionals adhere to communicative foreign language teaching in theory, the actual teaching in the classroom might not be classified as such. An article by Sharon DiFino and Linda Lombardino on learning disabilities in a foreign language classroom serves to illustrate this observation. When discussing the greatest difficulties encountered by students in foreign language classes, DiFino and Lombardino list memorization (memorizing gender, retaining meanings of nouns, remembering grammar rules), anxiety (fear of making mistakes, high affective filters), and lexical and grammatical confusion.[36] Their list implies that the main focus of foreign language courses lies in the *analysis*, rather than the *use* of language. Their own focus is clearly on the memorization of grammar rules and vocabulary lists in order to demonstrate language proficiency.[37] Once foreign language educators shift the focus from a grammar-driven curriculum to one that stresses language acquisition in a meaningful context—a curriculum that combines communication and cross-cultural exploration—instructors might find that students are motivated to communicate and interact with the target culture(s) while at the same time improving their language proficiency.

In addition to course content and methodology, many factors converge in every language class that can affect the learning process. According to Eve Leons and Christina Herbert, world language teachers at Landmark College in Putney, Vermont, an institution designed specifically for students with learning disabilities, the structure of every element of the course curriculum, daily activities, classroom management, materials management, materials design, and assessment will affect whether a student with a learning disability will be able to interact effectively with the material to be mastered.[38]

A study at Landmark College, funded by a U.S. Department of Education Fund for the Improvement of Postsecondary Education grant, tracked sixty-seven students in beginning and intermediate Spanish courses, testing their oral proficiency level after the first and second semesters. Leons and Herbert report that "80 percent of the students in the program achieved the targeted level of proficiency" (novice-mid to novice-high after one semester, and novice-high to intermediate-low after a second semester), that "student enrollment doubled in Spanish courses subsequent to implementation of the program," and that all students surveyed "either disagreed or strongly disagreed with the statement 'research says LD students can't learn foreign languages.'"[39] The authors supply a list of best practices that they believe lay the groundwork for the success of the program. These practices include teaching for mastery, motivating students to use available technology, and providing time for individualized instruction and learning. The main tenet of all practices mentioned is Universal Design—using practices and materials that will benefit all students in the classroom. The authors conclude that many of the students in their classes "developed entirely new meta-linguistic understanding" that had a positive impact on their first language; others "developed cross-cultural interests and traveled to Spanish-speaking countries as a direct result of their studies"; and many of the students "experienced a tremendous boost to their confidence when they were able to be successful at something . . . [at which] they had been told they would never be successful."[40]

Foreign language learning opens new doors and opportunities for all students. Students with learning disabilities can become successful language learners given the right learning atmosphere and conditions. We should take advantage of the ongoing research in the cognitive sciences and lobby for foreign language instruction at a much earlier age. All students, regardless of whether they have been diagnosed as having a learning disability, should be encouraged to pursue foreign language study. High schools that waive a language requirement for students "at risk" or with a learning disability put these students at a disadvantage compared to other students. Not only are these students deprived of an integral part of their education, they also face the possibility of having to take a foreign language at the university level with no previous exposure or experience. Instead of defaulting to a policy of waivers at the high school level (or even earlier), administrators, teachers, and parents should advocate the implementation of effective and successful teaching methods and techniques.[41]

Models to Educate Foreign Language Faculty

In recent years, foreign language faculty have worked closely with their campus disability support service providers to formulate guidelines for teaching foreign languages to students with disabilities. We highlight the following three examples to demonstrate differing motivations, processes, and outcomes of endeavors to do so.

The first is at Baylor University, where, in light of the 1996 Boston University lawsuit, the director of the Office of Access and Learning Accommodation approached the Department of Modern Foreign Languages to collaborate in the decision-making process regarding accommodations for students with learning disabilities. A committee was formed comprising one member from each of the foreign languages, the associate dean of the College of Arts and Sciences, and the director of the Office of Access and Learning Accommodation. The committee undertook an extensive review of literature, including pertinent legal precedents and general as well as discipline-specific research about learning disabilities, and case studies of methodologies that have proven successful in enabling students to learn a foreign language. As a result of their research, the committee members were unanimous in their recommendation to reverse the Baylor precedent of granting course waivers as standard practice; course waivers are now a rare exception. When a waiver is granted, the dean of Arts and Sciences, the director of the Office of Access and Learning Accommodation, and the Modern Foreign Language Committee develop an individual education plan. The committee also examined the place of foreign languages within the Baylor curriculum and developed a rationale for their importance in undergraduate education at Baylor. This rationale prompted the foreign language faculty to collaborate in drafting a mission statement for the Department of Modern Languages, a process that has renewed its sense of purpose and prompted an examination of objectives and methodology.[42] Moreover, this process guarantees the individual rights of a student with a learning disability while at the same time respecting the academic standards established by the university.

A second initiative, Project PACE (Postsecondary Academic Curriculum Excellence), at the University of Arkansas at Little Rock, is funded by a U.S. Department of Education grant. PACE is a campus-wide faculty and staff development program designed to ensure that students with disabilities have access to the full spectrum of educational opportunities. The foundation of this initiative is the Faculty Resource Council on Disability, which includes members from each academic discipline. Representatives from the Division of International and Second Language Studies created a *DISLS Faculty Handbook for Teaching Students with Disabilities*. The *Handbook*, distributed to DISLS faculty members in 2002, provides strategies for engaging disabled students in meaningful ways and describes pedagogical practices that benefit all students. The *Handbook* also addresses physical accommodations (classroom space, the layout of the Language Resources Center), accessible course materials, and information about adaptive equipment, computer technologies available on campus, and Web accessibility.[43] Finally, DISLS produced a brochure, "A Guide to Foreign Language Learning at UALR," to be distributed to all students.

Landmark College offers a third model for facilitating the learning of students with disabilities. Founded in 1983, the college is one of only a handful of institutions in the United States whose unique mission is to serve students with disabilities (primarily learning disabilities). Faculty members from various disciplines at Landmark—including the visual arts, psychology, literature, communication, mathematics, and history—contributed to discussions of how best to address the needs of students with learning disabilities. The publication that resulted from these discussions, *Teaching in the Disciplines*, is the first to address inclusive teaching from various disciplinary standpoints. Experienced foreign language teachers and trainers from the School for International Training's Master of Arts in Teaching program worked together with Landmark College professors to identify various "best practices" for teaching foreign languages to students with learning disabilities.

These are only a few initiatives created to foster a better understanding of issues involved in teaching students with disabilities. For a variety of reasons, colleges and universities nationwide are examining curricular objectives and methodologies with the aim of fuller inclusion. Earlier diagnosis of learning disabilities combined with the cost-driven trend to trim high school foreign language programs means that an increasing number of students may graduate from high school without exposure to a foreign language. It is crucial for faculty in foreign language departments to be informed about disability research and effective teaching methodologies. Because the students of today will be the teachers of tomorrow, it is important for today's foreign language educators to incorporate best practices, Universal Design, and methodologies that have proven to be effective for all learners.

Notes

1. National Joint Committee on Learning Disabilities, "Learning Disabilities: Issues on Definition," *Asha* 33, suppl. 5 (1991): 18–20. This committee, made up of representatives from various organizations concerned about issues related to individuals with learning disabilities, was founded in 1975 and has representatives from the following organizations: American Speech-Language-Hearing-Association (ASHA), Council for Learning Disabilities (CLD), Division for Learning Disabilities (DLD), International Reading Association (IRA), National Association of School Psychologists (NASP), Association for Higher Education and Disability (AHEAD), Division for Children's Communication Development (DCCD), International Dyslexia Association (IDA), Learning Disabilities Association of America (LDA), and National Center for Learning Disabilities (NCLD). See http://www.ldonline.org/njcld/ for more information.
2. Kenneth Dinklage, "Inability to Learn a Foreign Language," in *Emotional Problems of the Student,* ed. Graham Blaine and Charles McArthur (New York: Appleton, 1971), 185–206.
3. Elaine K. Horwitz, "It Ain't Over 'til It's Over: On Foreign Language Anxiety, First Language Deficits, and the Confounding of Variables," *Modern Language Journal* 84, no. 2 (2000): 257.
4. Tsai-Yu Chen and Goretti B. Y. Chang, "The Relationship between Foreign Language Anxiety and Learning Difficulties," *Foreign Language Annals* 37, no. 2 (2004): 284.
5. Initially Sparks, Ganschow, et al. used the term Linguistic Coding Deficit Hypothesis. Compared to their earlier version of the hypothesis that suggested that weak foreign language learners have overt language *deficits,* the authors now believe that these learners exhibit subtle *differences* when compared to successful foreign language learners. Hence the term used is now the Linguistic Coding Differences Hypothesis (LCDH).
6. Richard L. Sparks and James Javorsky, "Section 504 and the Americans with Disabilities Act: Accommodating the Learning Disabled Student in the Foreign Language Curriculum (An Update)," *Foreign Language Annals* 33, no. 6 (2000): 646.
7. See, for example, Richard L. Sparks, Leonore Ganschow, James Javorsky, Jane Pohlman, and Jon Patton, "Test Comparisons among Students Identified as High-Risk, Low-Risk, and Learning Disabled in High School Foreign Language Courses," *Modern Language Journal* 76, no. 2

(1992): 142–59; Leonore Ganschow, Richard L. Sparks, Reed Anderson, James Javorsky, Sue Skinner, and Jon Patton, "Differences in Language Performance among High-, Average-, and Low-Anxious College Foreign Language Learners," *Modern Language Journal* 78, no. 1 (1994): 41–55; and Richard L. Sparks, Marjorie Artzer, James Javorsky, Jon Patton, Leonore Ganschow, Karen Miller, and Dottie Hordubay, "Students Classified as Learning Disabled and Non-Learning Disabled: Two Comparison Studies of Native Language Skill, Foreign Language Aptitude, and Foreign Language Proficiency," *Foreign Language Annals* 31, no. 4 (1998): 535–51.

8. Sparks, Artzer, et al., "Students Classified as Learning Disabled and Non-Learning Disabled," 535–51, and Richard L. Sparks, James Javorsky, and Lois Philips, "Comparison of the Performance of College Students Classified as ADHD, LD, and LD/ADHD in Foreign Language Courses," *Language Learning* 55, no. 1 (2005): 151–77.

9. Ann Sax Mabbott, "An Exploration of Reading Comprehension, Oral Reading Errors, and Written Errors by Subjects Labeled Learning Disabled," *Foreign Language Annals* 27, no. 3 (1994): 293–324. It should be noted that not all of these students were tested for having a learning disability.

10. Examples of two such testimonies are: Charlann Simon, "Dyslexia and Learning a Foreign Language: A Personal Experience," *Annals of Dyslexia* 50 (2000): 155–87, and Ann McGlashan, "'Tell Me I'm Not Dumb!' Helping the ADD Language Learner," Conference of the American Association of Teachers of German, Salt Lake City, 24 Nov. 2002.

11. Noam Chomsky, *Syntactic Structures* (The Hague: Mouton, 1957).

12. Susan Curtiss, *Genie: A Psycholinguistic Study of a Modern-Day "Wild Child"* (New York: Academic Press, 1977).

13. Steven Pinker, *The Language Instinct* (New York: Morrow, 1994).

14. Ibid., 278.

15. William H. Calvin and Derek Bickerton, *Lingua ex Machina* (Cambridge, Mass.: MIT Press, 2000), 195.

16. Elena L. Grigorenko, "Foreign Language Acquisition and Language-Based Learning Disabilities," in *Individual Differences and Instructed Language Learning,* ed. Peter Robinson (Amsterdam: John Benjamins, 2002), 96–112.

17. *Standards for Foreign Language Learning in the 21st Century* (Lawrence, Kans.: Allen Press, 1999).

18. *Guckenberger et al. v. Trustees of Boston University et al.,* 974 F. Supp 106 (D. Mass., 1997). The full text of the *Guckenberger v. Boston University* opinion can be found at the following Web site: http://www.nacua .org/documents/Guckenberger_v_BostonU.txt.

19. "Portals and Pathways to Inclusive Instruction," Office of Faculty Re-

sources for Disabilities, Emory University, 26 April 2007, http://www.portals.emory.edu/faq/index.html.

20. *Guckenberger v. Boston University*, 1997.
21. Leonore Ganschow, Richard L. Sparks, and Robert Shaw, "The Issue of Accommodations, Waivers, and Course Substitutions for Students Who Have Difficulties Learning a Foreign Language: An Interview," *ADFL Bulletin* 32, no. 3 (2001): 61–62.
22. Ganschow et al., "Issue of Accommodation," 63.
23. Ibid., 60.
24. Although the term "at risk" is commonly applied to students who have difficulties learning a foreign language, we use the term in quotation marks in order to point out the danger of stigmatizing students through the use of such a label.
25. "AHEAD Best Practices: Disability Documentation in Higher Education," *Association on Higher Education and Disability (AHEAD)*, 26 April 2007, http://www.ahead.org/resources/bestpracticesdoc.htm.
26. In the Boston University case the judge ruled against the requirement of the university that only experts with a Ph.D. were eligible to diagnose a learning disability. However, in the case of ADHD/ADD she agreed that a Ph.D. indicates more experience and knowledge of advances in diagnosis. For all other cases she ruled an M.A. degree for an evaluator to be sufficient.
27. See Sparks and Javorsky, "Section 504," 647, for a more detailed discussion of this issue.
28. These observations of trends are based on our Web survey and personal exchanges with faculty in various institutions. A survey with responses from 166 colleges from 1987, which was conducted prior to the Boston lawsuit, found that 24 percent of the colleges and universities responding to the survey had no standard procedure regarding possible substitutions or waivers of a foreign language requirement at that point. It is safe to speculate that, as a result of the Boston lawsuit, most colleges and universities have established a standard procedure. For the 1987 study results, see Leonore Ganschow, Bettye Myer, and Kathy Roeger, "Foreign Language Policies and Procedures for Students with Specific Learning Disabilities," *Learning Disabilities Focus* 5, no. 1 (1989): 50–58.
29. An excellent example of a modified course is the Haddad Center intervention program, which focuses on building English language proficiency in an academic context in an attempt to help students with reading disabilities pass their exit-level university English requirement. The program focuses not only on linguistic skills but also on the development of cognitive and metacognitive strategies. These courses explicitly introduce and teach foreign language reading strategies, something that does not necessarily come naturally to students in a foreign language,

especially students with reading disabilities. As the focus of this chapter is on foreign language learning in the U.S. context, we have chosen not to include a discussion of this program here. For further information, see Rachel Shiff and Sharon Calif, "An Academic Intervention Program for EFL University Students with Reading Disabilities," *Journal of Adolescent and Adult Literacy* 48, no. 2 (2004): 102–13.

30. For more details on the program at the University of Colorado at Boulder with a discussion of phonological processing problems, see Doris M. Downey and Lynn E. Snyder, "Phonological Core as Risk for Failure in Foreign Language Classes," *Topics in Language Disorders* 21, no. 1 (2000): 82–92.

31. See, for example, Richard L. Sparks, Leonore Ganschow, Silvia Kenneweg, and Karen Miller, "Use of an Orton-Gillingham Approach to Teach a Foreign Language to Dyslexic/Learning-Disabled Students: Explicit Teaching of Phonology in a Second Language," *Annals of Dyslexia* 41 (1991): 96–118; Richard Sparks, Leonore Ganschow, Jane Pohlman, Sue Skinner, and Marjorie Artzer, "The Effects of Multisensory Structured Language Instruction on Native Language and Foreign Language Aptitude Skills of At-Risk High School Foreign Language Learners," *Annals of Dyslexia* 42 (1992): 25–53; Richard L. Sparks and Leonore Ganschow, "The Effects of Multisensory Structured Language Instruction on Native Language and Foreign Language Aptitude Skills of At-Risk High School Foreign Language Learners: A Replication and Follow-Up Study," *Annals of Dyslexia* 43 (1993): 194–216; Richard L. Sparks, Marjorie Artzer, Jon Patton, Leonore Ganschow, Karen Miller, Dorothy J. Hordubay, and Geri Walsh, "Benefits of Multisensory Structured Language Instruction for At-Risk Foreign Language Learners: A Comparison Study of High School Spanish Students," *Annals of Dyslexia* 48 (1998): 239–70; and Richard L. Sparks and Karen S. Miller, "Teaching a Foreign Language Using Multisensory Structured Language Techniques to At-Risk Learners: A Review," *Dyslexia* 6 (2000): 124–32.

32. Peter D. Macintyre, "On Seeing the Forest and the Trees: A Rejoinder to Sparks and Ganschow," *Modern Language Journal* 79, no. 2 (1995): 245.

33. Elke Schneider, *Multisensory Structured Metacognitive Instruction: An Approach to Teaching a Foreign Language to At-Risk Students* (New York: Peter Lang, 1999).

34. Mabbott, "Exploration of Reading Comprehension," 312.

35. Ann Sax Mabbott, "Arguing for Multiple Perspectives on the Issue of Learning Disabilities and FL Acquisition: A Response to Sparks, Ganschow, and Javorsky," *Foreign Language Annals* 28, no. 4 (1995): 492.

36. Sharon M. DiFino and Linda J. Lombardino, "Language Learning Disabilities: The Ultimate Foreign Language Challenge," *Foreign Language Annals* 37, no. 3 (2004): 390–400.

37. This becomes evident when looking at table 2 of their article, in which they list teaching and learning strategies pertaining to mastering the structure of a foreign language.

38. Eve Leons and Christina Herbert, "World Languages and the Student with Learning Disabilities: Best Practices," in *Teaching in the Disciplines: Classroom Instruction for Students with Learning Disabilities, A Landmark College Guide,* ed. Lynne Shea and Stuart W. Strothman (Putney, Vt.: Landmark College, 2002), 60.

39. Leons and Herbert, "World Languages," 56.

40. Ibid., 82.

41. Besides the resources in this volume, see Ann Sax Mabbott, "Students Labeled Learning Disabled and the Foreign Language Requirement: Background and Suggestions for Teachers," in *Faces in the Crowd: The Individual Learner in Multisection Courses,* ed. Carol A. Klee (Boston: Heinle and Heinle, 1994), 335; and Leons and Herbert, "World Languages," 63–82.

42. For the text of the mission statement and further discussion of legal issues regarding course substitutions, see Sheila Graham Smith, "Considerations in the Development of Foreign Language Substitution Policies at the Postsecondary Level for Students with Learning Disabilities," *ADFL Bulletin* 33, no. 3 (2002): 61–67.

43. The *Handbook* draws primarily on the work of Linda Jones at the University of Arkansas at Fayetteville. See, Linda Jones, "Lab Management," *IALL Journal of Language Learning Technologies* 29, no. 1 (1995): 53–57; 29, no. 2 (1995): 43–47. Contact pace@ualr.edu to obtain copies of the *Handbook* or for further information about the project.

Technology

CHAPTER 7

Incorporating Foreign Sign Language in Foreign Language Instruction for Deaf Students: *Cultural and Methodological Rationale*

PILAR PIÑAR, DONALDA AMMONS,
AND FACUNDO MONTENEGRO

Introduction

This chapter discusses the methodological advantages of incorporating foreign sign language into the instruction of written foreign languages for Deaf students.[1] The case study is a Spanish reading program for beginners, specifically designed for American Deaf students, which combines written Spanish and Costa Rican Sign Language through the use of video and caption technology. The program consists of a video containing ten Costa Rican legends narrated in Costa Rican Sign Language (Lengua de Señas de Costa Rica, or LESCO) and captioned in Spanish. The videotape is coordinated with a booklet containing written Spanish versions of the same stories that appear on the video. The written stories range from the basic to the basic-intermediate level of Spanish, and they feature many of the key grammatical structures that are typically covered in a first-year Spanish course, such as regular and irregular verbs in the present tense or the preterit and the imperfect. The stories are part of Costa Rican folklore. Some are related to Costa Rica's strong Catholic tradition, some are myths related to Costa Rica's Indian and colonial history or to its natural phenomena, and some are ghost stories that include a moral. We begin our discussion in this chapter by explaining the rationale for producing such a combined reading program. Subsequent sections provide theoretical background on reading strategies by Deaf readers and on the cognitive processes that are engaged through this program. Finally, we discuss our experimental design and the results of the assessment of our program that we conducted at Gallaudet University in the spring of 2001.

Rationale for the Approach

The natural approach to second-language learning promoted by Leonard Newmark and David Reibel, Stephen Krashen and Tracy Terrell, and many others, has been the most influential method in second-language teaching for thirty years. The premise of this approach is that the process of acquiring a second language should replicate as closely as possible the way in which one's first language is learned, that is, through natural exposure and interaction, rather than through explicit grammar instruction. These ideas are based on Noam Chomsky's views about first-language acquisition, which claim that the child's innate language ability allows him or her to acquire language by deducing and generalizing the grammar from the input that he or she receives, rather than through a stimulus-response process or through explicit instruction from adults. Research shows that the way in which certain grammatical structures are acquired in a second language in fact replicates the pace and manner in which they are acquired by the child in the first language. In spite of the constraints that a classroom setting imposes on the natural approach to second-language learning, most programs now emphasize direct exposure and meaningful communication in the target language rather than time spent solely on explanations of grammar and practice drills.[2]

While hearing students have greatly benefited from this approach, using the natural method to teach a spoken/written language in a Deaf environment raises a special challenge. The essence of this challenge is how to expose Deaf students to a spoken language in a direct, natural way. In the absence of a resolution to this problem, foreign language classes in Deaf environments still spend much time on explicit grammar instruction and guided practice drills, which in turn produce less than optimal results and often erode the students' motivation.

The only way to expose Deaf students directly to the authentic, meaningful use of a spoken language is through the written form. However, unlike spoken or signed language, the written form of a language is not a natural manifestation of an inherently human ability. Learning how to read involves a set of cognitive abilities different from those needed to process language presented in an oral or signed form. Thus, whereas children acquire their first language—be it spoken or signed—naturally, without explicit instruction, learning how to read is a skill that must be taught. It can be concluded, then, that there is "no" natural way to teach literacy skills. There are, however, natural tools that can be used to decode the written form of a language. When hearing students learn how to read a foreign language (or any language for that matter), they bring to the process a wealth of previous knowledge based on their direct use and perceptions of the spoken language. Thus, an effective strategy for developing literacy skills is to establish links between the spoken and the written language via phonological coding, a process by which the written words are parsed and kept in working memory by mapping their segments onto their phonological counterparts. Although it is true that some people develop reading skills in a language that they don't speak, they will transfer their first-language-based phonological coding abilities as a strategy to process the second language. Direct, natural exposure to the spoken language acts as a key that opens the door to deciphering the written language, and it creates a linguistic context against which the written language can be interpreted. As it is impossible to expose Deaf students directly to the spoken form, we explored the alternative of using foreign sign language as a natural bridge to access the spoken/written language. Our discussion here centers on Deaf foreign language classroom environments where the focus is reading and writing, not speaking and listening.

Before we proceed, it is important to understand that sign languages are naturally occurring languages that develop within Deaf communities, much as spoken languages develop within hearing communities. Although sign language is often in contact with the spoken language of the surrounding community and might be lexically and grammatically influenced by it, it is not an artificially created code based on spoken language. The grammar and vocabulary of signed and spoken languages are fundamentally distinct. As a result, just as there is no universal spoken language, there is also no single universal sign language; in fact, each country may have more than one distinct sign language. This is clearly illustrated by the fact that countries and communities that share one spoken language, such as all the Spanish-speaking countries, do not share one sign language. Instead, there are many individual and discrete sign languages worldwide, and they exhibit the same complexity and expressive power as spoken languages. Given these differences between spoken and sign languages, it may seem puzzling that successful Deaf foreign language learners, including one of the authors of this chapter, perceive that exposure to a foreign sign language facilitates the acquisition of the written language of the same community. Why should this be the case? The answer might be that the sign language, to which Deaf learners do have direct, natural access, provides a linguistic context that helps them decipher the vocabulary and grammar of the spoken language. We will argue that contextual links between signs and written words provide the beginning Deaf reader with a key for accessing the target written language.

By combining foreign signs with written texts, our program provides students with an alternate tool for decoding the written vocabulary through access to linguistic visual cues. Our claim is that the LESCO presentation of the stories allows students to make associations between foreign signs and written words that facilitate vocabulary decoding and retention. In addition, watching the signed stories before reading the full Spanish texts allows students to approach the written texts in a more holistic and contextual manner. In the next section, we provide background on reading strategies. We will then discuss in more detail how a combined program can help Deaf learners utilize some of these strategies.

What Strategies Do People Use When They Read?

Readers use a variety of strategies for temporarily storing written information in their working memory. As we mentioned earlier, one such strategy involves phonological coding, a strategy that is commonly used by Deaf readers, too.[3] For some Deaf readers, the coding may correspond with the actual pronunciation patterns of the language, and for others the phonological coding may be idiosyncratic but, nevertheless, quite effective in segmenting the basic units of the text.[4] Another strategy commonly used by Deaf readers in order to keep information in their memory buffer is to associate specific signs from the reader's sign language with specific printed words.[5]

While it is possible that, over time, Deaf readers will develop a phonological coding mechanism in an unfamiliar foreign language, it is unlikely that this strategy will be successful for beginning learners, when they first encounter an unfamiliar spelling system and have no access to the sound system of the foreign language to assist them in decoding the spelling. Fostering associations between the unfamiliar written words and linguistic visual cues (in the form of foreign signs) might provide an alternative decoding strategy at the initial stages of literacy acquisition. In particular, our program fosters sign-written word associations by carefully timing the Spanish captions that the students see at the bottom of the screen while they watch the storyteller signing in the LESCO video. The captions are simple and short, and they highlight key Spanish vocabulary that the students will later encounter in the written texts. Classroom use of the videotapes indicates that, in fact, the students make quick connections between signs and captions, a process that helps them deduce the meaning of the captions and retain their written form. After just one viewing, the students are able to recall the spelling and meaning of an impressive list of new Spanish words. Most foreign language teachers working with beginner Deaf students would agree that obtaining the same results after a reading unaccompanied by video is highly unlikely. As we will discuss in our assessment results section, sign-written word connections enhance vocabulary retention (both spelling and meaning) and global text comprehension.

Why Costa Rican Sign Language?

Costa Rican Sign Language was chosen primarily because it is closely related to American Sign Language (ASL), as a result of continued historical and educational links between the two communities. In fact, it is estimated that in educated settings LESCO shares about 70 percent of its vocabulary with ASL. However, as a result of language contact with the spoken language of the community and oral training practices for the Deaf, certain signs might be accompanied by specific oral movements that partially match the articulation of the corresponding word in the spoken language. Shared signs in ASL and LESCO might therefore occasionally be accompanied by different mouth movements, matching English and Spanish, respectively.

LESCO thus provides a perfect balance for our purposes. On

the one hand, its signs and some aspects of its grammar are different enough from those of ASL so as not to give the stories away to students completely before they approach the full, written texts. On the other hand, the similarity of LESCO to ASL allows students to understand enough of the stories to contextualize the Spanish vocabulary presented by the captions. Thus, rather than adding an extra burden by presenting the students with foreign signs and foreign written vocabulary simultaneously, the LESCO signs provide the students with a tool for accessing and decoding the Spanish captions on their own.

The reading program is implemented as follows. Students begin by watching one of the stories on videotape. Two viewings are recommended in a regular classroom setting. Students are asked to focus on the signs during the first viewing and on making connections between signs and captions during the second viewing. Having acquired some familiarity with the vocabulary and with the essence of the story, students proceed to read the full written text in their booklets. The method is successful because the signed versions are not 100 percent accessible to students, which would not be desirable for obvious reasons: if the students could understand all the signs, they would have no incentive to pay attention to the Spanish captions or to read the printed Spanish texts afterward. The relative unfamiliarity of the LESCO signs allows the students only a general, and not complete, understanding of the story, and this in turn activates their curiosity and motivates them to read the Spanish texts in order to achieve a more complete understanding.

In sum, using LESCO for our program has several advantages: (1) it would be culturally and linguistically awkward to match—artificially—ASL with Spanish captions; (2) using LESCO compels students to pay attention to the Spanish captions, since LESCO is not completely accessible to them; this, in turn, drives them to make sign-written word associations, a process that assists them in decoding and retaining vocabulary; (3) by using LESCO, we do not give away the story, which is meant to encourage students to work through the written Spanish text later; using ASL as the sign language accompanying the captions would not achieve any of these goals.

Cognitive Processes Engaged through This Approach

Our approach assumes the theory that the reading process that takes place is simultaneously "bottom-up" and "top-down." That is, on the one hand, the reader focuses on the bottom, or more basic, units of the texts (letter combinations, vocabulary, syntax) and builds the meaning of the text from these; on the other hand, the reader also builds the meaning of the text from previous, general knowledge and expectations (about the subject, about the world, about the language) and deduces "from the top" the meaning of the "bottom" units of the text. Providing a format as a first step to approaching written texts is consistent with recent theories and methodologies on literacy development.[6] It is also consistent with the strategies adopted by proponents of the natural approach to second language acquisition. As pointed out by Krashen, learners reach the next level of comprehension by using context to figure out new material.[7] Without a frame of reference that the beginning reader can utilize, a bottom-up reading process yields less than optimal results, especially when dealing with a foreign language, in which most elements of the text (vocabulary, spelling, word order) are unfamiliar and uncodifiable by the reader. Watching the LESCO stories before approaching the written texts helps beginning readers in two ways: as discussed above, it assists them in decoding and retaining vocabulary, thus enhancing vocabulary recognition during the reading task and facilitating the bottom-up cognitive process. In addition, watching the videotapes provides the readers with some background knowledge about the story, which serves as a top-down frame of reference.

In sum, this approach enhances vocabulary deduction through associations with the foreign signs, and provides a context for the readings. The beginning reader is then able to focus on vocabulary and larger units of meaning first, rather than on linear, decontextualized syntactic structures. The methodology of focusing on vocabulary and meaning more than on syntactic structure at this beginning stage is also consistent with natural approaches to language acquisition. According to Terrell, the key elements that aid comprehension of either spoken or written materials at the early stages are context, gestures or body language cues, a comprehensible message, and knowledge of the meaning of key vocabulary in the text or utterance.[8] The LESCO videotapes provide all of these elements to the students.

Assessment

We assessed the effectiveness of this program by comparing the reading performance of three first-year Spanish classes at Gallaudet University. The results indicate that the LESCO videotapes are an effective and motivating tool for developing reading skills in Spanish among Deaf students. The assessment of this approach addresses the following questions: (1) Do the LESCO videotapes enhance global comprehension of the written texts by facilitating the top-down cognitive process? (2) Do the captioned LESCO videotapes improve Spanish vocabulary recognition and retention by helping students establish contextual connections between signs and captions? Our hypothesis was that watching the videotapes prior to reading the texts would in fact help the students' reading task by familiarizing them with the vocabulary and, thus, reducing dictionary dependency and frustration. In addition, we hypothesized that the videotapes would provide a context that would help the students deduce the basic units of the text.

Evaluation Design

A total of thirty Deaf students were enrolled in three classes of second-semester Spanish. At the time of the assessment all three groups were taking Spanish 112 with the same professor. The students read four of the Costa Rican stories at different points in the semester. Each text was presented twice in class with an interval of about ten days between readings. All the groups first read each story without watching the videotape. Then they answered comprehension questions and completed a fill-in-the-blank vocabulary retention exercise. Both the texts and the students' answers were collected, and the number of correct answers was calculated for each student. Ten days later, the students read the same story again. This time, two experimental groups watched the LESCO version once, immediately before reading the text. The control group simply read the story again without ever watching the videotape. Students in all three groups were again asked to complete the same comprehension and vocabulary exercises. Each student's scores from the first and second readings were compared.

Results

As shown in figure 7.1, the scores of all students improved during the program. The solid color bars show the mean score improvement, between the first and second readings of each story, for those students who watched the video before reading the story a second time. The striped bars show the mean score improvement for those students who did not watch the tape before reading the story the second time.

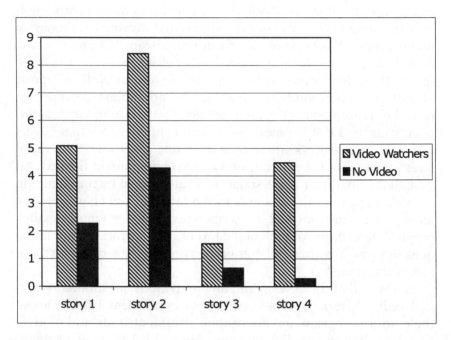

Figure 7.1. Score improvement averages

As the graph indicates, the mean score improvement for each reading was higher for the students who were in the two experimental groups than for the students who were in the control group. That is, the students who watched the videotape before reading the text for the second time showed a larger score improvement than the students who simply read the text twice. Scores improved both in the comprehension questions and in the vocabulary exercise. We attribute this to two factors. First, the captioned videotapes associated written words with signs and aided vocabulary decoding and retention. Second, we believe that the videotapes stimulated the top-down cognitive process.

One might argue that the improvement of scores in the experimental groups is the result of greater exposure to the vocabulary through the captions and through the written texts. This is unlikely, however, because all students answered the comprehension questions with the texts in front of them and had unlimited access to both the texts and the vocabulary. The experimental groups seem to have done better because they were better able to decode the vocabulary and comprehend the text globally. The text was more comprehensible to students who watched the videos first. Again, we emphasize that because LESCO is sufficiently different from ASL the students do not understand the story completely before they read the texts. In addition, the comprehension questions were carefully designed to test comprehension of the written texts, not of the videotapes. In fact, the written texts contain some details that do not appear explicitly on the LESCO tapes. For example, in one story that begins with two young lovers sitting by a river, one of the comprehension questions is about the description of the characters in the text. Although the character impersonation strategy used by the signer on the videotape cues the students to the fact that the characters are ideally young and innocent, the written text includes a more detailed physical description of each of the lovers. An accurate answer to the question thus requires full comprehension of the written text, not just of the video.

At the end of the assessment, an anonymous questionnaire elicited feedback from the subjects in the two experimental groups about the reading program and about their overall attitude and motivation regarding the reading task (see Appendix 7.1). Answers reveal that the majority of students felt that the videotapes enhanced their comprehension and their vocabulary retention and, no less important, they confirm that the LESCO videotapes motivated them to read the stories and made the reading task more culturally relevant and enjoyable.

Conclusions

As we hypothesized, the video component of our combined LESCO/ Spanish reading program enabled our beginning Spanish learners to access the vocabulary of the Spanish texts through contextualized connections with the LESCO signs. The improved results of the experimental groups over the control group on the vocabulary task indicate that these connections enhanced vocabulary retention and this, in turn, helped bottom-up processing of the written texts.

In addition, the results pertaining to global comprehension of the text indicate that the videos provide a framework that also helped students approach the texts in a top-down fashion (using their general grasp of the story to understand specific vocabulary and grammatical structures). Enhancing top-down cognitive processing in reading is particularly relevant in a situation in which the bottom information is in a foreign language to which the readers have had limited exposure. As reported by Leonard Kelly, average Deaf readers seem to compensate for their limited ability to process texts in a bottom-up fashion by relying on top-down processing.[9] This is in contrast to skilled Deaf readers, whose bottom-up and top-down processing is more balanced. While one would not want to make students dependent on a top-down-only reading strategy, given Kelly's findings, it seems unrealistic to expect beginning students of a foreign language to employ a bottom-up strategy before they become familiar with the vocabulary and the spelling system of that language.

Finally, in addition to the practical advantages of incorporating foreign signs as a way to access the written language, our program recognizes the cultural and linguistic value of the sign languages associated with foreign Deaf communities. One cannot emphasize enough the importance of motivating Deaf students to learn a written foreign language. Because a considerable number of American Deaf students have struggled with English throughout their school years, they do not always welcome the task of learning a written foreign language. Skepticism about the practicality of teaching foreign languages to Deaf students often evokes a defeatist attitude even among students themselves. In contrast to this, Deaf students do not demonstrate the same negative attitude toward foreign sign languages. Combining foreign signs with the target language makes the students more optimistic and interested in learning the foreign written language. In addition, Deaf students are often interested in other Deaf communities. They should, therefore, be given opportunities to develop awareness about how their community might be similar to and different from Deaf communities in other countries.

Materials are scarce that exploit the combined reading strategy promoted in this chapter. The motivated teacher of Deaf students might be able to produce his or her own basic vocabulary collection of foreign signs by videotaping a foreign signer signing a word list that corresponds to vocabulary typically taught at a beginning level, such as "the house," "the classroom," "the family," and so forth. Learning the signs along with the corresponding written words will motivate Deaf students to learn the words in the written language and will facilitate retention. Alternatively, if a fluent foreign signer is available, the students themselves can help collect and videotape the signed vocabulary under the teacher's supervision. Bear in mind that one should always pair the target written language with a sign language that is culturally related, such as Spanish and Costa Rican Sign Language, or French and French Sign Language. Also, it is just as important to incorporate cultural information about the related foreign Deaf community as it is to incorporate cultural information about the target spoken language. Most national Deaf associations have Web pages with a wealth of information related to the history and current situation of their communities. These Web sites often contain contact information for obtaining sign language materials.[10] So far as we know, our program is the first of its kind to integrate written texts in a foreign language with foreign sign language stories. Copies of the program can be requested from the Department of Foreign Languages, Literatures, and Cultures at Gallaudet University.

Appendix 7.1: Questionnaire

The subscript number after each letter indicates the number of students who circled that letter as their answer. A total of twenty students from the two experimental groups answered the questionnaire.

Please answer the following anonymous questionnaire by circling one of the letters (A, B, C, D). A is the most positive and D is the most negative.

1. Do the Costa Rican Sign Language (LESCO) videotapes make the Spanish readings easier to understand?
     Very much so A_{12} B_4 C_4 D   Not at all

2. Do the LESCO videotapes help you understand the Spanish readings more in-depth?

Very much   A$_{10}$ B$_4$ C$_5$ D$_1$ Not at all

3. Do the LESCO videotapes help you deduce the Spanish vocabulary on the written texts?

Very much   A$_9$ B$_9$ C$_2$ D   Not at all

4. Do the LESCO videotapes help you remember the Spanish vocabulary better?

Very much   A$_8$ B$_9$ C$_3$ D   Not at all

5. Do the LESCO videotapes help you understand the Spanish grammar in the readings?

Very much   A$_5$ B$_{12}$ C$_2$ D$_1$ Not at all

6. Do the LESCO videotapes motivate you to read the Spanish stories?

Very much   A$_{13}$ B$_3$ C$_4$ D   Not at all

7. Do the LESCO videotapes help you appreciate the cultural information in the stories?

Very much   A$_{14}$ B$_6$ C   D   Not at all

8. Does the combined approach to reading (LESCO videotapes and Spanish texts) make the reading experience more pleasant or more burdensome?

More pleasant A$_{11}$ B$_8$ C$_1$ D   More burdensome

9. How much LESCO could you understand?

100% A$_1$ 80% B$_{15}$ 50% C$_2$ less than 50% D$_2$

10. Did the Spanish captions help you understand the signs?

Very much   A$_{10}$ B$_7$ C$_1$ D$_2$ Not at all

11. Would you recommend the use of this approach for other foreign language courses?

Strongly   A$_{16}$ B$_3$ C$_1$ D   Not at all

Notes

1. The convention of writing Deaf with a capital *D* indicates that the individuals being referred to are part of a cultural and linguistic community where deafness is a sign of identity and is not viewed simply as a condition. Because the students who would benefit from our program would need to be familiar with sign language, we assume that they would be part of the Deaf community and we will therefore refer to them as Deaf.

2. Leonard Newmark and David A. Reibel, "Necessity and Sufficiency in Language Learning," *International Review of Applied Linguistics* 6, no. 2 (1968): 145–64; Stephen D. Krashen and Tracy D. Terrell, *The Natural Approach* (New York: Pergamon and Alemany, 1983); Noam Chomsky, *Aspects of the Theory of Syntax* (Cambridge, Mass.: MIT Press, 1965); Nathelle Bailey, Carolyn Madden, and Stephen D. Krashen, "Is There a Natural Sequence in Adult Second Language Learning?" *Language Learning* 24 (1974): 234–44.

3. Donald P. Shankweiler and Stephen Crain, "Language Mechanisms and Reading Disorders: A Modular Approach," *Cognition* 24 (1986): 139–68; Rudi Conrad, *The Deaf School Child* (London: Harper and Row, 1979); Vicki Hanson, "Recall of Order Information by Deaf Signers: Phonetic Coding in Temporal Order Recall," *Memory and Cognition* 18, no. 6 (1990): 604–10; Vicki Hanson, Elizabeth W. Goodell, and Charles Perfetti, "Tongue-Twister Effects in the Silent Reading of Hearing and Deaf College Students," *Journal of Memory and Language* 30 (1991): 319–30.

4. Vicki Hanson and Carol Fowler, "Phonological Coding in Word Reading: Evidence from Hearing and Deaf Readers," *Memory and Cognition* 15 (1987): 199–207.

5. Harlan L. Lane, Robert Hoffmeister, and Ben Bahan, *A Journey into the Deaf World* (San Diego, Calif.: Dawnsign Press, 1992).

6. Peter Paul and Stephen P. Quigley, *Language and Deafness* (San Diego, Calif.: Singular/Thompson Learning, 2001).

7. Stephen D. Krashen, *The Power of Reading* (Englewood, Colo.: Libraries Unlimited, 1996).

8. Tracy D. Terrell, "The Natural Approach to Language Teaching: An Update," in *Methods That Work: A Smorgasbord of Ideas for Language Teachers*, ed. John W. Oller and Patrica A. Richard-Amato (Cambridge, Mass.: Newbury House, 1983).

9. Leonard P. Kelly, "Processing of Bottom-Up and Top-Down Information by Skilled and Average Deaf Readers and Implications for Whole Language Instruction," *Exceptional Children* 61, no. 4 (1995): 318–34.

10. In addition, a variety of books, videos, and CD-ROM materials on Deaf issues, including materials pertaining to other sign languages, can be found through the on-line store http://www.forestbooks.com.

CHAPTER 8

In Dialogue with Michelle N. Abadia: *My Life Journey Studying and Teaching with Adaptive Technology*

INTERVIEWED BY ELIZABETH C. HAMILTON
AND TAMMY BERBERI

EH: Professor Abadia, you refer to your experiences with adaptive technology as a "life journey." How did the journey begin?

MA: I was always taught to rise above any obstacle that stood in my way, to respect myself, to stand up for my rights and for what I believed in. I was taught to persevere, to try as hard as I could to achieve my goals, regardless of any prospect of failure. Basically, I was taught to be fearless. However, I have a confession to make: I have always been afraid of computers, electronic gadgets, any computerized system that would make weird noises, sounds, and whistles. As a child, they used to scare me to death. I remember that sometimes while I was playing electronic games, the batteries would go low, and when I heard a noise that I knew did not belong in that particular game, the whole experience would turn into a nightmare for me. I guess I just could not see computerized games as inanimate objects.

As it happened, reality set in very early on in my life. By the age of five, I had completely lost my sight. Due to my supposed "great intellect and talent," the question became not whether or not I would be able to function in school and in life, but how would we make this a reality? What tools, instruments, means would we use for little Michelle to succeed in school, in music, in society as a whole, in life itself?

TB: It sounds as though you could count on lots of support from your family. How was your introduction to school?

MA: At first, things looked awfully bleak: I think I came close to being the first little girl ever to fail kindergarten. I decided that I would not learn how to read Braille. I learned to type it very well with the Braille typewriter; however, I refused to read it. For weeks I fooled my teachers into thinking that I could read all the short stories we were covering in class, when in fact I simply memorized them as we went along. Thanks to my very observant mother, however, my days as a so-called skilled Braille reader came to an abrupt end. I reluctantly learned how to read and subsequently went on to teach Braille to other children.

EH: Were other resources available to you as a young child?

MA: In the summer of 1978, I was introduced to the Opticon. The Opticon was my very first experience with real adaptive technology. The Opticon is a system with which a visually challenged person can read printed text through pulsating, electric sensations through his or her fingers. Several issues made this Opticon course a bit problematic for me, six years old at the time. First, I was a young child taking the class alongside young adults. Second, and most importantly, the positioning of the hand inside the system was quite tiresome. I was soon ready to quit. My mother encouraged me along, however, promising me a nice, big toy if I completed the class successfully. By the end of that summer, I had basic knowledge of assistive technology and a shiny, new doll.

TB: Reading does have its rewards! What other interests did you have as a child?

MA: As I grew, I continued to pursue the main interests I had developed after losing my sight: music and literature. In the fourth grade, I was mainstreamed from a school for the blind into a regular Catholic, parochial school. Around this time, I began writing stories taken from my own imagination. Some were for fun. Others were transcribed in print by special education teachers or by special printing machines at the local library for academic purposes, which made it possible for me to hand in my materials to my teachers with little trouble. In addition, I participated in various literary competitions. Both Braille and the Opticon allowed me to proofread my writings so that, in turn, I could share them with the rest of the world. These systems also helped me to keep up with my reading and to further develop my writing skills.

EH: You were clearly developing several talents and not just getting by. What were some highlights of your junior high and high school years?

MA: As an eighth grader, I competed in and won Puerto Rico's Spelling Bee competition, while placing decently in Washington, D.C.

TB: Congratulations! How did you prepare for that?

MA: Of course, the spelling books were not accessible in Braille. Our local library helped with some of the transcriptions. At times, I myself transcribed the printed pages with my mother's assistance. In addition, I was able to scan text with the Opticon and was also aided by recordings of the printed text.

EH: When did foreign language study enter your life? How accessible were your first materials?

MA: As a high school student, I started learning the French language. As a speaker of English and Spanish, I found it fascinating to be able to compare the similarities and differences between the languages. I really wanted to understand it, to read it, write it, and to be proficient in it. At the same time, I had access to a new line of reading machines called the Kurzweil Readers. These reading systems are named after the great inventor Dr. Raymond Kurzweil. This equipment was introduced in its most primitive form in the mid-seventies, and at first these systems were quite expensive. Since I could not afford one at the time, I would go to local libraries where they were available for public use. The Kurzweil also used to be very bulky, consisting of a huge speaker, a keypad, and a full scanner. The machine scanned text automatically while the user controlled the functions with the keypad. The user could choose one of nine humanlike voices to give life to the text. The Kurzweil gave me a sense of freedom and great independence in the way I studied and in the way I was learning a new language. It was much more fun to read several books at a time with this kind of reading aid. School, foreign languages, music, literature, life; all this was slowly becoming more and more accessible to me.

TB: That's good to hear. When you think about it, this is what teachers and parents want for all young people, isn't it?

EH: It certainly is. Schools should open up new opportunities for students and enable them to develop all of their talents. Michelle—if I may—what prospects did you have after your high school graduation?

MA: While developing my musical interests, I did want to attend college. I had decided to major in French literature, with a minor in international relations. Not only was I looking for a good school, I also wished to attend a college which would have the technology I needed to be able to study independently and to be my own free spirit. I wanted so much to prove my independence to myself and to the world.

I remember interviewing for some colleges in the Northeastern United States. I came across very good ones who offered good language and music programs. They had many questions for me, and I certainly had a few questions of my own. I was offended, almost insulted at the lack of adaptive technology at many of these institutions. They would not even apologize for the lack of accessibility. They would say, "Well, we don't really carry those types of things."

"Those types of things?!" It was as if I and many others did not have the right or as if we did not deserve that "royal privilege" of gaining access to a higher education in their midst.

TB: This dismissive attitude is probably the biggest barrier to students with disabilities. What did you eventually decide to do?

MA: Well, after much consideration, I decided that Boston College, in Chestnut Hill, Massachusetts, was the perfect fit for me. This school had a wonderful language program, great musical opportunities, and a complete and recently renovated adaptive technology center. Upon entering the computer room for the first time, I found printers, computers with speech input, Braille embossers—which are just printers that print in Braille—and a Kurzweil Reader with a French adapter. Kurzweil Readers come with an English language cartridge that can be easily replaced by cartridges in most Western languages and some Asian languages as well. The cartridges are in the shape of credit cards. Once installed, the system changes to the correct pronunciation and vocabulary of the desired language.

So many gadgets! The possibilities seemed endless. I felt like a kid in a candy store!

It became clear to me that Boston College always made sure (and still does today) that all its students have equal access and opportunity to as much as they wish to take advantage of, regardless of disability or situation. In addition, I was very fortunate to have very smart, distinguished professors with a high degree of common sense. Most of them made sure that all class activities were accessible to me. They were aware of my presence without being overly intrusive. I truly appreciated that.

I can still remember when, during a German class, my professor decided to play a very fun visual identification game. Luckily, I have always been shameless. I think I said something along the lines of: "Wait just a second; let's try this again." He did have a sense of humor and quickly adjusted the game.

EH: What exactly did your German professor do to modify the game?

MA: As the professor would point at each object to be identified, I was handed the item so that I could actually "see" what it was.

TB: Very nice! It sounds as though you took on a big responsibility for educating your professors. It's impressive that you were able to do this with good humor as well.

EH: It's important, though, for teachers to ask themselves in advance how they might make their courses accessible. Boston College had apparently taken many steps to do this. Would you tell us about some others?

MA: As a college student, I was also assisted by the high-quality recording of textbooks by Recording for the Blind, which today is known as Recording for the Blind and Dyslexic. These recorded textbooks were of particular assistance when it came to very long, complex literary works, especially while I was still getting used to the French adapter on the Kurzweil Reader. It was also during my college years that my rehab counselor at the Massachusetts Commission for the Blind in Boston introduced me to a writing tool that made my life so much easier: the Braille'n Speak, a product manufactured by Blazie Engineering. The Braille'n Speak is a speech-based notetaker with a highly complex file system, which allows the user to organize documents in a series of folders. It also contains a calendar, a spell-checker, a clock, a stopwatch, and a calculator. With the Braille'n Speak, I was able to quietly take notes in class, as well as prepare and organize all my course work in separate electronic compartments. Because of its printing capabilities, I was also able to write papers and essays with no difficulty.

What I truly liked about this new piece of equipment was its portability. I had always wished for a computer-type product that I could take with me everywhere I went. As the Braille'n Speak continued to be updated, more features were added. Among the most significant ones for me was the addition of French language software, which allowed the system to switch languages with the press of two keystrokes. This new functionality served to improve even more the way in which I studied the language.

EH: What did you decide to do after college?

MA: My life continued to evolve. Upon completing my studies at Boston College, I embarked on the graduate phase of my studies in French literature at Tufts University in Medford, Massachusetts. In order to obtain my degree, I was expected to read many books spanning various genres of French literature: novels, essays, theater, poetry, and journalistic articles. In addition, I needed to complete a month-long independent study, which required the reading, comprehension, and analysis of fifteen to twenty books covering the narrative prose genre.

As I entered the language department's laboratory, I realized that its Kurzweil reading machine did not have a French language adapter. I politely spoke my mind and stated my case: "I'm sorry; I just don't think I'll be able to complete my master's degree under these conditions. It would be a rotten shame if we were to throw away the eighteen-thousand-dollar scholarship the university has awarded me. Any thoughts?" With the assistance of the language laboratory, a French adapter to the Kurzweil Reader appeared within days. I love it when people get the point.

TB: Yes, accessibility is in everyone's best interest. In your case, this ultimately meant that a university scholarship was not wasted and that a degree was awarded to a qualified candidate.

EH: In addition to that, having the French adapter in place now means that future students at Tufts will be able to read French literature and complete their studies. But there is probably no singular device or application that can do it all, is there?

MA: No, not really. However, we are fortunate nowadays to have a variety of assistive software that can assist a person with any physical or cognitive disability to succeed as a person and as a professional. Students should not be afraid to ask for the technology necessary to make their studies easier. Along those same lines, academic institutions must do everything in their power to obtain such technology and to make reasonable accommodations so that all students may have equal access to a high-quality education.

　　As my life continued to undergo some changes, so did mainstream technology. Blazie Engineering kept up with the times, and I was able to upgrade from a Braille'n Speak to a Braille Lite. The Braille Lite is quite similar to the Braille'n Speak. The two main differences are the much bigger memory capacity of the Lite and the addition of a Braille display. The Braille display works just like your regular computer screen. A visually challenged person can rely on written text in Braille at the bottom of the notetaker or computer to see where the cursor is. The person can also read and edit text using the cursor buttons on the display, without always having to rely on electronic speech. Graduate school is not easy for anyone. As for me, I would have never been able to complete my master's degree in French literature without the availability and assistance of this kind of adaptive equipment.

TB: How did computer technology and music intersect in your life?

MA: As I went on to pursue my master's degree in vocal performance at the New England Conservatory, in Boston, Massachusetts, my Braille Lite assisted me in the completion and printing of theory and music history papers. Its Braille display allowed me to input music notation and text and then be able to read it comfortably and without disruption during lessons and rehearsals. I still kept my old Braille typewriter. If my computer was not available, it was always good to have instant Braille available for me to prepare music sheets to bring for practice times.

　　But enough with school. The big test was yet to come. I mean: real life had to begin some time.

EH: Employment! What was your plan?

MA: My two most cherished dreams in life have always been to be a concert singer and a college professor; but at least the latter would have to wait a bit. Having completed my master's degree in music, I became a judicial language interpreter and translator for the Massachusetts court system. For four years, I interpreted criminal, civil, juvenile, and probate proceedings to all parties involved who spoke either Spanish or French. My job also required the accurate written translations of depositions, police reports, restraining orders, and other such legal documents. In order to further my quest for independence, I decided to purchase the latest product by Kurzweil: The Reading Edge. This product was conceived to be similar in concept to prior Kurzweil Readers; however, it is far more compact and definitely more affordable. In October of 1997, I stopped having to go to libraries to use their computing services in order to read legal documents. I could now just stay home, make a nice, big pot of coffee, and read at my leisure with my Reading Edge, which I still own today. I continued to use my Braille Lite to edit, paste, translate, and print all my legal and other documents.

TB: When did you decide to enter college teaching?

MA: In July of 1999, I chose to leave the court system and to pursue my dream of becoming a college professor. I truly wished to enlighten others, not only in the acquisition of and proficiency in a foreign language but also in the understanding of other cultures and ways of thinking. Because of my experience as a linguist and interpreter in the judicial system, I felt that I could start sending my information to several colleges. I do remember sending résumés pretty much all over creation. My job interviews went quite well in general. Of course, I went to each interview equipped with whatever piece of adaptive technology I could carry and with a full description in mind of whatever I could not take with me. I had to. I needed to be prepared for those all too frequent questions: "So tell us, how do you read papers? How do you grade them? How much assistance will you need? Do you perceive what's going on around you? How do you write?"

EH: Were these interview questions bothersome to you?

MA: No, I did not mind the questions too much. I do not mind them today. I prefer that people know how I get things done. I would not wish to be denied employment simply because someone didn't believe I could actually do the tasks required of me.

My career as a professor of languages began on January 20, 2000, at Framingham State College in Framingham, Massachusetts. I taught there for five years. I shall always be grateful to Framingham State for being the first school to grant me the opportunity to teach in a college setting. This institution also made its Office of Disability Services available to me as a resource, if ever I was in need of assistance.

TB: What new experiences did you face now that you were on the faculty?

MA: No longer was I a student of foreign languages, I had now become the instructor. Now I had to be sure that my instructional handouts and all my work were in a format that sighted students could understand. I had to use my own adaptive technology to cater to the learning needs of your average sighted student. I know this may not seem like a big deal. But you see: I am blind. Suddenly, I had to appeal to students who learn languages visually. It was up to *me* to adjust to *them*.

At first, this notion was hard for me to reconcile. It became a constant struggle for me, which turned into a challenge that I have come to enjoy to this day. Have I truly reconciled myself to this notion? I guess so. I must have. Some students have actually said to me: "Professor, you are so visual in your teaching. Do you realize how ironic that is?" I love it!

TB: Would you share with us some of your most successful teaching activities?

MA: Well, I am a firm believer that speaking and oral comprehension are two of the most important components of language acquisition. The most successful exercise in my classroom has to be "Creative Dialogues." Students get together in groups of two, three, or four; and based on the grammar we may be covering at the time, they prepare dramatizations that must be no less than five minutes in length. This activity gives them an opportunity to work together, to help each other with the understanding of certain topics, and to put into practice what they have learned in class. As a professor, it gives me a chance to evaluate their proficiency and their ability to create real life situations using a foreign language. It is such a thrill for me to see how students seek to incorporate a lot of the things I have mentioned in class and how eager most of them are to become actors for a day. I always come out feeling very proud of them and quite confident that I must be doing something right!

EH: All new teachers face challenges they hardly expected. Would you tell us about one of yours?

MA: Just a couple of years ago, and as I continued teaching college students and adults alike, I was faced with one of my biggest issues yet. Both as a student and as a professor of foreign languages, I have always believed in the absolute inclusion of students in class activities, regardless of which subject is being taught, regardless of any disability or any other circumstance. I had taught dyslexic students, students who suffered from various emotional disturbances, and physically disabled students. But I had never had the priceless opportunity to encounter a *blind* student in my classroom!

When you meet, befriend, and engage in conversation with so many sighted people on a daily basis, you sort of forget that you cannot really see. Well, I'm speaking from my own personal experience, of course. At any rate, one beautiful September morning, I received a phone call from the academic dean: "Good morning, Professor Abadia. I have been advising a student who is visually challenged and who would very much like to enroll in your course. I just wanted to give you a heads-up." So, just how good was I at practicing what I preached? And actually presenting the course material in a format that would be feasible and comfortable for this student? Would I rise to the challenge as a professor? I have another confession to make: I was so scared of blowing this one! Well, I transcribed my syllabus and all other handouts to Braille. The next day, my student received her own materials in a format that she could readily access. She did not have to wait to get home in order to read what had been given to her. She could just follow along with the rest of the class. She seemed so excited when I presented her with the Braille transcriptions. She was very gracious: "Thanks so much; you don't know what this means to me!"

To which I replied: "Oh, but I do! I so do!"

TB: What a terrific story! You really put your principles to work.

EH: Are there other new developments in technology that have made your life easier?

MA: In the summer of 2004, I once again upgraded my technology. As I said earlier, I truly enjoy computers that are portable and with which I can accomplish major tasks on the go. The PAC Mate, manufactured by Freedom Scientific, became that computer. The PAC Mate is the first PDA [personal digital assistant] and portable computer for the visually challenged that works on the PocketPC platform. It uses a Windows operating system and performs most tasks like a regular computer. It comes with either the Braille keyboard or the regular Laptop keyboard—user's choice—as well as with an optional Braille Display.

TB: The Internet has become an indispensable tool in education. How easy was it for you to gain access?

MA: In fact, surfing the Web, sending and receiving e-mails, reading, editing, and printing documents, and performing mathematical calculations are easy to accomplish on a PAC Mate BX or QX. Although the PAC Mate was introduced in 2002, my childish fear of technology got the best of me, and I did not upgrade until two years later. As it turns out, it was not such a bad idea. By that point, the PAC Mate had upgraded according to the advancements in mainstream technology. By the time I purchased it, the PAC Mate had undergone some changes in design that turned it into an even more powerful tool. In order to address the needs of an increasingly global market, the PAC Mate has been upgraded to include Language Modules, which can be downloaded into the actual computer from the PAC Mate Web site. Of course, I have downloaded both the Spanish and French modules for teaching purposes, and in order to better read Web pages in such languages while using speech. The PAC Mate's nine English voices give rise to those same nine voices in the clear phonetics of the desired language.

As a professor of languages, I can attest to the multiple ways in which this latest technological enhancement has truly expanded my capabilities. Now, students can easily e-mail me questions, concerns, and even whole papers and drafts for me to review. I am able to give Internet research assignments,

having viewed the Web sites myself on given topics. I can organize my schoolwork, my personal documents, and my music
files with much greater ease. I don't even bring textbooks to
school anymore. I transcribe most textbooks from my Reading Edge to the storage card I install on the PAC Mate. With
the aid of the Braille display, I can now explain a given page
on a textbook while the students have a visual reference. I felt
so proud of my seemingly great ease with technology when a
student majoring in computer science said: "Gosh, professor,
you're so techno!"

TB: Do you also teach music or incorporate music into your French
       courses?

MA: I do not teach music, because what I truly love is to perform
       on stage. I do, however, incorporate music into my language
       courses. Some days, I bring my guitar and copies of printed
       text for the students. Whether it be in French or Spanish, I
       make them sing. I think that live music works so much better
       than just a simple recording. Students really get to participate
       in the song and to understand how language, music, and cul-
       ture relate to one another.

EH: Where are you working now?

MA: I am currently a professor of languages at Babson College
       and at Massachusetts Bay Community College, both located
       in Wellesley, Massachusetts. I thank both institutions for giv-
       ing me new challenges and responsibilities that have greatly
       enriched my teaching experience. I also continue to give con-
       certs, performing classical art songs, jazz, American standards,
       and Puerto Rican/Latin American folk songs.

TB: What else would you like readers to know about your journey
       with adaptive technology?

MA: I would like them to know that my journey continues. I am
       about to receive a new reading machine called the Kurzweil
       1000. This reader is Windows based and will provide me and
       many others with even more flexibility in the way we can read
       and organize documents.
            The fact is that every new technological advancement has
       given me independence, freedom, worth and dignity—not only
       as a student, professor, and vocalist but as a total human being

who has always wished to be as much of a positive force in the world as I can be. At age thirty-five, I can honestly affirm that my life has been quite interesting so far. I can describe my experiences with adaptive technology as one crazy whirlwind of a ride. Considering how fearful I have always been of strange computer noises and the like, it is a shocking wonder that I have become as comfortable with complex technology as I have.

I am in no way related to Kurzweil or Freedom Scientific, nor am I a paid spokesperson for their products. However, I must give credit to wonderful breakthroughs that have and will allow me, I hope without fear or hesitation, to continue on my journey with adaptive technology.

TB and EH: Michelle, thank you for sharing your story with us.

Appendix 8.1: Some Web Sites Related to Technology for the Visually Impaired

http://www.freedomscientific.com

This Web site provides detailed information about the newest technology for individuals with low or no vision. Information includes availability, technical support, and pricing.

http://www.pacmategear.com

This is the Web address for the PAC Mate and all its features. One can find availability and pricing information on this product, as well as frequently asked questions about the PAC Mate.

http://www.rfbd.org

This Web site for Recording for the Blind and Dyslexic provides detailed information about books, periodicals, and other material on tape for people with visual disabilities.

http://www.kurzweiltech.com

This Web site offers information related to the history and latest innovations of the Kurzweil reading machines. It also features biographical information on their inventor, Dr. Raymond Kurzweil.

CHAPTER 9

New Technologies and Universal Design for Learning in the Foreign Language Classroom

NICOLE STRANGMAN, ANNE MEYER,
TRACEY HALL, AND C. PATRICK PROCTOR

Introduction

As Professor Garcia prepares for her Spanish language class of twenty students, she faces the same significant challenge that nearly all her colleagues do: how to teach effectively a diverse group of learners with wide variations in background knowledge, literacy skills, academic preparation, and, in some cases, physical or sensory ability. William is hard of hearing and sometimes finds it difficult to follow classroom discussions. Jacqui excels in most subjects but not in Spanish: she hates memorizing vocabulary and does not see how the foreign language requirement is relevant to her major in biology. Cheryl has dyslexia, making it hard for her to decode both English and Spanish texts. Professor Garcia considers what goals, strategies, and materials would help each student learn in the way that is best for him or her. What barriers do the usual classroom materials and tools present? What supports and additional resources would help students overcome those barriers so they can focus on learning? What would make Professor Garcia's instruction more engaging? What options can she provide students to accommodate their individual styles and interests while still allowing her to focus on learning content? What performance criteria are appropriate? What assessments will guide her efforts? Today's instructors face a significant challenge in trying to raise academic standards and improve outcomes for increasingly diverse populations of students. In addition, providing the opportunity to learn at both the K–12 and the postsecondary level is increasingly recognized as a civil right of all citizens, especially those with disabilities. New approaches to planning and executing instruction are needed to ensure that all students have such opportunities. A single classroom may have students with very different backgrounds, skills, knowledge, and interests. Instructors know that each student is unique, and they want their students to succeed. They want to respond to individual differences by providing flexible and supportive learning environments. The question is how to accomplish these goals.

Universal Design for Learning: A Blueprint for Teaching Every Student

Of course, there are no simple answers. But educators can learn to develop and use flexible goals, methods, materials, and assessments to reach more learners without compromising high standards. Universal Design for Learning, an emerging approach to educational reform pioneered by the educational research organization CAST (the Center for Applied Special Technology), provides a blueprint for accomplishing this through the development of flexible, supportive learning environments. By referring to this new approach as Universal Design for Learning, or UDL, CAST's researchers echo the universal design movement in architecture and product development, which calls for designing structures—from office buildings to television sets—that accommodate the needs of the greatest possible variety of users from the outset, without expensive or cumbersome retrofitting.[1]

Drawing on new understandings of the complexities of individual learning and how the brain processes information, the UDL framework suggests guiding principles for the design of learning opportunities (table 9.1). These principles provide flexibility with respect to three primary areas of learning: recognition of the information to be learned, application of strategies to process that information, and engagement with the learning task.[2]

Table 9.1. Three Primary Networks of the Learning Brain and Corresponding UDL Principles

Brain Network	UDL Principles for Anticipating Differences in Brain Networks
Recognition networks, which make it possible to receive and analyze information—i.e., to recognize patterns, concepts, and relationships; the "what" of learning	Provide multiple, flexible methods of presentation; give learners various ways to acquire information and knowledge
Strategic networks, which make it possible to generate patterns and develop strategies for action and problem solving; the "how" of learning	Provide multiple, flexible methods of expression and apprenticeship; offer students alternatives for demonstrating what they know
Affective networks, which fuel motivation and guide the ability to establish priorities, focus attention, and choose action; the "why" of learning	Provide multiple, flexible options for engagement in order to help learners get interested, challenged, and motivated

Source: Meyer and Rose 2000; Rose and Dalton 2001; Rose and Meyer 2002

UDL Teaching Methods

CAST has also developed UDL teaching methods that provide teachers with some broad strategies to customize curriculum for individual learners by mapping instructional design according to the three networks (table 9.2). Each UDL principle is supported by a set of teaching methods, as described in the following sections. UDL calls for providing:

1. Multiple, flexible methods of presentation in order to support diverse recognition networks. Providing students multiple examples of a pattern helps them to extract the key features and offers them the chance to select and focus on the examples that are most effective for them. Students vary in their ability to process different patterns, making it essential that teachers use different media and formats during instruction. This might mean showing students text, images, and video as well as immersing students in field experiences. For example, the content of a lesson on food in France could be presented as printed text, text in digital format (with an option

for text-to-speech, Braille, and variable display formats), images, and video—or by actually preparing and eating French food.

2. Multiple, flexible methods of expression and apprenticeship in order to support diverse strategic networks. Students' strengths, weaknesses, and preferences in the area of strategic learning vary as widely as they do for recognition learning. Thus, it is equally important to offer multiple, flexible opportunities and methods for expression and apprenticeship when students are figuring out what they are expected to learn and demonstrating what they know. Just as students can extract critical features of a pattern from multiple examples, they can also extract the critical features of a process from multiple models. In addition, complex skills and texts are easier to master when their component steps or parts are presented. Offering students the chance to practice with scaffolds can facilitate that process. Depending on the learner's level of need and preferences, scaffolds may take many forms, including graphic organizers with clusters of related vocabulary words to demonstrate their relationship visually; one-on-one review with the teacher; or access to peer expertise through cooperative work, such as developing a story. As students continue to practice, it is also essential to provide ongoing, relevant feedback. This, too, takes a variety of forms to meet different students' needs and preferences: one-on-one teacher or peer feedback; a group discussion to reveal gaps in knowledge, misconceptions, or skill deficits; or perhaps a self-test. When it comes time for assessment, it is essential to ask students to demonstrate their skill and knowledge in ways that reveal what they actually know and can do, rather than how good they are at, say, taking a test. For example, when testing understanding of Spanish vocabulary, a teacher could offer students a variety of options, such as answering multiple-choice questions, composing essays or writing their own Mexican folk song, selecting critical features from a picture series, composing scrapbooks, or giving an oral presentation.

3. Multiple, flexible options for engagement in order to support diverse affective networks. Students vary widely in their preferences and inclinations; it is important to offer them the flexibility of pursuing their own interests and to provide different options for engagement. Although by design the content area is often restricted, offering choices of content and tools is one way for teachers to fuel every student's enthusiasm. For example, students might be given the option of working with many different media: during a lesson about the history of German-speaking regions

in Switzerland students might read oral histories, watch a documentary, explore relevant Web sites, interview an expert from another university via teleconference, or conduct a scavenger hunt to collect clues to the region's development. Challenge is another factor influencing students' motivation to learn. When challenged too much or too little, students tend to disengage. Providing adjustable levels of challenge can help ensure that each student is optimally motivated.

Table 9.2. Teaching Methods to Support UDL Principles

To support diverse recognition networks:
Provide multiple examples
Highlight critical features
Provide multiple media and formats
Support background context

To support diverse strategic networks:
Provide flexible models of skilled performance
Provide opportunities to practice with supports
Provide ongoing, relevant feedback
Offer flexible opportunities for demonstrating skill

To support diverse affective networks:
Offer choices of content and tools
Offer adjustable levels of challenge
Offer choices of rewards
Offer choices of learning context

Source: Rose and Meyer 2002

Digital Technology and UDL: A Potent Combination

Though not a technology-based approach per se, digital materials such as electronic texts offer indispensable support for UDL implementation because their inherent flexibility enables them to be modified in a host of ways. This flexibility makes it possible to customize learning materials and methods to each individual, depending on his or her needs. Although providing multiple representations might be challenging in a course that depends predominantly on printed text and hard copy images, digital materials enable the assembly, storage, and maintenance of a large collection of examples in the form of digital text, images, sound, or video.

In contrast with fixed formats of print, electronic text can easily be transformed in its visual presentation (the size, color, shape, or layout of text elements) and even be transformed into other modalities and languages (for example, from text to speech, to refreshable Braille, to American Sign Language, to second language). Digital content can contain media elements other than printed text, including images, audio, video, and so forth. Some of these, like video, which cannot be included in printed text, add great variability to learning materials. Also, the "associative" quality of digital material—as compared with the "linear" quality of printed text—makes learning richer for a greater variety of students. Printed elements appear in a fixed sequence, whereas digital materials, including electronic text, can be "linked," creating many alternative sequences and structures.

Of course, not all digital formats are flexible. For example, image-based PDF files are formatted to preclude the common transformations (like text-to-speech) and presentational options that are essential for accessibility. Some others are embedded within images and are therefore not available for transformation. Web pages often display this type of inflexible and inaccessible content. Others, like ASCII, lack sufficient structural markup to provide an adequate basis for the kinds of customization needed by many students with disabilities. But in general, digital materials offer formidable advantages over the kinds of printed curricular materials that predominate in most classroom settings.

Technology-Enriched UDL and Second-Language Learning

Do technology-enriched UDL approaches offer a helpful framework for current foreign language teaching and learning? An informal survey of recent literature on second-language learning (L2)—combined with observations from CAST's two decades of UDL research, including the development of digital learning environments to support English Language Learners (ELLs)—suggests that it could be useful.[3]

Already many teachers of foreign languages have moved toward the sort of individualized, highly contextualized learning approaches that UDL has been shown to support effectively. For example, foreign language practice, especially computer-based practice, has moved away from isolated skills instruction—such as drill and practice in vocabulary, grammar, and pronunciation—toward a greater focus on communicative proficiency and the use of culturally authentic texts or learning in culturally relevant contexts. Meei-Ling Liaw writes that while computers were originally used in L2 courses primarily to provide practice in languages, this paradigm shifted with the advent of advanced communications technologies, so that computers and computer networks now fulfill a "primary function as enablers of authentic and natural language use."[4]

Knowledge of vocabulary is integral to the acquisition of reading, speaking, and listening skills. Although traditional direct instruction of individual words has not been shown to be a powerful means of generating high degrees of word knowledge, richer, technology-based techniques have proved successful in increasing L2 vocabularies of foreign language learners. For example, in a series of experiments with adolescent and adult learners of English as a foreign language, Batia Laufer found that students who were required to work with words (through writing) were significantly more likely to understand and retain a word's meaning after a delay in testing. The conclusion is that for second language learners (and perhaps for most readers), the amount of cognitive energy expended to understand a word's meaning is directly related to its retention.[5]

Twenty-first-century communications technologies offer powerful means to provide contextualized language use through local and global student-student and student-teacher interactions. E-mail, blogs, chatrooms, and other such tools and venues provide powerful connections among students and teachers across the globe, mediating geographic and linguistic barriers, and facilitating communicative proficiency.[6] Other technologies for L2 include interactive games with speech recognition technology so students can hear how they sound; reference packages with dictionaries, atlases, and encyclopedias; and programs that help teachers to develop multimedia language materials that leverage audio, video, and satellite technologies.[7]

These tools are having an impact on foreign language instruction around the globe. Ingrid Pufahl, Nancy Rhodes, and Donna Christian surveyed teachers in nineteen countries outside the United States about elementary and secondary foreign language instruction. In answer to the question, "What do you think are three of the most successful aspects of foreign language education in your country?" teachers stressed the importance of a "comprehensive use of technology: technology as a way to provide access to information, give students an opportunity to interact with speakers of a foreign language, and to engage students."[8] These technologies can all be used to support the three brain networks identified in the UDL framework—recognition, strategic, and affective—by providing multiple means of representation, expression, and engagement. UDL's emphasis on ensuring the relevance of learning goals and contexts, providing multiple media options for learning, and supporting students' individual learning needs and preferences is compatible with the changing L2 field, particularly as it relates to technology use.

Digital texts have several advantages. First, they make it possible to embed strategy instruction and metacognitive supports directly into texts, potential that Andrew Cohen has identified as effective for teaching L2 learners reading comprehension strategies. Cohen identifies the goals of strategy training as helping students to (1) identify strengths and weaknesses; (2) develop metacognitive knowledge of what helps them learn a foreign language effectively; (3) develop problem-solving skills; (4) experiment with familiar and unfamiliar learning strategies; (5) make decisions about how to approach a language learning task; (6) self-monitor and self-evaluate; and (7) transfer strategies to new contexts.[9]

Second, digital multimedia can be an efficient and effective way to support vocabulary acquisition. For example, Dorothy Chun and Dan Plass found that the use of multimedia vocabulary annotations, including audio, graphics, and animated pictures or video, contribute to vocabulary acquisition and to overall text comprehension. In one study of 160 university students learning German, Chun and Plass found that the inclusion of multimedia annotations—visual and verbal—facilitated reading comprehension more than verbal annotations alone.[10]

An Example: Universal Learning Editions

The UDL framework and teaching methods complement and support the National Standards for Foreign Language Education established in 1999.[11] For example, the Standards call for student communications that are conversational and contextual—in which students provide and obtain information, express feelings and emotions, and exchange opinions in ways that engage them. The Standards also call for students to "reinforce and further their knowledge of other disciplines through the foreign language" (Standard 3.1).

Such an interdisciplinary approach is compatible with the call for multiple means of representation, expression, and engagement because it extends the variety of contexts, methods, and approaches to foreign language learning. The Standard calling for students to "show evidence of becoming life-long learners by using the language for personal enjoyment and enrichment" (Standard 5.2) is especially consonant with UDL, which emphasizes engagement as well as the development of usable knowledge and knowledge-building strategies.

In recent years, CAST has researched and developed the use of digital texts called Universal Learning Editions (ULEs), which have embedded scaffolds that support diverse learners' literacy achievement. While this work has focused on K–12 learning environments, the demonstrated value in providing just-in-time, individualized learning supports is relevant to learners of all ages, including those at the postsecondary level. ULEs are digital learning environments that make high-quality literature truly accessible and useful for learners across a wide spectrum of ability and disability. In developing them, CAST applied research on reading comprehension instruction, specifically reciprocal teaching and UDL, to the design of interactive digital texts with embedded strategy instruction.[12] Students with decoding and fluency problems can use text-to-speech to have individual words or passages read aloud with synchronized highlighting. To support the development of reading comprehension, strategy instruction prompts are embedded in the digital text and hints, think-alouds, and model responses are provided on demand by animated, virtual coaches. Strategy support is leveled so that students move from high to low support, with the goal of independent application of strategies. For example, at level 1, students select a good summary from three multiple-choice options; at level 2, students review a list of points from the passage and identify the "important" ones; at level 3, students construct a summary using highlighted text in the passage and complete a self-check rubric; at level 4, students create an original summary and complete the self-check rubric; and at level 5, students choose a strategy that they feel would be most helpful. Students' on-line responses are collected in a computer work log for review and evaluation by the student and the teacher.

Engagement is addressed in multiple ways. Key factors include using on-grade level texts so students are reading at their interest level, rather than at their decoding level (text-to-speech makes this possible); allowing students to choose which supports to access, such as computer agent strategy coaches, hyperlinked vocabulary, and background knowledge; providing students with frequent opportunities for self-reflection; and situating the ULE within the larger classroom context by giving students opportunities to discuss the ULE texts and share their insights about strategic reading.

Table 9.3 offers further examples of how the ULEs can support the development of essential background knowledge in struggling readers, including Spanish-speaking English language learners.

Table 9.3. UDL and Background Knowledge Applications of a Universal Learning Edition Prototype

UDL Teaching Method	Supportive Lesson Feature(s)
Provide multiple examples	The multimedia glossary offers multiple photo illustrations for vocabulary words; Web links to resources offer students multiple examples of key facts and concepts
Highlight critical features	The Maps, Timeline, and Character Journey highlight critical features of the text related to setting and characters; the PowerPoint and Web links to resources highlight other critical features related to the text
Provide multiple media and formats	The multimedia glossary offers text and illustrations; the video and photo essay provide redundant information in multiple media and formats; Maps and Character Journey present story information in another medium and format; vocabulary support is provided in English and Spanish
Provide opportunities to practice with supports	All the background knowledge aids provide optional support for students, who can access them or not, as they wish
Offer adjustable levels of challenge	Students can adjust the level of challenge by varying their consultation of the background knowledge supports
Offer choices of content and tools	The variety of background knowledge aids provide students with the opportunity to choose among different content and tools

Bridget Dalton and colleagues compared traditional classroom-based strategy instruction with a comparable condition that made use of ULE versions of the texts. In the three-year study, 102 middle school students in both conditions used the reciprocal teaching strategies of prediction, questioning, clarification, and summarizing, as well as visualization.[13] After controlling for gender and initial reading achievement, students in the ULE condition demonstrated significantly greater gains on a standardized measure of reading comprehension than did their peers in the traditional strategy instruction condition. Improvement was moderate, equating to a reading achievement gain of approximately half a grade level. For struggling students who read at or below the twenty-fifth percentile prior to intervention, however, this was a meaningful increase. The finding that students with relatively greater initial vocabulary demonstrated greater gains in comprehension was particularly important, and suggests the need to improve the quality of the ULE vocabulary learning.

Extending this work to Spanish-speaking students of English, researchers have refined the ULEs to target vocabulary enrichment supports and Spanish language translation options. C. Patrick Proctor, Bridget Dalton, and Dana Grisham piloted a combined vocabulary and strategy ULE in a classroom of thirty fourth-grade students consisting of fourteen Spanish-speaking ELLs and sixteen monolingual English speakers.[14] The tested ULE had an event usage log tracker that recorded and stored each student's interactions with the ULE supports. Of particular interest to the proposed work was the finding that lower-performing students, including ELLs, were more likely to access important vocabulary (clicking hyperlinked vocabulary words and posting them to "My Glossary") and comprehension supports (accessing strategy coach support). Correlational analyses indicated that the use of vocabulary and strategy coach supports were positively associated with vocabulary and comprehension gain.

In a new study funded by the U.S. Department of Education's Institute of Educational Sciences, researchers at CAST and Harvard University are exploring ways to enhance vocabulary supports for ULEs with the goal of improving students' reading comprehension and vocabulary knowledge. Of particular interest is whether the use of embedded comprehension supports is associated with vocabulary and comprehension outcomes over the course of the intervention. In addition, the researchers are assessing learner characteristics to determine if students who typically struggle with text comprehension, such as struggling readers or bilingual students, are more likely to access the various supports as found by Patrick Proctor and colleagues. These data will yield critically important information relevant to the design and use of individualized digital learning environments for second-language learning.

Conclusion

Universal Design for Learning provides a potent framework for teachers like Professor Garcia as she works to meet the needs of diverse learners. In this framework, educational technologies can provide a wide range of opportunities to customize curriculum and instruction to meet individual differences. Of course, this will require new thinking about the role of the textbook in higher education, for although printed text surrendered its cultural dominance in high-impact fields, such as entertainment and commerce, its predominance in the academy continues. The result is that powerful multimedia tools are often relegated to supplementary status, while printed text—which is not easily adapted to meet individual needs—remains the core tool of teaching and learning in foreign language learning and other subjects. A book requires learners to "fit the mold" of what "good" learning is—a stricture that stifles those who want to, or have to, take diverse learning paths to the same curricular objective. On the contrary, graduates of a universally designed environment will, as David H. Rose and Anne Meyer have written, "know their own strengths and weaknesses, know the kinds of media, adaptations, strategies, and external technologies they can use to overcome their weaknesses and extend their strengths, and the kinds of colleagues who are likely to complement their own patterns of learning and performance."[15] They will be prepared to succeed in the world, on their own terms and in their own way.

Acknowledgment

This chapter draws on and develops material previously published by the authors as "UDL Implementation: Examples Using Best Practices and Curriculum Enhancements," in *The Universally Designed*

Classroom: Accessible Curriculum and Digital Technologies, ed. David H. Rose, Anne Meyer, and Chuck Hitchcock, 149–97 (Cambridge, Mass.: Harvard Education Press, 2005). Adapted with permission of Harvard Education Press. All rights reserved. For more information, please call Harvard Education Press, 617-495-3432.

Notes

1. Anne Meyer and David H. Rose, *Learning to Read in the Computer Age* (Cambridge, Mass.: Brookline Books, 1998); David H. Rose and Anne Meyer, *Teaching Every Student in the Digital Age: Universal Design for Learning* (Alexandria, Va.: Association of Supervision and Curriculum Development, 2002).
2. David H. Rose and Anne Meyer, "Universal Design for Individual Differences," *Educational Leadership* 58, no. 3 (2000): 39–43; Lev Vgotsky, *Thought and Language* (Cambridge, Mass.: MIT Press, 1962).
3. Lucinda E. Branaman, Nancy Rhodes, and Jeanne Rennie, "A National Survey of K–12 Foreign Language Education," *ERIC/CLL News Bulletin* 6, no. 1 (1998): 13–14.
4. Meei-Ling Liaw, "Using Electronic Mail for English as a Foreign Language Instruction," *System* 26 (1998): 336.
5. Batia Laufer, "Vocabulary Acquisition in a Second Language: Do Learners Really Acquire Most Vocabulary by Reading? Some Empirical Evidence," *Canadian Modern Language Review* 59 (2003): 567–87.
6. Jean LeLoup and Robert Ponterio, *Meeting the National Standards: Now What Do I Do?* (Washington, D.C.: ERIC Clearinghouse on Language and Linguistics, 1998); Kristi Rennebohm Franz and Edwin H. Gragert, "Global Education for Today's World: Creating Hope with Online Learning Communities," in *Better Teaching and Learning in the Digital Classroom,* ed. David T. Gordon (Cambridge, Mass.: Harvard Education Press, 2003).
7. Samantha Earp, *More Than Just the Internet: Technology for Language Teaching* (Washington, D.C.: ERIC Clearinghouse on Language and Linguistics, 1997).
8. Ingrid Pufahl, Nancy C. Rhodes, and Donna Christian, *Foreign Language Teaching: What the United States Can Learn from Other Countries* (Washington, D.C.: ERIC Clearinghouse on Language and Linguistics, 2000).
9. Andrew Cohen, *Strategy Training for Second Language Learners* (Washington, D.C.: ERIC Clearinghouse on Language and Linguistics, 2003); Bridget Dalton and Nicole Strangman, "Improving Struggling Readers' Comprehension Through Scaffolded Hypertexts and Other Computer-

Based Literacy Programs," in *The Handbook of Literacy and Technology*, vol. 2, ed. Michael C. McKenna, Linda D. Labbo, Ronald D. Kieffer, and David Reinking (Mahwah, N.J.: Lawrence Erlbaum, 2006), 75–92; see Rose and Meyer, *Teaching Every Student;* Nicole Strangman, "Strategy Instruction Goes Digital: Two Teachers' Perspectives on Digital Texts with Embedded Learning Supports," *Reading Online* 6, no. 9 (2003). http://www.readingonline.org/articles/art_index.asp?HREF=/articles/voices/winslow_previte/ (accessed October 14, 2005); Nicole Strangman and Bridget Dalton, "Technology for Struggling Readers: A Review of the Research," in *The Handbook of Special Education Technology Research and Practice*, ed. Dave L. Edyburn et al. (Whitefish Bay, Wis.: Knowledge by Design, 2005), 545–69.

10. Dorothy M. Chun and Jan L. Plass, "Effects of Multimedia Annotations on Vocabulary Acquisition," *Modern Language Journal* 80 (1996): 183–98; Chun and Plass, "Facilitating Reading Comprehension with Multimedia," *System* 24 (1996): 503–19; Chun and Plass, "Research on Text Comprehension in Multimedia Environments," *Language Learning and Technology* 1 (1997): 60–81.

11. *Standards for Foreign Language Learning in the 21st Century* (Lawrence, Kans.: Allen Press, 1999).

12. Bridget Dalton, Bart Pisha, Maya B. Eagleton, Peggy Coyne, and Susan Deysher, "Engaging the Text: Reciprocal Teaching and Questioning Strategies in a Scaffolded Learning Environment," Final Project Report to the U.S. Office of Special Education Programs (Peabody, Mass.: CAST, 2002); David T. Gordon, "Curriculum Access in the Digital Age," *Harvard Education Letter* 18, no. 1 (2002): 1–5; Rose and Meyer, *Teaching Every Student;* Annemarie S. Palincsar and Ann L. Brown, "Reciprocal Teaching of Comprehension-Fostering and Comprehension-Monitoring Activities," *Cognition and Instruction* 1 (1984): 117.

13. See Dalton et al., "Engaging," and Palincsar and Brown, "Reciprocal Teaching"; Michael Pressley, *Reading Instruction That Works: The Case for Balanced Teaching* (New York: Guilford Press, 1998).

14. C. Patrick Proctor, Bridget Dalton, and Dana Grisham, "Scaffolding English Language Learners and Struggling Readers in a Digital Environment with Embedded Strategy Instruction and Vocabulary Support," *Journal of Literacy Research* (forthcoming).

15. David H. Rose and Anne Meyer, "The Future Is in the Margins: The Role of Technology and Disability in Educational Reform," in *The Universally Designed Classroom: Accessible Curriculum and Digital Technologies*, ed. David H. Rose, Anne Meyer, and Chuck Hitchcock (Cambridge, Mass.: Harvard Education Press, 2005), 30–31.

Disabilities Abroad

CHAPTER 10

Cédez le passage: *A Chronicle of Traveling in France with a Disability*

ELIZABETH EMERY

Traveling to a country where one is not proficient in the language is a daunting experience. This is particularly challenging for students who may not have traveled before and may not know what to expect of a foreign culture. The extensive literature dedicated to study abroad emphasizes that false expectations or fears about other countries are the primary barriers to studying abroad.[1] Until arriving in a foreign country, even those students who do choose to travel tend to be preoccupied by immediate needs, such as food, shelter, and communicating in the foreign language.[2]

Studying abroad with a disability presents the same challenges, compounded by questions about barriers and services in the host country. Concerns about lodging, health, and communication are complicated by questions surrounding the accommodation of a disability. Surveys conducted with students at Pennsylvania universities reveal that it is precisely such issues as family support, faculty and staff resources, expense, and lack of accessibility or accommodations at host institutions that most often discourage students with disabilities from studying abroad.[3] Similar reasons seem to dissuade study abroad directors and institutions from encouraging students with disabilities to apply to their programs. While administrators can monitor the accessibility and services provided at their own institutions, partnerships with overseas universities involve a loss of control and unknown costs. It is often impossible to anticipate the conditions that will prevail in another school or another country.[4]

These concerns, however, are like those of students who choose not to travel abroad because of their fears of the unknown. Misconceptions about the difficulty of studying abroad with a disability cause students, faculty members, and administrators to see such trips as insurmountable obstacles and to discourage students from giving serious thought to the elements involved. This chapter argues that good communication, combined with determination on the part of the study abroad director and the student, can correct such misconceptions, the primary barriers to studying abroad. As its title—*Cédez le passage*—suggests, the chapter contends that study abroad with a disability is far from impossible; indeed, we must simply encourage travel professionals and administrators to make way for it. Once students travel abroad, they are surprised to find that other countries, even those with a reputation for poor accessibility, warmly welcome travelers with disabilities, opening the way for rich opportunities for international exchange and communication.

As Peter Matthews and his colleagues have shown, there are a great number of factors associated with individuals and their study abroad experiences: mobility concerns are not all alike. They are not the same as hearing or sight impairments, nor are they like learning disabilities. Planning and close consultation between student, campus accessibility specialists, and international education staff are essential. Because the type of travel planned and the students involved render each study abroad trip unique, this chapter does not aim to propose a model for study abroad. Instead, it is intended as a case study to help others contemplating group study abroad in France. I describe a summer study abroad experience in France for which I served as faculty leader. Kristin, a student with a mobility impairment (whose name has been changed for the purposes of my discussion here), joined thirty other students as we traveled to Paris and Nice. I provide a description of the logistical challenges I faced as program director in organizing group travel to accommodate the needs of a student with a disability; an overview of the experience itself, including its rewards and pitfalls; and an analysis of lessons learned. In the Appendix I offer a resource guide for those seeking information about traveling in France.

Logistics and Planning

The program in Paris and Nice is administered by the study abroad center at my university. French faculty members develop the academic content and run the program in France, while the center is responsible for managing finances and booking travel. When I led the trip, the summer program was in its second year, so planning to accommodate a student who regularly uses a wheelchair took place alongside other adjustments to the program. Four days of excursions in Paris were followed by a month of study and cultural visits in and around Nice. Staff included the program director, two students who would serve as resident assistants, and faculty members from the University of Nice, with whom we have a partnership.

This was the first time a disabled student from my university would study abroad. While supportive of Kristin's desire to go to France, the study abroad office cited an Office of Civil Rights ruling stating that universities are not responsible for making accommodations for disabled students choosing to study abroad on optional trips. They made it clear that we were under no obligation to admit Kristin to the program and that it was my choice to accept or reject her application. I argued that we should include her because she was actively involved in the French program and was enthusiastic about participating. I had known Kristin for two years, she had taken several language classes with me, and she had served as secretary and president of our French Club. She talked often about visiting France, especially after her friends returned from studying abroad and spoke nostalgically about their experiences.

Kristin and I discussed her needs and researched the problems she was likely to encounter in France. I cannot insist enough on the importance of this step. Students who have not yet traveled abroad lack the tools to anticipate what awaits them. Indeed, studies such as those of Rohrlich, Martin and Rohrlich, and Barrows have shown that students tend to focus on immediate concerns such as food and health because they cannot anticipate the ways in which culture shock and homesickness will affect them.[5]

For students with disabilities, it is particularly important for the director to spell out clearly and extensively both the highlights and the challenges of studying abroad and to place them in the context of the student's needs. For a student with a mobility impairment, this might involve looking at pictures and videotapes showing streets, sidewalks, and transportation systems, while a student with a learning disability would benefit from a detailed description of pedagogical methods and materials used in the foreign classroom. National attitudes toward accessibility constitute an important cultural difference of which all students should be aware; this is a good topic to introduce at group orientation sessions. Realizing that other cultures and different countries have radically varying public policies for and attitudes about people with disabilities becomes part of the study abroad experience itself.

In Kristin's case, we were worried primarily about mobility. On campus, she relied on a motorized electric scooter for transportation, but used crutches to walk very short distances. As anyone who has traveled to Europe knows, old city infrastructures do not lend themselves well to wheelchairs: Metro stations are rarely equipped with elevators, few buses have electric lifts, and narrow sidewalks and cobblestones or sand paths make transportation challenging at the least and impassable at the worst. A related issue was the unwieldy nature of her heavy two-hundred-pound machine, which we would need to lift in and out of buses and trains, especially in Paris.

In conducting research for the trip, we read Internet horror stories about the airlines' rough handling of scooters as they were dismantled for transport or dropped from the conveyer belt, and about the difficulties of voltage compatibility—melted batteries and burnt-out motors. Getting equipment repaired abroad seemed time consuming at best and impossible at worst. First-hand accounts from on-line discussion groups convinced us that it was better to give up the autonomy of the motorized scooter for the mechanical simplicity and flexibility of a manual wheelchair.[6] We decided that we could rent a scooter in Nice if it was too difficult to rely on other students to push the chair when necessary.

Although one might think that buying a new wheelchair is an expensive proposition, there are models for every budget, ranging from $150 for reasonably lightweight (twenty-pound) "transporter" or "companion" chairs that fold, to ultralight and titanium models ranging in price from $500 to $1500 (see Appendix 10.1). Kristin hesitated to adopt a new mode of transportation, and at the last minute she borrowed an Invacare manual wheelchair (like those found in most hospitals) weighing nearly fifty pounds. It was incredibly heavy for one person to lift and not collapsible, but at least it was solidly built, with thick rubber tires that could not be punctured. Because Kristin had borrowed the wheelchair from a friend, she did not spend any more money on this trip than any other student in the program.

Kristin was fortunate; depending on the nature of the disability, finances can play an important part in the decision to study abroad, especially if assistants or translators are required. Mobility International USA (MIUSA) has published a very helpful article pointing out inexpensive substitutes for such accommodations and arguing that cost does not have to be a major factor when deciding to study abroad.[7] This is true; however, the situation fluctuates according to each student's needs. Even modest costs can seem prohibitive to students.

Originally, Kristin and I had estimated that she might need to budget as much as $1,000 for buying or renting equipment, whereupon we decided to pursue outside funding options. I asked Kristin to work with the University Office of Disabilities, MIUSA, and other organizations to which she belonged to obtain grants to cover the cost of purchasing or renting equipment for the trip. I approached the staff members of our study abroad office to see whether they could contribute money or locate organizations to which we could apply for funding. Although their office supported my decision to include Kristin on the program, they presented it as her choice and stated that they were not required to provide support services for an optional program. Their budget did not include a provision for disabled students, and thus they were able to offer little financial assistance. Kristin was awarded a $500 scholarship for study abroad, but this sum was ostensibly for her excellence as a student and not a grant for equipment. The study abroad center was nonetheless helpful in providing me with links to disability offices in France, and to the National Clearinghouse on Disability and Exchange (NCDE) and MIUSA, but they took no part in arranging accommodations. Services for Students with Disabilities did not provide any financial support, either, and went so far as to question Kristin's motives for studying abroad. Kristin and I were thus responsible for making all the arrangements, and she was to be solely responsible for all costs related to accommodation of her disability. Because Kristin was able to borrow a chair, our lack of success in fundraising did not critically impact the program.

In addition to discussing Kristin's needs, locating equipment, and searching for grants, other advance preparations included finding accessible lodgings, arranging transportation and excursions in Paris and Nice, and preparing for the difficult conditions at the University of Nice. Dealing with both French and American travel agents was frustrating because of misconceptions surrounding travel with a disability. They questioned the notion of taking a student with a mobility impairment on the trip at all. Like staff members in Services for Students with Disabilities on my own campus, these travel agents asked, "Why would she want to do that?" and answered their own question with a firm, "That's simply not possible." These were the two most common responses to requests for information about accessibility. Here is an excerpt from one of the e-mail exchanges with a travel agent regarding planning for accessibility: "Regarding the handicapped person, unfortunately the hotel does not have any handicapped equipment. Unfortunatly [*sic*] only a few 3 star hotel [*sic*] in France are equipped but only 4 star may have handicapped rooms. Also the coaches can accept a folding wheelchair if the person does not need too much assistance but are not equipped to receive a motorized cart. Is this person really handicapped or can she move with help of some persons around? In that case a simple wheelchair can be fine."[8]

I will not comment on this quotation, which speaks volumes both about attitudes toward traveling with a disability and about the roadblocks inherent in the planning process. This was fairly typical of nearly every exchange about accommodations we had with professional travel agents. On the other hand, we found individuals in France to be surprisingly welcoming throughout the transatlantic planning process. The director of the summer program at the University of Nice was extremely apologetic about the difficulties we would soon face on the disability-unfriendly campus. She made things as easy as possible for us, choosing classrooms that would be accessible by ramp and elevator, and when we arrived, she personally guided us on the best routes through buildings to avoid stairs. She apologized often about the state of affairs and looked forward to reforms that were under way to make the school more accessible to those using wheelchairs and crutches.

Instead of selecting the Nice dormitories, which are far from public transportation and do not have elevators, I made arrangements for all students with a semiprivate student residence. Fairly modern, it was equipped with a large elevator and handicapped accessible private studio apartments; the staff promised to help in any way necessary. Although there was a step up to the main entrance, the back entrance had a ramp. It was only a few blocks from bus transportation, stores, shops, and tourist attractions.

A final step involved researching the accessibility of the monuments we planned to visit in Paris and making advance phone calls to verify the accuracy of the information. Expecting the worst, I was surprised to find that nearly every Parisian monument had some kind of provision for at least partial handicapped access. The Web site published by the Paris Tourism Office (see Appendix 10.1) provides a brief description of the accessibility of each monument, in addition to phone and fax numbers and e-mail addresses. It is possible to call ahead for more detailed information. Employees were universally cordial and helpful, and most offered free admission to those using wheelchairs. Although one is supposed to have an official French card to receive such benefits, the unofficial practice appears to be to waive admission fees. When Kristin asked why, she was told that it was because they were so embarrassed by the lack of accessible facilities.

Traveling in France

Although I had worried a great deal about the initial flight from Newark to Paris, it was among the easiest parts of the trip. We had alerted the airline, Air France, ahead of time, and once Kristin had checked her luggage (and wheelchair), the airline assigned her a porter who took her through security and met with us at the boarding gate. Airlines are well equipped for travelers with disabilities. Luggage, however, was another story. Although I had warned everyone to bring no more than they could comfortably carry for two blocks, our luggage caused consternation among the many bus drivers and train porters we saw and provoked a fit of anger in one driver, who exclaimed, "C'est pas normal! C'est pas des bagages normals!" Oversize and overweight suitcases seem to be a universal study abroad phenomenon, and Kristin's cases were no different. It was not easy to negotiate both wheelchair and luggage once we left the airport.

Paris

Upon our arrival in Paris after a sleepless red-eye flight, the travel agent sent to meet us expressed surprise at seeing the wheelchair and told us we could not put it in the bus. Although we had clearly spelled out our needs several times before arrival, the local travel agent had not informed the subcontracted bus company. When I insisted that we were not going to leave the chair at the airport and that there was absolutely no reason why we could not fold it and put it in the bus with our hand luggage, the driver grudgingly agreed. We thus hefted the chair into the bus, balancing it in the aisle, as we would for every subsequent bus trip.

Other communication was similarly problematic. Despite the fact that I had called the hotel to confirm that we could check in early in the morning, when we arrived at 10:00 A.M., we were informed that rooms would not be available until noon. We thus stowed our luggage and traipsed down the street to a café, where the students had their first French coffee. When the rooms did become available, we discovered that the hotel was not wheelchair accessible, as the travel agent had told us it would be. The elevator was minuscule, and the rooms were small and cramped. I offer these examples to illustrate the vagaries of the study abroad experience in general. Even the best-planned trip has its share of unexpected surprises and inconveniences, and students should be told to expect these kinds of situations.

Our system for touring was very simple, yet effective: groups traveled together, on foot, using buses, the Metro, or taxis. Because of the intractability of most of the travel agents we had contacted, I planned the excursions myself, designing them to allow maximum flexibility. We purchased a *carte musées et monuments* for each student as well as a book of Metro tickets. I then set up printed itineraries that followed a circuit of trips to various monuments with "rendezvous points." Students could thus travel as a group to each of the sites or explore on their own, meeting the group at the places that most interested them. In this way, anyone who was tired or who wanted to linger could do so while knowing where to find the rest of us.

I will describe one such day of touring in the interest of showing how a wheelchair can be incorporated smoothly into excursions. This particular day included visits to Notre-Dame de Paris, the Latin Quarter, and Montmartre. Everyone was to meet at 8:45 A.M. in the hotel lobby. Once assembled, we went down the street to the Metro station around the corner. While one of the students or I folded the wheelchair and carried it down the steps, Kristin used her crutches and the railing to descend. She would get back into the chair at the bottom and continue through the corridors of the Metro until we encountered the next set of stairs (the bane of our existence; there is staircase after staircase in the Metro). Nonetheless, the Metro itself was a tourist attraction: Kristin had never taken a subway before.

Once we arrived at the Ile de la Cité station, we continued down the street to the Sainte Chapelle. Prior to departure, I sent—in accordance with Web site instructions—a fax alerting the museum to our arrival. Security guards took Kristin through the Palais de Justice and into the upper level of the Sainte Chapelle, thus avoiding stairs. To reach the lower level of the chapel, however, she had to negotiate the winding and slippery stone steps with her crutches, while one of us brought down the wheelchair.

After our visit to the Sainte Chapelle, we continued down the street to Notre-Dame de Paris and visited the inside of the cathedral, which is perfectly accessible from street level. Next, we crossed the Seine and explored the Latin Quarter, stopping for lunch. We then took a bus to the Place des Vosges and the Maison Victor Hugo for a tour related to a class on nineteenth-century theater. The bus had a kneeling function, but a large step remained, so one student helped Kristin, while another two lifted the wheelchair. Other passengers also assisted and gave up their seats; it was very much a team effort. We repeated the process when leaving the bus, nearly getting shut in the doors when we could not exit quickly enough. This was typical of nearly every bus ride in Paris and Nice.

The garden in the Place des Vosges is lovely and accessible at ground level. We found that the Maison Victor Hugo did not have an elevator (though it has one now), and we were required to leave the wheelchair at the coat check, "for security reasons." Kristin said she wasn't tired, so she used her crutches to visit the exhibit, which was spread over three floors of the house. After this trip, we took the Metro back to the hotel.

That night, we met in the lobby at 7:00 P.M. and took the Metro to Montmartre, wandering up and down the steep hills, through the Sacré Coeur (not particularly accessible, because of the stairs at its entrance) and around the Place du Tertre, where we had dinner. Montmartre was particularly challenging because of the hills, but we were heartened to see two other travelers in wheelchairs negotiating the narrow sidewalks and hills (they both had lightweight chairs). As a safety precaution, two or three people walked in front of our heavy chair to make sure it did not get away, and two or three pulled or pushed it as we went uphill or downhill. Just as Kristin and I had planned her accommodations in advance of the trip, other students had done similar pre-reading; we thus ended the evening at the Lapin Agile cabaret, singing along to some of the songs the students had learned in preparation for our visit. We returned to the hotel via taxi, exhausted by the end of the day, but having enjoyed ourselves immensely.

The system of rendez-vous points gave students flexibility and choice (between English- and French-language guides, monuments to visit, and time of day), while breaking the group into a manageable size (two groups of ten to fifteen instead of one group of thirty-one). Because of the number of hands, there was always someone to push or carry the wheelchair up or down stairs, ramps, or sidewalks, and we were able to take the Metro, buses, and the funicular (at Montmartre) as a group. The great advantage of this was that the group moved together. Occasionally, we would run into snags with public transit (negotiating steps in the Metro station or the buses, for example), in which case one person would stay with Kristin and meet up with the rest of the group a bit later.

Much to their delight, students discovered that wheelchairs provided free entry to the Metro and to most monuments for the person with a disability and his or her companion. There was thus some competition as to who would accompany Kristin through the wheelchair accessible gates found at many Metro stations. When Kristin wanted to strike out on her own, she took a taxi and met up with us at the rendez-vous points. One or two students could lift the manual wheelchair in and out of buses, trains, taxis, and the Metro. It was, however, very heavy and difficult to get in and out of taxis; the footrests had to be detached each time so that it would fit. We quickly learned to order "breaks"—minivan taxis—which could easily accommodate the chair without our having to dismantle it.

Overall, the Paris trip worked more smoothly than I could have imagined. The good nature and camaraderie of the group turned the difficulties of Paris transportation into veritable adventures. The wheelchair worked marvelously for the group as a whole because we could move quickly and easily from one tourist site to another, carrying the wheelchair up or down stairs or into buses as we encountered them, while Kristin used her crutches. The drawback, of course, is that Kristin forfeited her autonomy from the rest of us by agreeing to bring the manual wheelchair, which she could not propel on her own. Kristin was very gracious about allowing us to push the wheelchair, but I know it was hard for her. She was accustomed to complete independence on campus, and as she told me in Paris, it was sometimes embarrassing to rely on others to get around. Renting a motorized wheelchair in Paris would have solved this problem but caused others. Kristin's unfamiliarity with the city, curbs without ramps, potential for theft or mechanical breakdown, and the impossibility of getting a motorized chair into buses or taxis made using one impractical for our brief visit.

Nice

The situation in Nice was much more complicated than had been the case in Paris. We traveled in large groups during the four days in Paris. In Nice, however, we stayed for a month, quickly settling into a pattern of classes and daily life. Students no longer kept the same schedule. The residence itself was marvelous, especially because it was equipped with an elevator and fairly spacious rooms. However, the University of Nice was a mile away, though accessible by bus. Buses in Nice do not have elevated lifts, and drivers tend to be somewhat impatient to leave on schedule. This is where I expected things to get very difficult for Kristin, and I felt that a motorized wheelchair would have been an easier mode of transportation. Streets in Nice are in better condition than streets in Paris, and the Promenade des Anglais provides a wonderful expanse of smooth sidewalk with tremendous views.

The University of Nice was extraordinarily helpful in making the most of conditions that can accurately be described as disability-unfriendly. From a few blocks from our residence, a local bus went to the main entrance to the school. None of the buses in Nice is designed to kneel, so getting in and out was a trial. This, however, was relatively easy in comparison to what came next. Once at the university, Kristin had to negotiate two steep flights of stairs before reaching the building itself, which has a circular staircase and no elevator. With great ingenuity, the director of the international summer program arranged classrooms that allowed us to circumvent this entrance. Instead, we arrived via a somewhat steep driveway, connecting through another building, which had an elevator. It was not ideal, but it worked.

The excursions in Nice functioned similarly to those in Paris: we all stayed together and moved the wheelchair up, down, and around, as necessary. We took tours of local museums and joined the University of Nice's excursions to Cannes, the Lérins Islands, Monaco, Eze, and La Turbie. The difficulties encountered here were minor, largely a product of the French guide's unwillingness to wait for the group. This French graduate student, hired by the university, moved at his own brisk pace, continually losing students who stopped to take photos. He told me that it would be categorically impossible to take a student with a wheelchair on his excursions, but we did it anyway. Equipped with maps and a cell phone, several of us would take our own routes when the guide's were impassable, meeting up with the larger group later on. The cell phone saved us on many occasions.

I worried that this leg of the trip would be difficult for Kristin and that she would suffer from the truly daunting transportation situation in Nice. This was not the case. There were many steep curbs and stairs, but one simply had to think about them ahead of time and negotiate them one at a time. With determination, these are easy obstacles to overcome. Everything else—courses, excursions, interaction with other students from all over the world—was a great adventure.

Lessons Learned

Traveling abroad with Kristin, who had long dreamed of visiting France, was a highlight of my experience with study abroad. There were many difficult moments, such as arguing with bus drivers or struggling to get the wheelchair in and out of tight spaces, but on the whole I could not have wished for a student more enthusiastic about the program and more willing to take risks. Kristin's appreciation of the things we saw, from her delight in experiencing the Metro for the first time to her excitement in taking the elevator up the Eiffel Tower—things she never thought she would be able to do—changed our perceptions. Instead of focusing on one monument after another, for example, as we might have done by taking the Metro, the slower pace of our trip encouraged us to focus on architectural details, cobblestones, the scent of food from restaurants or markets, the play of light on the Seine or the Mediterranean. Walking, the easiest method of transportation with the wheelchair, focused more attention on the urban fabric of both Paris and Nice. Kristin's stream of commentary and her excitement at seeing things she had only dreamed about visiting in person made other students realize how much they took their own mobility for granted. They also gained much greater sensitivity to life with a disability from this first-hand experience.

I was surprised to discover that Kristin's disability actually gave her an advantage over other students, linguistically speaking, because it afforded her privileged access to the French. The wheelchair became a conversation piece, a way of breaking the ice. Locals tended to strike up conversations with Kristin—asking her where she came from, what she was doing, what she thought of Nice—as they did not with other members of the group, who were dismissed as mere tourists. It is perhaps no surprise that Kristin's French improved dramatically over the month and that she even talked about moving to France after graduation.

Above all, the trip was a tremendous learning experience. I left home with the determination to make it work, but without fully understanding the obstacles in our way. During the month, I gained many insights into organizing a program to include a student with a disability. Contrary to what one might think, it is not significantly more difficult than planning any other study abroad trip. The key is good communication and advocacy: one must begin planning early, clearly identifying student and group needs and obtaining funding for accommodations.

First of all, it is critical to consult with the student early in the process—at least a year before departure—to establish needs and to raise funds, if necessary. One of the best organizations for such planning is Mobility International's National Clearinghouse on Disability and Exchange (see Appendix 10.1). Its Web site provides an up-to-date listing of organizations that provide financial support and personal chronicles of study abroad experiences, as well as a number of international organizations that welcome students with disabilities for home stays or that organize accessible local transportation.

Above all, it is important to communicate clearly and unambiguously about the expectations of both the student and the program director and to outline the responsibilities that each will assume. Until she arrived in France, Kristin did not understand why I had advised her so strongly to find a lightweight manual wheelchair. Despite extensive verbal descriptions of the difficulties we would encounter with a wheelchair in streets, residences, universities, and public transportation in France, Kristin was surprised by differences in accessibility in France. This misunderstanding demonstrates that verbal descriptions are not enough to present an accurate picture. There is a fine line between being realistic and being discouraging, but it is crucial for the student to understand exactly what challenges

he or she will face in the host country and to present them as con-
cretely as possible. Looking closely at pictures of the locations to
be visited will help the student anticipate the barriers he or she will
face in the target country.

Similarly, it is extremely important for students to take the initiative in planning the trip and to state their needs and preferences
clearly. Much as an American student may not be able to anticipate
life in a foreign country, a faculty member cannot always imagine
what a student will require to maintain quality of life abroad, from
clothing and voltage compatibility for computers and hair dryers to
prescription medicines and wheelchairs. Each student has different needs, and it is important to weigh them against the objectives
of the program and the constraints of travel. While true of every
student studying abroad, this is particularly important for students
requiring accommodation for a disability. Good communication is
capital. In Kristin's case, it was difficult for her to imagine a mode
of transportation other than the one she was used to. Even if the
university had provided a lightweight wheelchair, would it have been
right to impose that model on Kristin without asking her opinion?
Moreover, who is responsible for specialized needs, such as a motorized scooter, which the student cannot transport from home?
The director may have no control of the budget and thus no means
of providing accommodations for the student. Yet it is the faculty
director who travels abroad with the student and must deal with the
repercussions of not having appropriate accommodations.

I would recommend that any study abroad advisor planning a
trip with a student with a disability lobby vigorously for institutional
funding to support accommodations, even if it takes time and energy.
Had I fully understood the difficulties Kristin would encounter in
France and the extent to which she would have to sacrifice her independence, I would have worked more strenuously to find or raise
money. We could have started earlier, applied for grants, and looked
for sponsors. These efforts are amply repaid once the trip begins.

In retrospect, many of our problems would have been solved by
working with a tour operator specializing in trips for people with
disabilities. Many agencies can anticipate needs and build them into
the cost of group travel. With services ranging from finding accessible hotels to renting an electric scooter and having it waiting at the
airport, or from arranging accessible tours to reserving accessible

buses and taxis, such travel agencies are relatively economical and they offer good advice (see Appendix 10.1).

In some respects, there is little to distinguish my experience that summer from the other years I have run our study abroad program. In the end, no matter how thoroughly one plans, unforeseen situations arise; this is the Murphy's Law of the study abroad experience. The key is to maintain composure, to accept each situation as it comes, and to make the most of every day. In this sense, what distinguishes traveling abroad with a student with a disability from any other study abroad experience is the anticipation of needs and equipment, greater patience, and a willingness to improvise when problems arise. Study abroad with a disability is not "impossible," as so many of the travel professionals with whom I spoke before leaving so bluntly put it; it is eminently possible. Such perceptions will change as more students and faculty members insist on the value of traveling abroad for everyone, thus persuading administrators and professionals to share the right of way.

Appendix 10.1: Resource Guide

There are a great number of books and Web sites about traveling abroad with a disability. The list below includes resources that were most helpful for us in studying abroad in Paris and Nice. In general, recent changes in European laws regarding accessibility render information given in books obsolete. We found Internet sites, which were frequently updated and featured recent stories from travelers, much more helpful. Sites available only in French are marked with a † at the end of the annotation.

General Information on Studying Abroad with a Disability

http://www.miusa.org

Mobility International USA hosts a well-organized and helpful site, full of excellent information about disabilities, advocacy, and international exchange. From information about various exchange programs to a host of free publications, videos, brochures, and tip sheets, the site continues to grow and is always up to date. Within the MIUSA Web site is a link to the National Clearinghouse on Disability and Exchange (NCDE), a site that also contains information about international exchange for disabled individuals, a searchable database of international exchange programs and internships, information about obtaining financial aid, student stories, and online discussion groups.

http://www.miusa.org/ncde/stories/

This is a list of anecdotes about experience abroad, organized according to a number of criteria, including type of disability, exchange program, and destination. These stories are accompanied by useful tip sheets for students and parents. Of particular interest is an article entitled "Helpful (and Low-Cost!) Tips for Accommodating Participants with Disabilities," which lists strategies for arranging sensible accommodations for a variety of disabilities using inexpensive devices, such portable ramps, wood blocks, and tape recorders.

http://www.miusa.org/ncde/tipsheets/lowcost
http://routesinternational.com/access.htm

This site has a variety of links to different resources sites throughout the world for disabled travelers.

People with Disabilities and International Law

http://www.miusa.org/publications/freeresources/RR%20book.pdf

"Rights and Responsibilities: A Guide to the Americans with Disabilities Act (ADA) for International Exchange Organizations and Participants" is a Mobility International publication that describes the act and its implications for those organizing and participating in study abroad trips and exchanges.

http://www.dredf.org

This Disability Rights Education and Defense Fund international site has links to a variety of countries and the text of their laws concerning disabilities.

http://www.edf-feph.org/

This European Disability Forum site posts links to various laws and organizations related to disabilities in Europe.

Travel Agents

http://www.access-able.com
http://dmoz.org/Society/Disabled/Travel/Agencies

Accessible Hotels

http://www.viamichelin.com

The Michelin red guide to hotels and restaurants reliably labels those that are accessible.

General Resources

http://www.pagesjaunes.fr

The French yellow pages allow one to search for services, organizations, and products available at stores in one's neighborhood (using a zip code). Many pharmacies and medical equipment stores in France rent out wheelchairs at extremely reasonable rates. In French and English.

http://www.cellularabroad.com

Cell phone service can be a lifesaver on study abroad trips. Europe uses the GSM standard, not compatible with most American cell phones. As a result, one must already have an American phone adapted to this standard and must speak with one's service provider in order to receive service in France. Most of the French companies support prepaid phone cards that allow one to purchase air time in lieu of signing a multiyear contract. Receiving calls is generally free, so this can be a fairly economical way to maintain an emergency phone abroad.

Travel Resources in France

See *Paris en fauteuil* by Lucie Fontaine and Jean-Baptiste Nanta, published in the "Paris est à nous séries" (Paris: Editions Parigramme, 2004). Primarily intended for those traveling by wheelchair, this book describes (in French) the accessibility of Parisian restaurants, theaters, concert halls, cinemas, museums, libraries, sports arenas, tourist attractions, toilets, and transportation. In addition, it provides an entire section dedicated to swimming and playing sports in the city, as well as helpful contact numbers and information for associations for the disabled.†

http://www.handicap.gouv.fr

The French government's Web site for people with disabilities, this site includes legal statements mixed with practical resources, covering various aspects of life for the disabled in France: lodging, transport, work, and medical and social resources.†

http://www.handiweb.fr

This site lists resources for a variety of different disabilities: resources, organizations, companies, travel services, and support groups, primarily in France and Canada.†

http://www.apf.asso.fr

The Association des paralysés français site offers access to a network of partners throughout the country. Local branches can make arrangements for home stays, transportation to school and back, often for a minimal cost, but it must be arranged ahead of time.†

IN PARIS

http://www.ratp.info/informer/accessibilite.php

The Paris transit system (RATP) publishes an Internet guide to accessibility. This portion of their site is full of extraordinarily helpful information and updates about current projects to improve accessibility. They have now installed many bus lines with kneeling stairs and ramps, incorporated hearing devices at counters, and raised warning bands along subway platforms, as well as equipped RER stations with elevators and ramps. This site is useful because it provides both lists of stations and services and phone numbers for each of the major bus or commuter rail lines, so that one can call before attempting to take public transit.†

http://www.infomobi.com

The Ile de France's Infomobi site for those with mobility, hearing, visual, or mental disabilities provides lists of transit maps and accommodations for the disabled and lists of independent companies catering to special needs. One can even obtain personalized itineraries through a designated hotline (not toll free).†

http://www.adp.fr

The Paris airport association (ADP) publishes a guide to accessibility at the airports as well as a number of helpful transit links. In French and English.

http://www.parisinfo.com

This site for the Paris Tourist Office contains many helpful links about activities, including phone numbers and accessibility information. One must click on the name of the museum or monument in order to get detailed information (phone numbers, accessibility information). They also have a lengthy list of Parisian associations dedicated to handicapped access. In several languages.

http://www.mobile-en-ville.asso.fr/Plans/Transports.asp

The Mobile en Ville Association Web site provides information about the accessibility of shops, restaurants, transport, parking, and accessible toilets. The association has also published a book, *Paris comme sur des Roulettes* (1999), that includes itineraries for those on wheels.†

TAXIS

Normal taxis have difficulty fitting a wheelchair into their trunk without dismantling it. If you order a "break," you will be driven in a small minivan, capable of holding a chair without the need to dismantle it. The Association des paralysés (see above) also arranges shuttle services, but they cost about as much as a taxi.

IN NICE

http://www.nicetourism.com/GB/frameset/pratique/frameset_handicap.html

The Nice Office of Tourism site offers a short set of links dedicated to information about accessibility in Nice.

http://handiloisirs.free.fr/

Handi-Loisirs Association in Nice organizes social gatherings and sporting events, and provides support to the disabled.†

http://www.ulysse-travel.com

Created in Nice to provide travel options for people with limited mobility, Ulysse Travel has now evolved into a full-service travel agency specializing in guided tours and packages for Paris and the Riviera.†

Checklist

There are a number of questions to consider when planning a trip to include students with disabilities. Ideally, the student would be willing and able (in terms of language skills, cultural knowledge, and initiative) to resolve many of these issues with guidance. However, trip leaders should follow the planning process closely and, realistically, undertake it themselves in close consultation with the student.

For the Trip Leader

- Discuss individualized needs with the student six months to a year prior to departure. What equipment does the student need to participate fully in daily life at the university?
- Research accessibility options for each leg of the trip and each visit, using the Internet resources listed above.
- Contact representatives involved with each phase of the trip to discuss accommodations for the student. Depending upon the student's needs, you may need to think about accommodation in transit to and from airport, in the airport, in local transit systems, in university facilities, for home stay or other lodging arrangements, and for all planned excursions.
- Consider buying a modular cell phone that takes a GSM (European) adapter, or investigate renting a cell phone abroad.
- Can accessibility equipment be repaired abroad if it breaks? Who will carry it on various legs of the trip, if the student cannot? Have you researched and noted the contact information for local repair shops?

For the Student

- Do you have the repair manual for all equipment you must bring with you? Are you bringing a tool kit to fix the equipment yourself? If your equipment is electronic, do you have the proper plugs and adapters for using it in the foreign country?
- If you need medical supplies or medications, have you obtained the proper documentation from your doctor showing that they are required? Can medications or supplies be obtained in the host country? Have you located a pharmacy or medical center where you could replace them in case of an emergency?
- How much luggage are you bringing? Can you carry it yourself? Can one other person carry it for you? In planes, trains, and buses, you may need to rely on the kindness (and physical strength!) of others. Pack as little as you can.

Notes

1. See, for example, the numerous articles, case studies, and testimonials published regularly in *Frontiers: The Interdisciplinary Journal of Study Abroad* and in the *Journal of Studies in International Education.* No-

table books that discuss student expectations about studying abroad are *Students Abroad, Strangers at Home: Education for a Global Society*, ed. Norma L. Kauffmann, Judith N. Martin, and Henry D. Weaver, with Judy Weaver (Yarmouth, Me.: Intercultural Press, 1992); T. S. Barrows, *College Students' Knowledge and Beliefs: A Survey of Global Understanding* (New Rochelle, N.Y.: Change Magazine Press, 1981); and the valuable compilation of student interviews published in Michael R. Laubscher's *Encounters with Difference: Student Perceptions of the Role of Out-of-Class Experiences in Education Abroad* (Westport, Conn.: Greenwood Press, 1994).

2. Beulah F. Rohrlich, "Expecting the Worst (or the Best!): What Exchange Programs Should Know about Student Expectations," *Occasional Papers in Intercultural Learning* 16 (July 1993): 3–10; Cornelius Grove, *Orientation Handbook for Youth Exchange Programs* (Yarmouth, Me.: Intercultural Press, 1989); and Newton E. James, "Students Abroad: Expectations versus Reality," *Liberal Education* 62, no. 4 (Dec. 1976): 599–607.

3. Peter R. Matthews, Brenda G. Hameister, and Nathaniel S. Hosley, "Attitudes of College Students Toward Study Abroad: Implications for Disability Service Providers," *Journal on Postsecondary Education and Disability* 12, no. 2 (Summer 1998): 67–77; Brenda G. Hameister, Peter R. Matthews, Nathaniel S. Hosely, and Margo C. Groff, "College Students with Disabilities and Study Abroad: Implications for International Education Staff," *Frontiers: The Interdisciplinary Journal of Study Abroad* 5 (Fall 1999): 81–100.

4. Alan Hurst, "Students with Disabilities and International Exchanges," *Higher Education and Disabilities: International Approaches*, ed. Alan Hurst 149–166 (Aldershot, U.K.: Ashgate, 1998), and B. P. Aune and H. Soneson, "Survey of CIC Institutions Concerning Study Abroad and Disability" (unpublished raw data, University of Minnesota, 1996).

5. See Rohrlich, "Expecting the Worst"; Judith N. Martin and Beulah F. Rohrlich, "The Relationship between Study Abroad Student Expectations and Selected Student Characteristics," *Journal of College Student Development* 32, no. 1 (1991): 36–49; and Barrows, "College Students' Knowledge."

6. For tips about bringing a scooter to France or renting one there, see the Internet links listed in Appendix 10.1.

7. See Mobility International's brochure "Helpful (and Low-Cost!) Tips for Accommodating Participants with Disabilities," posted to its Web site: http://www.miusa.org/ncde/tipsheets/strategiesinclusion/lowcost

8. Name withheld, e-mail to the author, October 25, 2001.

CHAPTER 11

Awaiting a World Experience No Longer: It's Time for All Students with Disabilities to Go Overseas

MICHELE SCHEIB AND MELISSA MITCHELL

As the world becomes more connected through globalization, studying abroad and learning a foreign language are acknowledged as integral parts of a university education. More workplaces are becoming diverse or multinational, and employers are looking for people who demonstrate ease with intercultural communication, strong adaptation skills learned from living in other cultures, and fluency in other languages. Employers consider interpersonal skills the top qualification when hiring, and when questioned they believe that these skills are likely to be strong in a candidate who has had an overseas educational experience.[1]

For many of today's students with disabilities, a postsecondary education is about increasing the likelihood of securing a job with career opportunities and benefits. While 21 percent of students with disabilities are now taking foreign language courses at the high school level, they still lag behind the general student population (50 percent).[2] As the number of students studying abroad at the college level increases, so does the number of college students with disabilities, who now make up 3 percent of study abroad participants, an improvement over less than 1 percent in 1998.[3] However, students with disabilities continue to be underrepresented in overseas study programs, representing 3 percent of students who study abroad and 9 percent of students on campuses. Participation is especially low among students with mobility and sensory disabilities.[4]

However, as universities seek to internationalize their curricula and increase participation in opportunities abroad, not only will students with disabilities be interested, their participation will also be necessary to reach these institutional goals. American University in Washington, D.C., offers a case in point. Collaboration between the international and disability offices focused on increasing underrepresented groups' involvement to encourage all students to participate in study abroad. The two offices began by implementing suggestions compiled by the National Clearinghouse on Disability and Exchange (NCDE), gathering assessments of overseas sites and cross-training staff on how to work with a more diverse population of students. By the end of the three-year project, they had succeeded in more than doubling the numbers of students with disabilities going abroad, which paralleled the increases among nondisabled students.

This chapter addresses numerous reasons why students with disabilities have yet to reach parity with their nondisabled peers in education abroad. Our discussion also challenges people leading these study abroad programs to embrace new concepts, question their preconceptions, and imagine possibilities for all students to go overseas.

Attitudinal Barriers

While students repeatedly hear the terms "global economy" and "globalization," they may remain unsure of what these terms mean for their future professions or their current educational paths. What attracts students with and without disabilities to study abroad is "a desire to experience another culture or to see another part of the world."[5] While nearly half of all college students express an interest in studying abroad, the number of students who actually pursue a program is considerably smaller.[6] Financial considerations, family commitments, inflexible course requirements, and a belief that going abroad will delay graduation are just some of the factors that hinder participation in study abroad for students, with or without disabilities.

For students with disabilities there may be additional factors that keep them from going abroad. Advisers and others involved with a student's academic planning may fail to mention the possibility of an international experience. Many well-meaning faculty or advisers have not participated in an international program or have limited knowledge of disability resources overseas, so they find it difficult to imagine a student with a disability living abroad in conditions that may be less accessible than those found in the United States. This may lead to what students with disabilities report as the number one barrier to their participation—a lack of awareness about study abroad opportunities.[7]

Those students who are aware of the international opportunities available to them may, however, hold the mistaken belief that their disability status precludes their participation in such programs. By all appearances, international exchange is reserved for those students who are typical. Students who use wheelchairs may see glossy ads of people climbing the pyramids, or taking in a mountain view from the top, and conclude that they are not eligible for such programs. Students who use a sign language interpreter or captioning services in the classroom might believe access is impossible to achieve academically on an international program. Others worry they will not be able to access transportation, repair equipment, have medical needs addressed, and maintain their independence. Couple these issues with concerns about how people in another culture will react to a disability, and the reasons why so few students with disabilities pursue study abroad are abundantly clear.

Students are often hesitant to voice these concerns for a number of reasons. Taken together, they may seem to pose an insurmountable obstacle. Students may assume that their fears will be simply dismissed or that they will be viewed as making excessive demands on various professionals involved in the program. They may be right: too often this is the reaction of study abroad professionals.

Suspending Disbelief for Both Students and Professionals

The terminology that we use to discuss disability issues may reflect an internalized bias against students with disabilities. We may believe that disease or impairment hampers one's ability to live independently, to pursue a variety of career options, or to study abroad. This can come from "disability spread," a phenomenon characterized by the assumption that a disability has a larger impact on the person's life than it really does.[8] In fact, the student with a disability in all likelihood characterizes herself as a well-rounded person with diverse interests, skills, and capabilities that define her identity—often the disabling condition represents only one aspect of her everyday life.

Whereas a study abroad professional or faculty leader may consider a student's psychiatric or health-related disability as a problem and may anticipate being called upon for help if differences in the host culture prove too stressful, a student who has a psychiatric or systemic disability understands it as only one aspect of existence that she can manage with the appropriate supports and strategies abroad. This student is likely quite accustomed to seeking out the support she needs at home, and with minimal help, can do the same in the host country. If one believes a student is "confined" to a wheelchair, then one also must wonder how this student will travel in a country with high street curbs, or participate in excursions to the country-side, or attend classes held in historical buildings without ramps or elevators. Yet the student may perceive the wheelchair as a tool to achieve independence rather than a burden. Because she transfers out of her wheelchair to sleep and shower, walk up stairs, move around inside her home, or get into her car, she does not consider herself to be "confined" to her wheelchair.

On the other hand, confinement does occur as a result of the physical environment. One may not believe it possible to overcome a more restrictive environment overseas, but necessity is the mother of invention, as they say, and all kinds of barriers can be mediated. Classes can be moved to lower floors, freight elevators can often be located, temporary ramps constructed, local hospitality accessed for assistance, alternative transportation modes (e.g., horses, golf carts) hired, and interior doors removed to create access. Study abroad professionals must examine their fears, take time to investigate concerns, and educate their partners abroad to find solutions that work. Various resources, such as the book *Survival Strategies for Going Abroad: A Guide for People with Disabilities,* by Mobility International USA/National Clearinghouse on Disability and Exchange, provide firsthand accounts by travelers with disabilities who achieved access abroad.[9] Suspending disbelief means avoiding assumptions about how a disability will limit, or be impacted by, the overseas experience until one has undertaken an evaluative process, examining the built environment and other aspects of the program objectively. Only then can one truly begin a comprehensive discussion of the feasibility of a particular scenario.

Disbelief may also define a disabled student's response to an adviser or parent who suggests that he study in another country. For faculty or exchange leaders who consider study abroad to be a worthwhile opportunity for students with or without disabilities, it may be difficult to encourage the students themselves to suspend their doubts that they will benefit from a study abroad experience.

These students may need to be challenged to reinterpret for themselves what independence would mean overseas, and to value the
opportunity for intercultural immersion. Not unlike the majority of
college students, disabled students may need to start envisioning
that they can survive and thrive in a culture and environment very
different from their own. Independence is how one perceives it, as
one Peace Corps Volunteer in South America who uses a wheelchair said: "There is an infrastructure in Paraguay that is even better
than any type of physical infrastructure—there's an attitude among
the people that is extraordinary. I knew what I was getting into in
Paraguay to some degree because of my previous international experience studying abroad and interning in Costa Rica. I did need to
have flexibility in my definition of independence. Is independence
always being able to do something for myself? I had to redefine that.
It wasn't necessarily that I did it, but that I accomplished a goal that
I had set forth with assistive technology or by human assistance. To
me that is independence as well."[10]

People with disabilities have the lived experience of navigating
inaccessible or unfamiliar places in the United States, and they are
likely to have developed a knack for arranging access in advance
and a capacity for problem-solving barriers or changes in conditions
as they go. Students with health-related conditions like diabetes
or anxiety disorders may experience disability-related barriers that
prevent them from exploring an unknown place abroad or reaching
out to support systems, such as a host family or other students on
the program. By involving others in the process early on, investigat-
ing resources overseas, talking with traveled peers who have similar
disabilities, and making contingency plans, this isolation can be
alleviated. Once the students are abroad, it becomes clear to them
that many fears were unfounded, and even those who do encounter
difficulties consider the rewards to far outweigh the challenges. A
student with juvenile rheumatoid arthritis who interned abroad in
Scotland explains, "After working at the Parliament, I would delay going home just so I could visit museums, shops, parks, buildings, bridges, gardens, and see views of the city that I wouldn't have
been able to find if I hadn't taken that leap of self-reliance and self-
discovery. If things looked inaccessible [in my wheelchair], I found
another way in. If a road ended in stairs, I turned around and tried
a different road. If the bus I had been waiting for was one without a
ramp, I pushed instead. Instead of cursing the city's inaccessibility,

I learned to love and appreciate its beauty and history. The reality of my situation forced me to learn how to do things I never thought possible and prepared me for the real world."[11]

Understanding Legal Obligation

The provisions of the Americans with Disabilities Act (ADA) are clear: international exchange programs that are based in the United States, or that conduct program admissions in the United States, cannot state that a program is only available to students without disabilities or institute admission criteria to prevent students with disabilities from meeting the standard of a qualified applicant. However, the ADA does not specify whether the ADA applies once the student is abroad. Different interpretations of study abroad case law are outlined in the on-line publication *Rights and Responsibilities: A Guide to National and International Disability-Related Laws for International Exchange Organizations and Participants.*[12] Legal application abroad is only explicitly stated in Title I of the ADA for U.S. employers engaged in activities overseas. The debate centers on extraterritoriality—whether or not the ADA applies to programs not on U.S. soil—as it applies to Titles II and III of the ADA or Section 504 of the Rehabilitation Act of 1973.[13] To adhere to the spirit of the law, a college, university, or private program of a certain size that is funded and operated in the United States should endeavor to meet the requirements of programmatic access defined to provide equal opportunity in a nondiscriminatory manner. However, the ADA cannot conflict with laws in other countries. Some of the critical factors in legal analysis may include:

1. The location of the program, or at least the program aspect (e.g., recruitment, courses, living arrangements) for which the student requires accommodation.
2. The location and nature of the entity that actually offers the overseas study program and the relationship between the home institution and the overseas institution.
3. The degree of control (e.g., financial, administrative, contractual, study content) exercised by the U.S. institution over the overseas program.
4. The nature of accommodation requested.
5. The overall difficulty (e.g., cost, administrative burden, special

contractual obligations, and so forth) to the U.S. institution of providing the requested accommodation.[14]

Accommodations include services, tools, or procedures that allow a person with a disability to participate equally in and have access to all aspects of the program. Programs must determine whether or not the accommodation the student is requesting is reasonable or appropriate. Three kinds of accommodations are not considered reasonable: (1) if making the accommodation or allowing participation poses a direct threat to the health or safety of others; (2) if it requires a significant change in an essential element of the curriculum or a substantial alteration in the manner in which services are provided; or (3) if it poses an undue financial or administrative burden.[15] Many believe that providing reasonable accommodation is, as a rule, expensive. In fact, 20 percent of all reasonable accommodations requested incur no financial cost. Another 51 percent cost less than $500.[16]

If the accommodation the student requests does not meet one of the above exclusions, then it is probably reasonable, and every effort should be made to provide for it or an equivalent alternative. Program administrators must actively engage the student in the process, and they cannot impose accommodation based on their own assumptions or what has been done in the past for other students. Likewise, programs cannot impose additional requirements on a participant due to fears of liability or notions of safety. On the other hand, students also cannot make specific demands on a program or show no willingness to explore other ways to meet an identified need. The student may have to accept an alternative that is more feasible or readily available in the host country, so long as it provides equivalent results.

The university is not solely responsible for accommodations arranged on campus, and the same is true of arrangements abroad. The entity arranging for accommodation in the United States may also be responsible for arrangements in an international program. Examples of common resources outside the university include Vocational Rehabilitation, the Social Security Administration, the Veterans Administration, and service clubs or disability organizations that provide scholarships.

A participant who has a disability may not have any disability-related concerns while abroad (especially with appropriate planning), and may be able to cope with less than ADA-compliant access in order to make the experience to a remote destination possible. Even if no analogous legal protections exist for people with disabilities in that country, or if no provisions have been made for accommodations in the past, it is possible to meet a student's needs and overcome obstacles. The presence of complications should not be taken as evidence that a student with a disability should not go abroad; myriad unexpected issues arise for nondisabled students as well.

Empowering Their Lead

In order to recruit students with disabilities, materials put out by international program offices typically include a nondiscrimination statement and have begun including disability images and quotes from students with disabilities. A school might consider inviting alumni with disabilities to speak as recruiters for various study abroad programs. A student with a disability often needs reassurance from people who understand her trepidation. Alumni can speak to students about the benefits of study abroad, such as increased foreign language skills, a better understanding of their skills and abilities, greater self-confidence, renewed commitment to their studies and goals, and new possibilities to consider for employment after graduation. They might also offer insights about how studying abroad improved skills specifically related to their disability. For example, research suggests that students with learning disabilities or attention deficit disorder possess increased academic curiosity, social success, improved time management skills, confidence levels, and language abilities as a result of the intensity and novelty of short-term study abroad programs.[17]

The National Clearinghouse on Disability and Exchange can connect exchange alumni with disabilities with students as requested through its peer network. The mission of the NCDE is to increase the participation of people with disabilities in the full range of international educational opportunities by educating people with disabilities, as well as disability-related organizations, about international educational exchange opportunities, and by providing international exchange organizations with practical how-to consulting and training on including people with disabilities in their programs.

Unlike secondary school, colleges and universities require students with disabilities to assume responsibility for requesting accommodations. Workshops on self-determination, leadership, and advocacy provided by campus, community, or national student organizations seek to empower college-age students. After years of having people speaking for them, many college students are learning to speak for themselves. Because not all students will have an opportunity to participate in such workshops before they go abroad, they must be encouraged to find their voices, practice diplomacy, and be resourceful in solving problems they may encounter at home and abroad.

While some students with disabilities choose not to disclose a disability and decide instead to compensate for disability-related barriers on their own, the study abroad program should be welcoming and provide opportunities for the participants to identify their access needs.[18] The program leaders can encourage disclosure in various ways. This includes creating an environment for all participants to feel comfortable sharing individual concerns in predeparture meetings, providing opportunities for participants to discuss accessibility requirements on postacceptance forms, offering scholarships for students with disabilities, or sharing information in orientation packets about planning for certain disability-related needs abroad that students may not have considered, and where they can learn more. Students may be asked to provide documentation of a disability and suggest appropriate accommodations. They can facilitate this process by simply exploring their options at least a year in advance of departure in order to allow time for documentation of their disabilities, which may include testing or researching and arranging accommodations. Students may also research options, an exercise that will enable them to learn about the host country. All parties involved should draw upon the wealth of information compiled over the past decade that describes suggested procedures and practices for college and university education abroad offices.[19]

A basic lesson for skeptics is to focus on a student's qualifications and avoid the impulse to protect or pity her, for fear of what could happen. The best way to begin is to ask the student how she does specific tasks or how she might navigate potential barriers. She may not have the specific answers at first, but does she seem open to the challenge or passionate about the experience? Including the student with a disability in planning and decision-making about issues that relate to her is one of the best strategies to making inclusion work and to having the student understand her responsibilities. Questions to consider include: How is a student with visible disabilities introduced to the group or to host families? Is the student defining her own needs as well as what she is able to contribute to the group? How are students who have disclosed disabilities referred between program advisors? Which safety concerns are realistic and which are unwarranted because of lack of familiarity with the individual or overseas site? Is the student included in all "what if" discussions to dispel any assumptions about what or how she can manage in specific situations?

Students with disabilities are no different from other students, and must be allowed to learn, grow, and make mistakes. Like other students, those with disabilities have the right take on challenges. Program leaders must be able to recognize the difference between internal and external reasons for nonparticipation. Does the student need encouragement to dispel doubts about his own abilities to try something new? Or does he need accommodations or services that the program failed to provide? Understanding this distinction will become easier with experience, an occasional reevaluation of expectations, and honest communication, as one student with cerebral palsy in a group program to Thailand explains:

> The orientation hike at Khao Yai National Park was listed in the program guide as a "90 minute not-too-rigorous walk through the jungle." That not-too-rigorous walk was one of the toughest hikes I have been on. I had to constantly tell myself that I was able to do this and that I did not want to turn back. Although I felt a little uncomfortable, there was always a helping hand. The experience taught everyone about the importance of group effort. After the hike, I was glad I had completed it and felt a real sense of accomplishment. Although leeches and log bridges were not in my comfort level, I realized I could handle them. The villages also presented a number of challenges: steps and stairways (railings are a rarity), bathing facilities and the overall design of the houses. I managed these obstacles by talking to the resident director and seeing what we could do about them. The solution we came up with was to pre-screen my houses to make sure there were no steep stairs and that the bathroom had amenities which would allow me to bathe easier. The program also has a safety net set up whereby participants who are sick, injured or otherwise unable to participate have the option of using alternative accommodations for the night. There were two

places that were too far beyond my comfort level, Thani Asoke and Mae Mun. My decisions not to stay at these locations were based on mobility and accessibility issues and safety concerns. At Mae Mun, I recognized that spending the night (it was raining buckets and the slippery conditions presented an added safety concern) would have been a flying leap rather than a small step. I was glad the safety net existed, but when I needed it, I felt guilty as I sat and thought of the other participants having sore feet at Thani Asoke and being water-logged at Mae Mun. I felt concerned that I was not contributing to the group process. At first I was not sure the group understood, but at the next group meeting, I was given a chance to explain. I think they began to understand my concerns and they also let me know that I had fourteen people I could depend on. During the program, I sometimes felt left out; while at other points I felt that the group worked well together.[20]

Normalizing Diversity

A person unfamiliar with the disability community rarely uses the term "nondisabled"; she is more likely to use the term "normal," thus reiterating exclusionary power dynamics.[21] Society has not come to terms with the view that diversity is normal and that preparing for and welcoming diverse participants benefits everyone. People with disabilities make up 10 to 15 percent of the world's population, according to the World Health Organization, and they constitute one of the minorities whose membership is constantly in flux. Anyone can become a person with a disability through a variety of situations, including aging, injury, crimes, and war.

Progress in the international arena is contributing to greater access for students with disabilities. For example, nondiscrimination disability legislation that has been passed in forty-five countries through the efforts of grassroots groups led by activists with disabilities.[22] However, these laws are often not enforced outside capital cities, and while an exchange leader could leverage services for a student with a disability by mentioning these laws, doing so may prove ineffective within a short time frame. Nonlegislative efforts, such as compiling listings on the range of disability services available in certain countries overseas, make it much easier to determine what will be available and to plan accordingly.[23] It is no longer surprising to find Braille services in Mexico, South Africa, and Hungary, or adaptive equipment in the bustling capitals of small island nations. While there are still regions and pockets within countries where it is realistic to assume that accommodations will need to be brought along or improvised, those with disabilities traveling to other countries can through example encourage more inclusive efforts and possibilities for access.

If one accepts diversity as the norm, then budgeting for inclusion is the best investment. Inclusion differs from integration in that it is not made to fit in an existing, normative structure. Rather, by its very design, inclusion offers a new vision that works for everyone and welcomes the participation of students with individual needs. Inclusion is an integral part of the day-to-day operation of a program, which makes interpreting laws or engaging in ethical discussions about a student's individual needs unnecessary. For example, a Deaf student may choose to be in a program in which everybody speaks sign language rather than one in which she always has to rely on an interpreter or captioner. Study abroad programs at universities may not offer these types of programs and so may choose to integrate the Deaf student with hearing participants by hiring a sign language interpreter. While this accommodation may satisfy ADA compliance, the Deaf student may feel isolated, singled out as the only one that needs an interpreter, and weary of asking everyone to rely upon the help of that interpreter. These inconveniences might be remedied by incorporating new technologies in the classroom. For example, allowing all students to use interactive typing in class means that discussion is instantly captioned during class time. Students might have e-mail pagers or text telephones, so that they can communicate with each other. Program leaders may learn and encourage others to learn simple American Sign Language (ASL) signs for communicating during pre-departure planning, as the student may be likely to prefer this method of communication. Deaf students may also have an interest in visiting Deaf schools or clubs while abroad to learn some of the host country's sign language, and all students on the program would benefit from such a site visit.

Strategies for Success

Because disability is culturally determined, in order to understand how people with disabilities are treated in the host culture one must explore history, religion, language, and local and national customs. For example, students with or without disabilities who transition from the individualistic culture of the United States, where people are expected to do as much for themselves as they can, to a highly community-based culture, such as Japan, may need to learn to accept more help. In doing so, students will experience what it means to live in a culture where the needs of the community are valued over those of the individual. An understanding of the host country includes exploring what it means to live life with a disability alongside what it means to be a man, woman, child, or senior citizen. People with disabilities are part of the fabric of every culture in this world—to exclude the perspective of people with disabilities from an intercultural experience is to ignore the life experience of 10 to 15 percent of a culture.

Students who have disabilities will encounter cross-cultural situations related to their disability that may require knowledge about culturally appropriate models of providing accommodations and familiarity with disability-specific terminology and language. Experienced travelers have increased their success abroad by:

1. Researching the host culture perspectives and values on disability issues.

2. Preparing a simple explanation of their disability in both English and the language of the host country.

3. Developing confidence to ask for or politely refuse assistance in both English and the language of the host country.

4. Being creative and proactive in identifying solutions to their accommodation needs; people in some cultures may rely on community and family supports more than on formal policies and procedures.

5. Recognizing that their feelings may be similar to what other students, with or without disabilities, are experiencing.

6. Identifying ahead of time available local resources, such as disability organizations, health care providers, and adaptive equipment for people who have a similar disability.

7. Balancing their disability-related needs with culturally appropriate behavior.

8. Listening to the advice of exchange program alumni, with or without disabilities: "Have the time of your life! It is so worth it!"

In everyday life, the options of people with disabilities are limited time and again by physical inaccessibility or exclusionary information. A Deaf person using a telephone relay service to inquire about an available apartment may not be given the same amount of information as a hearing person using a conventional telephone; a wheelchair user may be forced to sit in a special section of the movie theatre. The situation is the same for a student with a disability studying a foreign language. One adviser told a Spanish major who used a wheelchair that she should go to England or Australia because Spain is not accessible. When this adviser was given the testimonials of wheelchair users studying in Spain and was provided with resources on where to find the relevant information about facilities in Spain, the adviser proceeded to determine which Spanish cities best suited the student's needs based on physical accessibility rather than other criteria, such as the best course offerings or internship options. Students with disabilities are entitled to the same range of options as nondisabled students. Trip leaders must strive for full inclusion even in the early stages of planning a trip. Inclusion is only possible once someone has suspended disbelief, empowered the student to take the lead, and normalized diversity.

Creative thinking about alternatives or a positive attitude toward traveling abroad can broaden available options and transform an inaccessible environment. Like everyone else, people with disabilities have a right to enjoy the pleasures and risks of new cultural experiences, to travel, and to experience the personal, sometimes painful growth of cross-cultural situations. People with disabilities do not need "experts" who are intent on limiting their potential and right to experience the world; they need allies who are ready and willing to embark on an exploration of all the possibilities. Dedicated study abroad leaders should spend two weeks to three months experiencing what people with disabilities encounter throughout their lives, promoting equal opportunity as the world works toward more inclusive environments. While it may require additional preparation, including students with disabilities on study abroad programs may bring new perspectives to home and host cultures, affording the program leader and participants a greater understanding of what it means to be a member of that culture, and what it means to be human.

Notes

1. J. Walter Thompson Education, ed., *An Exploration of the Demand for Study Overseas from American Students and Employers* (The Institute of International Education, the German Academic Exchange Service, the British Council, and the Australian Education Office, 2004), 2, http://www.iienetwork.org/file_depot/0-10000000/0-10000/1710/folder/10528/JWT+Study.doc (accessed on April 26, 2007).

2. Renee Cameto, "The National Longitudinal Transition Study-2," presentation on October 19, 2005, to the National Capacity Building Institute, Albuquerque, New Mexico. Cameto's sources: *National Longitudinal Transition Study (NLTS)-2, Wave 1, Student's School Program Survey* (Menlo Park, Calif.: SRI International, 2002); *1998 NAEP High School Transcript Study* (Washington, D.C.: National Center for Education Statistics, 2001); *NTLS School Record Abstract, 1985–87* (Menlo Park, Calif.: SRI International).

3. Michele Scheib, "How Are We Doing? A Survey on Students with Disabilities in Study Abroad," *IIE Networker Magazine* (Fall 2004): 52–54.

4. Ibid.

5. J. Walter Thompson Education, *An Exploration*, 2.

6. Higher Education Research Institute (HERI), raw data from 2004 national student survey; HERI staff member, e-mail to Richard Goldberg, April 22, 2005. See the HERI Web site at http://www.gseis.ucla.edu/heri/heri.html; Commission on the Abraham Lincoln Study Abroad Fellowship Program, *Global Competence and National Needs: One Million Americans Studying Abroad* (Washington, D.C.: Commission on the Abraham Lincoln Study Abroad Fellowship Program, November 2005), 31–32, http://www.lincolncommission.org/LincolnReport.pdf.

7. Peter R. Matthews, Brenda P. Hameister, and Nathaniel S. Hosley, "Attitudes of College Students toward Study Abroad: Implications for Disability Service Providers," *Journal of Postsecondary Education and Disability* 13, no. 2 (1998): 67–77.

8. Brenda P. Hameister, Peter R. Matthews, Nathaniel S. Hosley, and Margo Coffin Groff, "College Students with Disabilities and Study Abroad: Implications for International Education Staff," *Frontiers: The Interdisciplinary Journal of Study Abroad* 5 (Fall 1999), http://www.frontiersjournal.com/issues/vol5/vol5–04_Hameister.htm (accessed on June 16, 2006).

9. Laura Hershey, *Survival Strategies for Going Abroad: A Guide for People with Disabilities* (Eugene, Ore.: Mobility International USA/National Clearinghouse on Disability and Exchange, 2005).

10. Christa Bucks Camacho, "Volunteering in the Peace Corps (Paraguay)" (Eugene, Ore.: Mobility International USA/National Clearinghouse on Disability and Exchange), http://www.miusa.org/ncde/stories/buckscamacho (accessed on June 15, 2006).

11. Cindy Otis, "Interning in Scotland" (Eugene, Ore.: Mobility International USA/National Clearinghouse on Disability and Exchange), http://www.miusa.org/ncde/stories/otis/ (accessed on June 20, 2006).

12. Susan Sygall and Michele Scheib, eds., *Rights and Responsibilities: A Guide to National and International Disability-Related Laws for International Exchange Organizations and Participants* (Eugene, Ore.: Mobility International USA/National Clearinghouse on Disability and Exchange, 2005), http://www.miusa.org/publications/books/rr (accessed on June 15, 2006).

13. Arlene Kanter, "The Right of Students with Disabilities to Equal Participation in Study Abroad Programs," in *Rights and Responsibilities: A Guide to National and International Disability-Related Laws for International Exchange Organizations and Participants,* ed. Susan Sygall and Michele Scheib (Eugene, Ore.: Mobility International USA/National Clearinghouse on Disability and Exchange, 2005), 41–50, http://www.miusa.org/publications/books/rr (accessed on April 26, 2007).

14. Silvia Yee, "The Presumption against Extraterritoriality: Case Studies," in *Rights and Responsibilities: A Guide to National and International Disability-Related Laws for International Exchange Organizations and Participants,* ed. Susan Sygall and Michele Scheib (Eugene, Ore.: Mobility International USA/National Clearinghouse on Disability and Exchange, 2005), 53–74, http://www.miusa.org/publications/books/rr (accessed on April 26, 2007).

15. Department of Justice, "28 CFR PART 35—Nondiscrimination on the Basis of Disability in State and Local Government Services" (Washington, D.C.: Department of Justice, July 1991) and "28 CFR, Part 36—Nondiscrimination on the Basis of Disability by Public Accommodations and in Commercial Facilities," *ADA Standards for Accessible Design* (Washington, D.C.: Department of Justice, July 1994), http://www.usdoj.gov/crt/ada/reg3a.html#Anchor-0001 and http://www.ada.gov/reg2.html (accessed April 26, 2007).

16. U.S. Department of Labor, "Low Cost Accommodation Solutions," Job Accommodation Network Survey (Washington, D.C.: Office of Disability Employment Policy, 1999), http://www.jan.wvu.edu/media/LowCostSolutions.html (accessed April 27, 2007).

17. Wendy Shames and Peg Alden, "The Impact of Short-Term Study Abroad on the Identity Development of College Students with Learning Disabilities and/or AD/HD," *Frontiers: The Interdisciplinary Journal of Study Abroad* (August 2005): 1–31.

18. See Michele Scheib, "Let's Talk about Disability: Issues of Disclosure," in *A World Awaits You: Students with Non-Apparent Disabilities Go Abroad* (Eugene, Ore.: Mobility International USA/National Clearinghouse on Disability and Exchange, June 2006), http://www.miusa.org/ncde/away/nonapparentdisabilities/disclosure (accessed on June 20, 2006).

19. Examples of such resources include the University of Minnesota's Access Abroad site: http://www.umabroad.umn.edu:16080/access and Mobility International USA: http://www.miusa.org.

20. Justin Brumelle, "Reflection: Being Part of a Group and Having a Disability in Thailand" (Eugene, Ore.: Mobility International USA/National Clearinghouse on Disability and Exchange), http://www.miusa.org/ncde/stories/Brumelle (accessed on June 16, 2006).

21. Simi Linton, *Claiming Disability: Knowledge and Identity* (New York: New York University Press, 1998).

22. Mary Lou Breslin and Silvia Yee, "International Law and Policy," in *Rights and Responsibilities: A Guide to National and International Disability-Related Laws for International Exchange Organizations and Participants,* ed. Susan Sygall and Michele Scheib (Eugene, Ore.: Mobility International USA/National Clearinghouse on Disability and Exchange, 2005), 29–38, http://www.miusa.org/publications/books/rr (accessed on April 26, 2007).

23. See the Mobility International USA Web site at http://www.miusa.org.

CHAPTER 12

Dis/Abling the Narrative:
The Case of Tombéza

SALWA ALI BENZAHRA

> We were told we were making the music of Satan. It
> wasn't just us Raï singers who were threatened, though.
> The fundamentalists used to kill all the journalists as well
> as the musicians. . . . They kept saying to me: "We'll kill
> you if you say anything and we'll kill you if you sing." In
> truth, they would have killed if I stayed quiet, too. The
> only thing I could do was sing. That was my weapon.
>
> —CHEBB KHALED, *Le Monde,* 2001

It was with much dignity and considerable courage that the writer
Rachid Mimouni labored fiercely for years to paint a grim picture
of a mutilated society. It is no secret that he battled with ill health
and fear until he died of cancer of the liver in Tangier in 1995. One
may attribute his success as a writer at least in part to that same
ill health, what Edward Said aptly called "illness as narrative." All
of this struggle, however, should not be allowed to detract from his
position as perhaps the most authentic voice that was determined
to tell of the predicament his protagonists must endure before they
liberate themselves from the instinctive life of an old, violent culture.
The protagonists disturb and unsettle the reader because they live
at the margin, the edge. It is the nature of their life.

My purpose in this chapter is to reflect not on the victims of terror, but on the other victims: the marginalized from within; in sum,
the physically disabled. *Tombéza,* by Rachid Mimouni, will serve as
my *exempli gratia* of rejection and ostracism. This elegant and haunt-
ing novel casts us deep into the underworld of perversity. Unlike its
author, it lives still in a country overtaken by a group of "insane"
people, a group that seeks to control every element of life according

to the laws of their stringent moral theology: no work of beauty created by human hands should rival the wonders of their God.

Silently holding his ground, Tombéza withstands the multidimensional oppression he is subjected to, using the narrative and his personal history as weapons against puritanical forces. In the process, the reader is taken into the abysmal depths of the protagonist's dreams, memories, hopes, and impediments and his now empty family life. The questions therefore arise: Why this violence (of the letter) that keeps being yanked back into the terror and drudgery of the daily routine by the vandalism, assaults, and death warrants that afflict the writer and the reader alike? How far can Tombéza go to maintain hope and renewal in a society that is running short of both? What are we to make of the allegory, bequeathed to the world by Mimouni, and can we read it as a humanistic testimony, gleaming from beyond the grave and beaming at the complacent conscience of the world? Without intending to answer all the questions raised here, I would like my views on the subject of writing against the knife and/or bullet in present-day Algeria to be clear from the outset.

Mimouni had an acute sensitivity to human suffering. He described the atrocities incidental to the Islamist action—prisoners shot, women raped, children and elders slain and mutilated, mosques burnt, even beehives torched—with an inarguable terseness. In a moving tribute to the outcasts, he sought to draw attention to their plight as well as represent their predicament. In doing so, he forces us to recognize the existence of an entire underworld of drifters and outcasts at "home," as it were. It is in this sense that he is unique because he allows broken individuals to lead in a narrative that teems with *half-made* lives. A case in point is *Tombéza*, where the writer paints a character handicapped by numerous social and physical disadvantages, to relate the difficulties of the Algerian society and to trace its disability to complex cultural causes. At the same time, Mimouni demonstrates that the role the female plays in shaping the experiences of such men is crucial to their survival.

Tombéza, a child of rape, is born unwanted and unloved into a peasant family in 1930s Algeria. His fifteen-year-old mother has been so savagely beaten by Messaoud, her father, for dishonoring the family that she is seriously and permanently injured. Further cruelty ensues when her pregnancy becomes obvious and an abortion is attempted: eventually she dies giving birth. Tombéza, who is born deformed, describes his appearance as follows:

Beau spectacle, en effet, que mon apparition offrait! Noiraud, le
visage déformé par une contraction musculaire qui me fermait aux
trois quarts l'oeil gauche . . . rachitique et voûté, et de surcroît affecté
d'une jambe un peu plus courte que l'autre.[1]

[Indeed, what a lovely sight my appearance presented! Swarthy, my
face distorted by a muscular contraction that three-quarters closed
my left eye . . . rickety and crooked and further hampered by one
leg being a little shorter than the other.]

Although raised in his grandfather's household, the child is effectively excluded from family membership by his grandfather's refusal
to recognize his existence or even to make eye contact with him.
He is also left without a formal name, although the children of the
village mockingly provide a nickname for him, "Tombéza," a word
play on the French verb "tomber" (to fall), which ridicules both his
appearance and the condition of his birth. His illegitimate status
also excludes him from the local Quranic School. The best that he
can possibly expect from life is to scratch a living running errands
or subsist on charity as the village freak. But the very characteristics
that alienate him from his fellow Algerians make him an attractive
prospect for the French who plan to exploit his bitterness against
his own society by recruiting him as a spy. This work provides him
with the opportunity to accumulate wealth, marry advantageously,
and exercise power over his compatriots, able and disabled alike.
When, over the course of numerous surveillance missions, he infre-
quently encounters other disabled individuals, his reaction to them
is interesting—sometimes empathetic, at other times callous. Ultimately, however, he is betrayed, wounded, and finally, to ensure his
silence, murdered by a policeman—a corrupt fellow Algerian and
Tombéza's partner in crime. The story, tragic in its own right, unfolds
against a backdrop of sweeping change and national tragedy as the
French continue to entrench their imperialist presence. Even greater
upheaval accompanies the onset of World War II with the influx of
American troops when Algeria forms part of the theater of war.

The male-dominated society that Mimouni depicts is founded
both on a gendered concept of honor and a forced separation between the sexes. In the Maghreb women are still considered inferior,
at a distinct disadvantage to men,[2] although society also requires
that they be both good-looking and strong enough to deal with the
demands of physical labor, particularly child-bearing. The birth of

a boy is cause for riotous celebration within a family. It is a much different matter, however, if paternity cannot be established, as under these circumstances a male child will not be accorded the societal advantages that his sex would normally assure him—he will be rendered effectively genderless, his masculinity negated—in fact his social standing might be even lower than that of a woman.

During World War II, the French forced tribal leaders to select the best physical specimens from amongst their men so that they could be sent to fight for *La Gloire de la France*.[3] As a result, Algerian society became sensitive to the reality that the quality of the local bloodstock was being depleted. It was also important that the remaining manpower should be robust and capable of resisting the colonial presence; accordingly, the disabled were viewed with increased intolerance. Tombéza's bizarre appearance, distressing in itself, is a constant reminder to his family and community of the condition of his birth; his physical disabilities are interpreted as a mark of divine punishment for the sins of his mother rather than as the result of the abusive treatment that she received. Tombéza explains:

> J'ai grandi sous la risée des enfants du douar. . . . [Leurs] mères en profitaient pour faire un peu de morale à leurs rejetons.
> —Regardez, disaient-elles, le fruit de la débauche et de la fornication![4]

> [I grew up as the laughing stock of the neighborhood children. Their mothers would make use of my appearance to lecture their offspring.
> —Look! They would say. The wages of sin and fornication.]

He also contests society's rationalization of his disabilities:

> Fruit de l'illégitimité . . . ! Allons donc, laissez-moi rire! Je rirai des siècles entiers. Plutôt le résultat de la fantastique rossée qui laissa ma mère idiote, sans compter ce qu'elle a connu de rudoiements, de coups, de bousculades au cours de sa grossesse, sans compter les infâmes breuvages qu'elle fut forcée d'ingurgiter, sans compter le manque de soin, la saleté . . . , la faim, les maladies qui furent mon lot quotidien.
> —La fornication! Hypocrite société! Comme si je ne savais pas ce que cachent tes apparences de vertu, tes pudibonderies.[5]

[Fruit of illegitimacy . . . ! Come on, allow me to laugh! I could laugh for whole centuries. More likely the product of the unbelievable thrashing that left my mother an idiot, not counting the bullying that she had been subjected to, the blows, the knocks during her pregnancy, not counting the vile brews that she was forced to swallow, not counting the neglect, the filth, the hunger, the diseases that were my daily lot.

—Fornication! What hypocrites! As if I didn't know what your facade of virtue and prudishness conceals.]

Generally, Maghrebian society tends to be more forgiving and accommodating when physical abnormalities are borne by a male,[6] but because Tombéza has been denied his masculine status, he is left at an additional disadvantage. Doubly handicapped by his uncertain paternity and his physical disabilities, Tombéza is alienated. He, however, becomes the scapegoat for all the ills of his country and a pariah within his own community. Despite this rejection, he continues to define his disabilities as culturally acquired and blames the deplorable sanitary conditions, scarcity of food, and the primitive traditional healing malpractices fostered by his community's superstition, which also had such a deadly effect on his mother.

Tombéza's lack of a name, almost a denial of his identity, could be a curious product of the prevailing culture of the time when male and female family members were discouraged from calling each other by name; married couples would refer to their spouse as "he" or "she." In his handling of his grandson, Messaoud chose to apply the social rules that were intended to govern a man's treatment of women rather than those that a family would normally employ towards a disadvantaged orphan boy in their midst.

It was also customary in those days when men chose to ignore the presence of women, to not look at them and therefore "not see" them. In Messaoud's refusal to gaze directly at his grandson, he could be deemed guilty of religious hypocrisy. Such an attitude could be interpreted as an extreme distortion and misapplication of the Islamic recommendation that men must avoid prolonged eye contact with women or that they lower their eyes when they interact with them. While Messaoud's behavior is strikingly similar to the way in which the men in his culture avoid looking at women out of (dis)respect for the other sex—although it is true that some Algerian/Arab/Muslim men do not look at women during conversation out of genuine respect and modesty and in the interests of listening more closely—the motive and impact of the grandfather's conduct is a far cry from any guiding religious principle. By refusing to name or to make eye contact with his illegitimate grandson he further reduces the child to a state of femaleness.

In traditional Islamic countries, it is also characteristic of the men to hold women responsible for all unwelcome changes to the world order and to vent their feelings of humiliation, frustration, and powerlessness on their female relatives. The beating that Messaoud administers to his daughter for having allowed his family to be dishonored is a violent manifestation of his sense of loss of control over the world as he used to know it. His disproportionate aggression expresses the rage, humiliation, and despair of a patriarch who finds himself a powerless spectator of the sweeping changes that are taking place around him at the hands of the colonizer. Faced with the reality that in truth he retains command over only a few small elements of his shrinking world, he singles out the most vulnerable female in his household for punishment on the pretext that as a victim of rape she was transformed into a woman without allowing him to control the transfer of her domination to another man. This honor-related brutality echoes the deadly real-life practices that are still taking place today in other patriarchal societies such as Jordan and Bangladesh.[7] The following passage describes the father's punishment:

> Sans mot dire, l'homme alla décrocher sa canne. . . . Ce bagarreur émérite des combats de *çofs* maniait en expert son bâton d'olivier à bout renflé, visant la tête, les articulations des membres, bien au fait des endroits sensibles du corps, où la douleur irradie jusqu'au cerveau, ou les coups laissent des séquelles indélébiles. La main tendue de la fille dans une muette et terrible supplication n'eut pour effet que de décupler la rage de l'homme, la violence et le rythme de ses gestes. . . . La fille ne put jamais se remettre de ce phénoménal tabassage. Défigurée à jamais. . . . Elle en sortit avec le regard fixe et l'esprit absent. Elle ne comprenait plus ce qu'on lui disait, ne savait plus parler. . . . Toute la famille se mit à attendre sa mort.[8]

> [Without saying a word, the man went to take down his stick. . . . This renowned combatant of the *çofs* wielded his clubbed olive-wood stick with expertise, targeting her head, the joints of her limbs, aiming precisely at the most susceptible areas of the body where pain

floods to the brain, where blows leave permanent scars. The girl's hand, extended in a mute and terrible supplication, served only to focus the man's rage, the violence and rhythm of his blows. . . . The girl could never recover from this terrible beating. Disfigured forever. . . . She emerged from it with a fixed stare, devoid of any spirit. She could no longer understand what anyone said to her, no longer knew how to speak. The whole family awaited her death.]

Cruel as is Tombéza's own predicament, he is also aware of the suffering of others. In one instance he draws attention to a woman who becomes "impotente" and is abandoned by her family at a hospital where subsequently she dies after being raped by a member of the staff.[9] That this young woman should be cast off by her family within a culture where the bonds of kinship are supposed to be so strong testifies to the devaluation that the female body suffers within the same society upon loss of health. Absence of the protection and dignity that she would naturally receive at home leaves her in an utterly vulnerable situation, and it is the very knowledge of her insignificance and defenselessness that enables the hospital worker to violate her in the confident expectation of impunity. In fact, it is her family and society's failure to protect and serve the woman that is the most crippling contribution to her condition. In dis/abling the narrative, Mimouni challenges his society's definition and management of disability.

The prevailing conditions of poverty and woefully inadequate medical care in pre-war Algeria were exacerbated by the onset of war and the increased Western presence. The Americans in particular introduced irreversible changes to the indigenous culture and created long-term dependencies in the Algerian economy. It is interesting to note that the sense of American superiority as experienced by Tombéza and many of his fellow Algerians also extends to their concept of aesthetic perfection; in fact Tombéza begins the description of his own infirmities with his color, "noiraud." This is illuminating not only of the fact that being dark-complexioned seems to worsen the condition of a disabled individual in the Maghreb, but also that imported beauty standards appear to have reinforced and strengthened the existing preference for white skin in the region. What if Tombéza's skin had been white? What if, albeit illegitimate, he had been born healthy and looked like a "normal" French child? His experience in life might have been a little less wretched, both at home with his grandfather and in the outside world.

The very disadvantages that ensure Tombéza's rejection by his own society, however, have an entirely opposite effect on the French who welcome him into their workforce as a highly prized "ressource humaine." Already well aware of the alienation of the disabled within the colony, the French agents recognize the rich potential within Tombéza of a suppressed and internalized violence and anticipate a bitterness against his own society, which they intend to exploit. Tombéza is assigned to surveillance and information gathering where as a spy he acts as the eyes of the colonizers, somewhat ironic given that he is partially blind.[10]

There is a poignant connection between elements of this narrative and the reality of violence in Algeria under Islamic extremism. An article recently appeared in a Tunisian newspaper, which dealt with the complex fundamentalist violence occurring in Algeria since the early nineties, and described an incident where a dwarf was responsible for the brutal butchery of a number of villagers. Irrespective of whether this is truth or fantasy, the article prompts the question of how much of a person's violence might be caused by oppression and exclusion from his own society as a result of his physical differences. Such an investigation could provide a valuable field of research for social scientists and statisticians who might be able to trace a correlation between those who espouse Islamist causes and the alienating effects of society's reaction to an individual's physical abnormalities and disabilities.[11]

Tombéza's recruitment by the French alters his relationship with his own people and in many respects sets him further apart from them, although it also provides some unexpected opportunities for human bonding. In one incident, Tombéza refuses to denounce a disabled and disfigured dwarf whom he glimpses in the dark during a surveillance mission.[12] Although he appears only fleetingly in the novel, this man evokes rare sensitivity and emotion in the protagonist. The dwarf's deformities were politically acquired, his scars the product of Algeria's struggle against French imperial might. While fighting as a guerrilla he was badly burned during an ambush, horribly disfigured by bombs that were dropped as a countermeasure by the French army. Tombéza identifies with this man and chooses to protect him from capture and torture since he can understand only too well the agony that he must have endured throughout his life as a result of people's reaction to his appearance:

Pendant combien de temps encore cet homme pourra supporter la répulsion que son apparition provoque chez ses semblables? Les jours passeront, s'émoussera lentement le prestige du maquisard, seront plus pénibles les humides nuits de l'hiver qui réveilleront la douleur, et les petits enfants effrayés que sa vision fera fondre en larmes, et la mère serrera dans ses bras son rejeton apeuré, cachant son visage contre son épaule, et devant cette scène mille fois répétée tu n'oseras plus sortir dans la rue qu'avec l'obscurité, la tête enfuie sous la cagoule de ta *kachabia,* et tu fuiras la lumière et les hommes.[13]

[For how much longer could this man endure the revulsion that his appearance evokes in his fellow men? Time will pass, the prestige of the freedom fighter will fade, the damp winter nights that reawaken sorrow will become more painful, small, scared children will dissolve into tears at the sight of him and a mother will clutch her frightened child in her arms, hiding its face against her shoulder. Before this scene can repeat itself a thousand fold, you will not dare to go out into the street except under cover of darkness, your head tucked deep into the hood of your *kachabia,* you will avoid light and humankind.]

This benevolence is gratefully rewarded when Tombéza later finds himself held hostage by villagers who are seeking revenge for their mistreatment at the hands of French collaborators. Tombéza describes his reunion with the dwarf:

Qui est cet homme? . . . C'est étrange, mais je n'ai pas peur de lui. Il se glisse derrière moi. . . . Mon libérateur détache aussi mes chevilles.
—Fuis, me dit-il. Va-t'en, et ne reviens jamais dans la région. Je le regarde, muet d'étonnement avant de reconnaître ces yeux que le faisceau de ma lampe avait cueillis sous une haie dans la nuit du camp de regroupement.
J'ébauche quelques gestes mais il m'est impossible de me relever. Je rampe vers la porte entrouverte. Alors, l'homme a eu ce geste que je n'oublierai jamais: son bras fraternel se place sous mon aisselle et me soulève. Pour la première fois de ma vie, j'ai pu m'appuyer sur une épaule offerte.[14]

[Who is this man? . . . It is strange, but I have no fear of him. He slides behind me. . . . My rescuer also frees my ankles.
—Flee! He tells me. Get going and don't ever come back here! I

stare at him in dumb astonishment before recognizing the eyes that the beam of my flashlight had caught under a hedge on the night of the rallying camp.

I try to move but it is impossible for me to get up. I crawl toward the half-opened door. It was then that this man made a gesture that I shall never forget, he places a brotherly arm under mine and raises me from the ground. For the first time in my life I could lean against a kindly shoulder.]

This expression of understanding, sympathy and acceptance is a touching episode in Tombéza's bleak existence.

Toward the end of the novel, another incident warrants examination. Tombéza's response to the blind man, Bismillah, is both interesting and significant. Bismillah, whose name is Arabic for "in the name of God," is so called not only because he is a religious man who faithfully attends prayers but also because he utters the expression frequently as he finds his way along the street with his olive-wood cane. Tombéza is intrigued by this person, but reacts to him with a puzzling combination of cruel superiority and reluctant respect, exemplifying the divided consciousness with which disabled individuals sometimes relate to each other. At the same time, Tombéza's depiction of Bismillah draws on a traditional image of the blind as visionaries, and it is, in fact, this insight that enables Bismillah to rationalize his own maltreatment when Tombéza threatens to push him over a cliff to force an admission from him that his life rests entirely in Tombéza's hands, thereby negating the will of Allah. Bismillah's response is astute:

> C'est ma cécité qui t'encourage à me tenir ce discours. . . . Tu n'oserais pas blasphémer ainsi si tu savais mes yeux fixés sur toi. C'est donc que tu n'as pas de regard intérieur.[15]

> [It is my blindness that encourages you to force this conversation on me. . . . You could not dare blaspheme in this way if you could see me staring at you. Therefore (I conclude that) you have no insight.]

However, Tombéza finally offers Bismillah's guidance as good counsel to their society: that a possible solution to the ills of Algeria is a return to the roots of the Islamic faith by following the teachings of Allah, not in a hypocritically selective, dogmatic, or violent manner, but in a poetic and merciful spirit. Tombéza had also been inspired by another teacher who believed that the Algerian people should reclaim the essential power of the Arabic language by combining Western education with the reading of canonical works like those of Ibn Sina and Ibn Rushd. But, above all, Tombéza hopes that his people should again learn the divine poetry and practice its teachings with compassion for their fellow humans, particularly the disabled.

Beyond his portrayal of the predicament of the Algerian society in the throes of transition, there is one theme which runs through everything Mimouni has written—human communication and the lack of it. In *Tombéza,* he shows us the impossibly complicated difficulties of one person speaking to another, attempting to make himself known to another, attempting to hear—really hear—what another is saying. One of the things that accompanies the throes of transition is the explosion of narratives that manage against all odds to tell of their experiences. The result of decolonization and the development of newly independent peoples, like the rise of the women's movement from subaltern to coeval status, like the appearance from obscurity of various and variously suppressed minority voices, these things have demonstrated that all forms of knowledge about human history are forms of engagement in it.[16] This is particularly true, of course, in the experience of writing back to the West, where we have come to realize—if not always to acknowledge—that the formation of such voices in emergent narratives like *Tombéza* occur within those sites of intensity and contest we have tended to associate only with political struggle. The scientific images of inferior races that marked the nineteenth century are, to use a notion elaborated by Edward Said, part of the production of these beings as second class, and hence as dominated by the wielders of the scientific discourse about blacks, Arabs, women, and primitives. Mimouni, on the other hand, brings forward another breadth to post-independence narrative. It teems with hitherto excluded voices, voices like that of Tombéza, which makes another topic, subject, and "matter" about which interest and knowledge have evolved, but like all other such knowledge they are implicated in the contest over and about Algeria.

This measure is nowhere more evident than in Mimouni's unblinking witness and electric, heroically wrought prose, of which a final measure of slangy pungency must inevitably shock his readers. He certainly could invent, and the forces that oppressed him were *interior* enough to be converted into giant fables, tragic representations of the brown man's burden and unease. There are other oppressors too. The ones standing on the outside or the *exterior*—the philistine censors and paranoid enforcers of the increasingly totalitarian revolution he initially supported and, to the end, sought to accommodate. But no imaginative conversion, and not even silence, once his talent had announced itself, could evade or placate them. His narrative and/or art flourished in Algeria's false dawn. As darkness fell, he became his talent's warder; his vitality became his enemy.

Acknowledgments

This chapter originally appeared in *College Literature* 30, no. 1 (Winter 2003): 124–34. It is reprinted here with the kind permission of *College Literature*.

I wholeheartedly thank Fran Devlin for reading and polishing the manuscript in its entirety as well as translating the quotations from French to English, and acknowledge her kind generosity. Heartfelt thanks also go to Carolyn Bryson for proofreading the text. Mustapha Marrouchi helped me coin a befitting title. To him I say many thanks.

Appendix 12.1: Francophone Maghrebian Works and Films Treating Disability

Books

Ben Jelloun, Tahar. *L'Enfant de sable*. Paris: Éditions du Seuil, 1985.
———. *The Sand Child*. Trans. Alan Sheridan. Orlando: Harcourt Brace Jovanovich, 1987.
———. *La Nuit sacrée*. Paris: Éditions du Seuil, 1987.
———. *The Sacred Night*. Trans. Alan Sheridan. San Diego: Harcourt Brace Jovanovich, 1989.
Mernissi, Fatima. *The Veil and the Male Elite: A Feminist Interpretation of Women's Rights in Islam*. Trans. Mary Jo Lakeland. Reading, Mass.: Addison-Wesley, 1991.
Mimouni, Rachid. *Tombéza*. Paris: Éditions Robert Laffont, 1984.
———. *L'Honneur de la tribu*. Paris: Editions Robert Laffont, 1989.
———. *The Honor of the Tribe*. Trans. Joachim Neugroschel. New York: Morrow, 1992.
———. *La Malédiction*. France: Éditions Stock, 1993.
Watts, Thelma L. "Perceptions of Present and Future Programming in Selected Centers for Disabled Persons in Morocco." Diss., University of Nebraska, 1986.

Films

L'Honneur de la tribu. Mahmoud Zemmouri, 1993.
La Nuit sacrée. Nicolas Klotz, 1993.
Vent de sable. Mohamed Lakhdar-Hamina, 1982.

Notes

1. Mimouni, Rachid, *Tombéza* (Paris: Editions Robert Laffont, 1984) 33.
2. Think of the period 1930s–1950s and the case will be clear enough. Women have evolved in spite of all the limitations imposed upon them.
3. Mimouni, *Tombéza*, 66.
4. Ibid., 33.
5. Ibid., 34.
6. A disabled man in the Maghreb can easily get married. The same cannot be said of a disabled woman. A good example is to be found in *The Wedding of Zein* by Tayeb Salih (1976). The bride is usually very pretty. This is the case with Tombéza's bride. It is worth pointing out that the manhood that is forcibly granted Tombéza in marriage is in another gesture taken away from him as a bogus medico-societal narrative sterilizes him and makes him unable/disabled to father a child, less of a man once again. This could also be read as a fictional representation of the forced sterilization that society has variously subjected disabled people to. For more on the subject, see Rachid Mamouni, *La Malédiction* (France: Éditions Stock, 1993).
7. I owe this insight to Barbara Walters, 20/20 ABC (November 1, 1999).
8. Mimouni, *Tombéza*, 30–31. *Note: Çofs* were guilds, unions of men carrying on the same profession or trade in the Kabylie region.
9. Ibid., 196.
10. Ibid., 101.
11. It may be useful to point to the blind Islamist sheik Omar Abdel Rahmen, who is serving a sentence in a New York jail for masterminding the first bombing of the World Trade Center.
12. Ibid., 138.
13. Ibid., 157–58.
14. Ibid., 159.
15. Ibid., 262.
16. Edward Saïd, *Culture and Imperialism* (New York: Knopf, 1993) 215.

CHAPTER 13

No One's Perfect: Disability and Difference in Japan

KATHARINA HEYER

> I'm told that when prenatal tests reveal a disability, the
> parents nearly always choose not to have the baby. . . .
> Even my mother says, "If I'd had prenatal tests and found
> out that the baby I was carrying had no arms or legs, to
> be honest, I can't say for certain whether I would have
> had you." All of which makes me want to say loud and
> clear, "Even with a disability, I'm enjoying every single
> day." It was to send this message—you don't have to be
> perfect to be happy—that I chose the English title, *No
> One's Perfect*. Some people are born able-bodied but go
> through life in dark despair. And some people, in spite
> of having no arms or legs, go through life without a care
> in the world. Disability has nothing to do with it.
>
> —OTOTAKE HIROTADA, *No One's Perfect*

Disability Has Nothing to Do with It

"Disability has nothing to do with it" is the line with which Ototake
Hirotada concludes his immensely popular autobiography, *Gotai
Fumanzoku*, translated into English as *No One's Perfect*.[1] Ototake,
born without arms or legs, chronicles his youth (he writes at the age
of twenty-two) with humor and gusto to convey the central message
that disability has nothing to do with it: it will not automatically
prevent you from living a happy life. His is the story of a regular
Japanese kid, going to school, learning *kanji* (Chinese ideographs),
making friends, joining clubs, and worrying about getting into college. The fact that he also has a severe disability comes almost as
an afterthought. Readers looking for an inspirational "overcomer"

or "supercrip" story, as the genre is critically termed in the field of Disability Studies, will be disappointed, although Ototake certainly has overcome tremendous barriers and has inspired an international readership.[2] In fact, when his book first came out in 1998, his publisher Kodansha did not think his story would sell and only printed six thousand copies. They not only flew off the shelves but also made *Gotai Fumanzoku* the No. 1 bestseller in Japan that year. The book has sold 4.5 million copies since its release.[3] It has been translated into Chinese, Korean, and English and turned Ototake into a TV personality and popular public speaker.

The reasons for his popularity are at once obvious and surprising. Ototake is a gifted communicator, speaking and writing with charm and ease in a personable and engaging style. His cheerful and fun-loving personality have won him the hearts of readers worldwide who feel compelled—despite his protests that he's just a regular guy—to read his story as one of overcoming handicaps and reaffirming the power of the human spirit. Yet, for Ototake, "being handicapped is a little inconvenient, but it does not make me unhappy. My physical disabilities are simply my unique traits. I live my life normally, just like anybody else."[4] The resolute de-emphasis of disability difference is what makes this book unique and its success such a surprise, at least for his publishers, who feared public discomfort with a topic that is rarely discussed in positive and optimistic terms in the Japanese media. Just by telling his story, Ototake challenges common Japanese assumptions of what it means to be born with a disability: living in isolation and fear, segregated from the mainstream, facing stigma and stereotypes. His story, then, becomes an illustration or case study about disability in Japan by representing not the norm but rather the unusual exception. For readers abroad, *Gotai Fumanzoku* illustrates a personal experience of disability in Japan, and in that process offers important insight into the educational system, family roles, youth culture, and treatment of difference in Japan.

This chapter proposes *Gotai Fumanzoku* as a teaching tool for instructors of Japanese as a foreign language, or for Japanese Studies faculty to introduce disability as a part of language or culture curricula. The book's personable and informal style will quickly make it as popular for American students as it is for the Japanese (as well as Korean and Chinese) public. It is immensely readable in all languages, the Japanese edition aided by *furigana,* small *kana* letters attached to Chinese ideographs (*kanji*) that provide readers with the proper

pronunciation of characters, making it easier to look up the meaning of all but the most basic *kanji*. American—or, rather, nonnative
Japanese readers—of the book will need some historical and cultural
background about the meanings of disability in Japan, the Japanese
special education system, and Japanese language issues surrounding
disability, to make sense of Ototake's story. This chapter will provide
the background needed to make *Gotai Fumanzoku* an effective teaching tool and a useful addition to language and culture classes. I will
highlight central themes in the book and place them in their cultural
context, based on my research on Japanese disability law and politics.[5]

An Inauspicious Birth

We meet Ototake, quite appropriately, at the moment of his birth.
His mother was told she couldn't see him right away, since the baby
was "too weak." Her husband, along with the doctors, had decided
that she might not be ready to face her child's disability, and so
kept coming up with more reasons, such as "severe jaundice," to
postpone the inevitable. As any mother might, she soon understood
that something serious was going on, but never questioned her doctor. Withholding information about a child's medical condition will
sound both cruel and irresponsible to the American reader. But in
Japan patients tend not to challenge their doctors, who today hold
tremendous cultural authority, and held even more in 1976, the year
Ototake was born. Anticipating this reaction by non-Japanese readers, the translator of the English language edition, Geraldine Harcourt, decided to add an explanatory note about the authority of
Japanese doctors and the fact that informed consent was virtually
nonexistent at the time.[6] Eventually, Ototake's mother was told that
a disability, not jaundice, was the reason she had not been allowed to
see her baby. After waiting for three weeks, she met her son for the
first time, surrounded by hospital staff fully expecting her to faint at
the sight of a baby born without arms or legs. "He's adorable" was
her immediate reply, and so, in Ototake's words, "at the age of three
weeks, I was born at last."[7]

The inauspiciousness of his birth is captured in the book's Japanese title, *Gotai Fumanzoku,* which literally means "without all limbs
satisfactorily in place." It is a pun Ototake invented on the Japanese
saying *gotai manzoku,* which captures the usual sentiment of expec-

tant parents, "We don't care if it's a boy or a girl, as long as the baby is born healthy with four limbs and the head in place." His mother's immediate embrace of her "unsatisfactory" baby cements her and her husband's resolve to raise him like any other child and de-emphasize his difference. Ototake tells us that, unlike other parents who will go to great lengths to conceal their children's disabilities, or to keep them hidden at home, "my parents did no such thing. In fact, they always brought me along on their walks in a concerted effort to make neighbors aware of my existence."[8] He does not have to tell his Japanese readers about the history of shame and stigma associated with disability to explain how unusual this choice was.

The stigma associated with having a disability is based on Japanese cultural beliefs about *kegare*, or impurity.[9] People with disabilities (and by extension, their families) were considered polluted and kept out of public view. Japanese law and tradition have reinforced this segregation, which exists in some form to this day. The history of mental illness in Japan sheds light on cultural practices surrounding a range of disabilities. Historically, Japanese heads of households were responsible for both isolating and confining members of their family who were deemed mentally ill. It was the family's responsibility to keep the community safe from the perceived threat of those with mental illness. Most commonly, the person was isolated in a kind of private prison (termed *zashikirô* or *nyûkan*), a locked cell or cage inside or near the family's home.[10] This custom, later regulated by law, provides the foundation of Japan's history of institutionalization of people with all kinds of disabilities and their segregation from the mainstream.[11]

This fear of contamination associated with disabilities persists in current practices that will often exclude people with disabilities from celebrations, such as weddings or New Year's Day ceremonies, for fear that the person's *kegare* might spoil the good fortune of the married couple or the new year. This fear also shapes cultural norms surrounding access to public facilities. A growing number of accessible bathrooms are available in Japan's metropolitan centers, but most of them carry a sign indicating that they are "for the disabled only." These are universally avoided by nondisabled users. Whereas in the United States a wheelchair-accessible stall is commonly located in a bathroom for general use, the Japanese tend to maintain completely separate facilities. It is therefore rare to see disabled and nondisabled people waiting for the bathroom together.[12]

Choosing Inclusion

It is against this backdrop that Ototake's parents resolved not to hide their son from public view and to send him to regular schools. Thus, when Ototake—or Oto-chan, as he was affectionately called at the time—turned four, his parents enrolled him in kindergarten; they did not send him to Japan's special schools for children with disabilities, which is still the norm in Japan. Instead, they selected a kindergarten that prized individuality over one that enforced sameness and group norms, ideals that characterize most Japanese schools. This was not exceedingly difficult to do, as Japanese preschools make up the most diverse, individualized, and lively sector of Japanese education.[13] Ototake's kindergarten experience was thus one in which children choose their own activities according to their interests and abilities. "This approach was perfect for me," he explains. "If we'd all had to do the same activities, there were bound to have been things I couldn't do." An outgoing child, Ototake soon became popular, attracting friends by sheer charisma and of course the novelty of his power wheelchair. He instinctively learned to take on leadership roles to avoid being left out of activities inaccessible to him. Thus, when children were at the playground and he couldn't keep up, he would call them over to the sandbox and then give them orders about what to build. "I said, 'We are making a castle today. If you don't like it, you can go play by yourself. Since I could already talk up a storm in those days, it seems no one was able to stand up to me.'"[14]

The choice to continue Ototake's education in a regular classroom seemed a natural one for his parents. Yet at the time, the prescribed choice by the segregated Japanese educational system would have been placement in one of Japan's many special education schools (*yôgôgakkô*). There are five different types of schools, each specializing in a particular disability: visual or hearing impairments, chronic illness, mental disabilities, and physical disabilities. Their origins date back to the 1880s with the foundation of the first public schools for blind or deaf students, which later expanded into a comprehensive special education system. Accordingly, deaf and blind students were the first to receive education rights along with nondisabled students in the postwar period. Education rights for children with other physical disabilities followed in 1956, but the education for children with mental disabilities was not made compulsory until 1979, after organized pressure and activism by parent groups.[15] To this day, children with disabilities attend segregated schools in their prefecture unless their disability qualifies them to attend their local public school's special education classes (*tokushu gakkyû*). These classes are subdivided by disability category, are held in separate classrooms, and are established by the individual school based on need and teacher availability.[16] Because Japanese compulsory education does not include high school, these classes are rare at the high school level. This means that most children with disabilities will at some point in their education attend a segregated, special school.

The very early separation between a disabled and a nondisabled world is now a source of intense criticism by parents of disabled children who might receive a pedagogically sound and disability-appropriate education in special schools but in the process remain segregated from the children of their neighborhoods. They argue that the interaction between disabled and nondisabled students is a basic requirement for future success in the workplace, which relies heavily on interpersonal relations and adherence to social norms. Parental activism today is primarily focused on the right to have access to high school education, something that is often denied to students who are academically qualified but whose inability to fulfill physical education requirements or to access school grounds is often used as a reason not to admit them. A typical case involved a student with muscular dystrophy who scored in the upper 10 percent on the entrance examination of Agagasaki Public High School. The school principal refused to enroll him because he was not able to fulfill the gym requirement and because he might have endangered himself using a wheelchair on school property. The case went to court in 1991, and the student was admitted to the school.[17]

Ototake's parents faced similar resistance when they insisted on sending him to a regular classroom rather than a special school. "I expect all parents feel a mixture of anxiety and hope when their children are about to enter a new environment," he writes. "For the parents of a child with a disability, though, chances are that the anxiety outweighs the hope. First of all, they run smack into the question, 'Is there anywhere that will accept our child?'"[18] In a chapter entitled "A Heavy Door," Ototake describes the many times his parents were turned away at the gates of both public and private schools as administrators refused even to meet with them. Just as they thought they were out of options, an elementary school principal agreed to interview Oto-chan. Seeing how bright and articulate the boy was, the principal admitted him to Yôga Elementary school. But Ototake's excitement was short-lived. The local Board of Education took the unusual step of reversing the principal's recommendation based on a "lack of precedent" (*zenrei ga nai*) for a severely disabled child's attending a regular school. Citing a lack of precedent is a common method used by Japanese administrators to enforce the status quo and reject change while denying responsibility for doing so.[19] Ototake's parents decided to fight back and arranged for a meeting with board officials. They assumed that if they could just educate officials about all the things that Oto-chan could do, rather than allowing the board to focus on what he could not do, then "permission would surely follow." Ototake staged a demonstration of his abilities in front of the entire board: writing by holding a pencil between his shoulder and his cheek, eating by using the spoon leveraged against the rim of the bowl, and cutting by holding scissors with one end in his mouth and the other against his shoulder while moving his head. In the end, even the administrators were not immune to his charisma and granted permission for him to attend the school.[20]

Mothers and Education

There was one condition, however. Ototake's mother was going to have to accompany him to school every day, waiting in the hallway during classes. This arrangement would be rejected as outrageous in today's American context, but Ototake finds it quite natural. He admits that the burden to his mother was colossal. It was a price the family was nonetheless eager to pay. Ototake's education in a regular school thus depended upon his mother's willingness to sacrifice any prospect of a career or a life outside the home. This assumption is deeply embedded in Japanese notions of motherhood, which assume a mother's tireless dedication to the lives of her children, and tie women's roles as mothers and housewives to the educational success of their children.[21] Both the Board of Education's ruling and Ototake's discussion of it thus rest upon the assumption that Japanese women with young children should not work outside the home and should be available at all times to attend to their children's needs. This assumption has contributed to, indeed, reinforced, the well-documented role women have played in the postwar Japanese economy: they are relegated to low-paying and dead-end jobs in a workforce that depends on their flexibility as they enter and leave the workforce in accordance with their childrearing responsibilities.[22] The fact that Ototake comes from an upper-middle-class family allows his mother to make her choice (which is hardly discussed as one) without many financial considerations, but it is a choice that merits more discussion in a Japanese language or culture classroom than the book suggests.

Inclusion and the "Oto-chan Rules"

Once he was in school, questions arose about how to deal with Ototake's difference. How were his teachers and fellow students to address his disability in a classroom emphasizing uniformity in curriculum, teaching, and student activities? As I mentioned earlier, there was no precedent at his school for his teachers to formulate a response. Although no one could have predicted it, Ototake would become a prominent—and even nationally celebrated—figure for setting the very precedent that the Board of Education had tried to deny. In the American educational context, students with disabilities have the right to be educated in the "least restrictive environment," in a manner integrated as much as possible into the regular classroom.[23] An individualized education plan charts the course for an education that balances a student's right to be treated as an equal member of the classroom with the right to have special needs addressed. This approach to equal treatment does not enforce a strict standard of sameness, but recognizes that equal rights for students with disabilities must incorporate a respect for difference. In Japan, the few students with disabilities who gain access to regular education do not receive individualized treatment, which occurs in special education classes.

In accordance with this rule, Ototake's first homeroom teacher, Takagi Sensei, instituted strict orders that Ototake was not to receive special treatment. Ever the popular student, Ototake had soon established a throng of followers who admired his power wheelchair and were eager to help him with difficult tasks. While this spirit of cooperation and helpfulness would be the pride of many teachers, Takagi Sensei issued a no-help rule for the class, fearing that Ototake would become too dependent on the help of others. At some point he even outlawed the use of the power wheelchair at school, forcing

Ototake to "scoot on his butt," because he viewed the wheelchair as yet another marker of difference that separated Ototake from his peers. In retrospect, Ototake describes how grateful he is for having received such tough teaching: "I believe the mobility I have today is entirely thanks to Takagi Sensei's guidance. If I'd been using the power wheelchair all the time from those first years, I would surely have become completely reliant on it. I try to imagine what my daily life would be like. . . . I'm sure it would be very different from the life I lead now in terms of freedom, mentally as well as practically."[24] With the benefit of hindsight, Ototake recalls his days in middle and high schools, which were not always physically accessible to him and often required him to abandon his wheelchair.

This pedagogical move was for the benefit of the class—teaching that children with disabilities are not as helpless as students are conditioned to believe—but also to accommodate Ototake's desire to be treated as a regular Japanese kid. He hated being thought of as different and did not want to be left out of activities. This arrangement truly integrated him as an equal member of the class, especially at recess, which he describes as the most painful part of the school day for students with disabilities, as they feel left out of the fun. Ototake decided that he, too, would play baseball, soccer, and dodgeball during recess: "There was no reason to give up on these games. All it took for me to be in on the action was some special rules. These were known as the Oto-chan Rules, and they were invented by my classmates." The Oto-chan rules allowed him to participate in sports with his peers. When playing baseball, for example, Ototake hit the ball while another player on his team ran the bases in his stead, as an "unorthodox pitch runner."[25] These rules, which were initiated and designed without any input from teachers, were not the result of charity. Rather, they were a natural consequence of shared cultural values: his classmates simply took it for granted that Ototake would be part of the team.

Takagi Sensei's approach to equal treatment and the class's development of Oto-chan rules demonstrate a form of inclusive education that is unique to Japan. Inclusive education, as theorized in the U.S. educational context and supported by the Individuals with Disabilities Education Act (IDEA), mandates that children with even the severest disabilities be included in all aspects of classroom life, with the use of aids, assistive technology, and adaptations to classrooms and curricula.[26] The underlying goal of inclusion is to welcome students with disabilities into the general education classroom and to educate them among their peers, rather than separating them into special education classrooms. To implement inclusion, schools must provide individually appropriate supports and services, as outlined in each student's Individualized Education Plan. The American context stresses the importance of an individualized approach to education, which stands in stark contrast to the collective values inherent in the Japanese model.

In the Japanese version of inclusion as practiced at Yôga Elementary School, there were neither aids, nor technology, nor disability-appropriate teaching methods; rather, there was a reliance upon cultural norms that value the participation and inclusion of every student. Students in the class did not have to be prompted by their teachers to include Ototake in their recess play; they would not have considered excluding him. His popularity and natural potential for leadership—if not bossiness, as he likes to call it—certainly helped with his integration, but there are structural aspects unique to the Japanese education system that facilitated Ototake's inclusion. Japanese elementary schools are known for fostering initiative and autonomy in students by delegating aspects of classroom management to them at a young age. Students are responsible for administering the morning's roll call, cleaning, making announcements, and, perhaps most important, for maintaining order and classroom harmony. Teachers rarely intervene in fights between students and instead leave it to the class to resolve conflict, for example.

The reasons for de-centering the role of the teacher in Japanese elementary school classrooms are part of larger socialization goals. When asked why school is important, Japanese parents respond quite differently from their American counterparts. In Japan, the importance of schooling, especially in the lower grades, is socialization rather than academic performance, which ranks highest with American parents.[27] Japanese schools will not separate students into different ability tracks, as this violates the assumption that every student can and should master the national curriculum as well as the larger socialization goals of Japanese education. Students who are academically gifted are commonly recruited to tutor their peers, but they are not placed on an advanced track as their American equivalents would be. Ototake's inclusion in the class community was thus a natural extension of this system. It took tremendous effort to gain entrance into a regular school, but once he had been admitted, joining the class became less of a struggle. Ironically, the very norms of group conformity (and disavowal of special treatment) that initially kept Ototake out of school ultimately allowed students to embrace him as an equal once he was in school.

Testing the Rules

The big test came in fourth grade when the entire class was to hike up Mount Kobo on their annual school outing. Because the excursion was not wheelchair accessible, Ototake's mother requested an exception from the equal treatment rules, asking that he be excused from the trip. Even this became a class discussion.

> *Teacher:* For our school trip we're going to Mount Kobo in Kana-gawa Prefecture. We'll be climbing the mountain. All right, everybody?
>
> *Class:* All riiiight!
>
> *Teacher:* I've just been there with the other teachers, and the going's really tough. What do you think? Still all right?
>
> *Class:* All riiiight!
>
> *Teacher:* But remember Ototake is in a wheelchair. The other day, his mother told me he won't be coming on the trip this time. What do you think?
>
> *Student:* Hey, that's cheating!
>
> *Student:* If it's such a tough mountain to climb, it's not fair that only Oto-chan gets out of going!

Cries of "That's right" went up from the other kids. They were the ones who would have to work extra hard if I went. It meant taking a wheelchair up a peak that was difficult enough to begin with. And yet, what they came out with was, "It's not fair that only Oto-chan gets out of going!" It just didn't make sense to them that this one member of the class can be excused from an event. Which is how, I, too, came to challenge Mount Kobo.[28]

This conversation demonstrates beautifully the impact of the Japanese-style inclusion mandate. Because Ototake was "just an-other member of the class," it was unthinkable for him to use his disability as a reason to get out of a difficult challenge, even if this meant that the climb would become more difficult for everybody. As Ototake describes in excruciating detail, the trip up the mountain was muddy and wet and exhausting for everybody as teachers and students took turns pushing and pulling the wheelchair up the mountain. Just as Ototake's mother agreed to accompany Ototake to school every day, so did his classmates push and pull his wheelchair up the mountain without question. By comparison, the American approach to inclusion would be more likely to dictate a choice of class outings that would not make participation prohibitively difficult for students with disabilities. Alternatively, an American school might provide the aides and supports that would enable the student's equal participation. Students would not be asked to provide the services themselves, or be expected to enable the student's participation in any material way, except of course to accept the student as an equally valuable member of the class. That Ototake's classmates assumed this responsibility without much thought for themselves attests to the importance of socialization in Japanese education.

Protection and Paternalism

Ototake's mother's request to let him skip the class trip was out of the ordinary. Her usual approach was to let the school make virtually all the decisions regarding Ototake's treatment. Ototake's parents were unique in that they fought hard to get him into school, but once he had been accepted, they had a hands-off policy. Takagi Sensei gratefully recalls how Ototake's mother, rather than making demands on the teacher as most parents of disabled children would, "entrusted everything to me, which made my job straightforward." He did consult her before banning the power wheelchair from school, but she never second-guessed his decision. Neither did she interfere, for example, when Oto-chan was first starting school and children were running up to him, touching him, asking what was wrong with him, imitating him by tucking their hands and feet inside their clothes. "My mother just said coolly, 'It's a problem he has to solve for himself.'" Similarly, when Ototake asked to go on a summer trip with friends, something he was sure his mother would consider too risky without an adult by his side, she surprised him by not only allowing it but also immediately booking a vacation to Hong Kong for herself and her husband. "There's a tendency for parents of disabled children to be overprotective," surmises Ototake. "Not the Ototakes, though: they gaily seize the chance to zip off on vacation while their son's away. Gee, a disabled person just gets no respect around here! But seriously, they had the right approach."[29]

In hindsight, Ototake appreciates his parents' relaxed attitude. He credits them with having the right approach because he—along with the Japanese readers of his books—is only too aware of how unusual it is. Typically, Japanese parents face strong expectations to protect, if not overprotect, their children from an inaccessible and disability-unfriendly world. Ototake alludes to the overprotective mother, a role shaped by cultural expectation and reinforced by policy.[30] The family is still the locus of much of contemporary Japanese disability policy that depends upon the unpaid work of women to care for their children, often far into adulthood, where the state fails to provide alternatives.[31]

Protected by their mothers and dependent on their families for a lifetime of care, people with disabilities in Japan now face considerable hurdles to approaching the goals of Independent Living (IL, or *ai-eru* in Japanese) as first conceptualized by the American disability rights movement.[32] The Japanese disability movement has worked to incorporate these ideals since the 1980s and now operates more than one hundred Centers for Independent Living in Japan.[33] Issues of paternalism and dependence, however, continue to play an important role. As an example, consider Atsuko Kuwana's essay describing her experiences of reverting to childlike dependence when she returns for a visit to her home country and suffers *sato-gaeri sutoresu* ("homecoming stress"). Kuwana, who now lives in the United States, describes her cultural readjustment when returning to Japan as a person with a disability who needs to be "protected by the able-bodied." For example, when she misses her regular train one evening to attend an office party, the station attendants are so concerned about her that they phone her office and her transfer station to inquire about her whereabouts. Kuwana likens this treatment to that of a missing child.[34] Her chronicle of such benevolent paternalism, coupled with the expectation that she be grateful for the special treatment she receives, are a powerful reminder of how easily Ototake could have experienced similar treatment, from both his parents and his school.

Equal Treatment, Modified

In fifth grade Takagi Sensei retired and Ototake got a new teacher. With the arrival of Ota Sensei, there was a new opportunity to reflect on the no-special-treatment doctrine. In Japan the first day of school is devoted to a schoolwide cleaning (*sôji*), a common custom, since Japanese schools typically do not hire cleaning staff. Ota Sensei saw Ototake struggling with both a wet and a dry cleaning cloth as he tried to mop the floor. Under the old regime, Ototake was not to be left out of communal activities, as the school cleaning is an especially important event to foster a sense of community and school ownership. But Ota Sensei decided to use Ototake's abilities in different, and to his mind more effective, ways. He put him in charge of the word processor, which Ototake had never used before, to produce class handouts, notices for bulletin boards, and whatever else needed to be printed. In essence, this new approach conveyed the attitude, "If he can't do the same things, we'll find a trade-off."[35]

Ototake describes the pride he took in mastering the word processor and eventually producing handouts for the entire school as the self-declared president of the "Otohiro Printing Company." In word processing, he found an outlet for his love for words and, most important, an equal opportunity to do his share for the class. Under the new regime, the strict equal treatment approach was modified into one of "different but equivalent" treatment. As Ototake explains, this was Ota Sensei's foresight that as Ototake's classmates matured physically, there were going to be fewer and fewer things that he would be able to do just as they did. As the effects of his physical difference increased—and as the gulf between him and his peers widened—Ototake would need more help from his classmates performing the exact same chores. "No doubt they would be happy to help," writes Ototake. "But how would I feel about having to ask all the time? What if I ended up feeling wimpy and helpless?"[36] The task was to find chores Ototake could perform without help, by using his abilities. Under the new regime Ototake had found an equivalent way to fulfill his responsibilities as an equal member of the class.

Ota Sensei did not stray too far from the equal-treatment mandate, however. When it came time for Sports Day (*undôkai*), he suggested that, for the first time, Ototake participate in a race. In previous years, Ototake had been excused from Sports Day, primarily, as he explains, because the school worried that spectators, mostly parents, would object to the view of him running by "shuffling [his] butt" and complain: "Why are they making a child like that run in front of everybody? The poor boy. It is very insensitive of the school." To Ototake, such paternalism is clearly discriminatory, but not surprising in light of the Japanese tendency to "think 'poor fellow' when they see a disabled person." In preparation for his first race (and in order not to make a fool out of himself), Ototake enlisted the help of his best friend Minoru to help him with "early morning training," which consisted of runs around the block—strolls for Minoru—before the beginning of school. What mattered to Ototake and his teachers was that he participate in an important school event, not that he perform well. Yet it is with no small measure of pride that Ototake describes his receiving his "last place" award: "I crossed the finish line over twenty seconds behind the others. But I felt an enormous sense of fulfillment at having gotten there. To the applause of the crowd, I lined up behind the banner that read 6th. I was probably the only child in sixth place who looked as thrilled as if he'd won first prize."[37]

Language and Disability

Gotai Fumanzoku is filled with such anecdotes as these, which allow Ototake to reflect on his participation in mainstream education. Reading his book is like following a video diary of his life with voiceover reflections of how his experiences have shaped him and his environment. He likes to comment on the irony of his situation— the fact that he became an international celebrity by stressing his normalcy. The relationship between normalcy and language merits closer inspection at this point. Ototake is very keen on downplaying his difference by representing himself as "just a member of the class" (*tada kurasu no hitori*). This approach has guided his integration into the mainstream and is reflected in his teachers', parents', and classmates' treatment of his disability. Accordingly, he is careful to avoid calling himself an "individual" (*kojin*), a term that guides the American approach to disability rights but would challenge the model of full inclusion he describes.

Language of course plays an important role in the ways that disability is conceptualized and constituted. The field of Disability Studies has paid close attention to the impact of language in generating the social, legal, and political responses to disability. Prominent in the United States is the evolution of accepted terminology related to disability, from terms like "handicapped" or "the disabled" to "individuals with disabilities." This shift toward what is called "people-first language" promotes the idea that others "see us as people first" rather than as conditions or diseases, or as "heroic cripples, struggling to be normal, people suffering the tragedy of birth defects, or victims who fight to overcome their challenges."[38] This attitude complements Ototake's frequent assurances that "disability has nothing to do with it," and that, while his disability certainly is part of his identity, his primary experience of life is not so different from that of his peers. Witness the glee with which he describes goofing off with his friends, getting into schoolyard fights, receiving his first love letter, and confessing his passion for designer shirts.

Language relating to disability has been similarly contested in Japan. In an article entitled "Language and Disability in Japan," Nanette Gottlieb chronicles the changing public use of language referring to disability. Gottlieb describes the growing awareness of disability issues during the 1990s as a result of international developments in disability law that pushed the Japanese government to formulate an Action Plan for People with Disabilities and that raised awareness about alternative, rights-based approaches to disability policy. Public recognition of discriminatory language played an important part in this development. For example, when Japanese students are asked about words they consider discriminatory, terms describing disability, such as *mekura* (blind), *tsunbo* (deaf), and *kichigai* (mad), constitute the overwhelming majority of those mentioned, more than racist language or terms describing the Burakumin minority, Japan's largest minority group, who were stigmatized by law and culture in the feudal period due to the polluting nature of their occupations (such as tanning and skinning hides); to this day they experience formal and informal discrimination on the basis of their ancestry. Buraku activism has, among others, drawn public attention to the power of stigmatizing language.[39] Partially as a result of the United Nations' International Year of Disabled Peoples (IYDP) in 1981, which drew attention to the power of language, the Japanese government began replacing terms like *fugu haishitsusha* (the lame and deformed) with *shôgaisha* (disabled person), *mekura* (blind) with *me ga mienai* (eyes don't see), *hakuchi* (imbecility) with *chiteki shôgai* (intellectual disability), and *kichigai* (crazy) with *seishin shôgai* (mental disability).[40]

Barrier-Free Hearts

The International Year of Disabled Peoples brought with it an influx of English-language terminology that was eagerly adopted by
Japanese disability groups as a sign of progressive politics.[41] Ototake dedicates an entire chapter to a discussion of the popular term
"barrier-free," which typically describes an environment that is
physically accessible. Ototake combines it with the term "heart" to
summarize his central message and cement his public role as an
ambassador for acceptance. For Ototake, the problem with growing up with a disability in Japan is not the disability per se but the
ignorance, misperceptions, and fears of the nondisabled. If more
people, particularly children, were in everyday contact with people
with disabilities, their hearts would indeed become barrier-free, and
bring about other forms of physical access and integration.

It is this emphasis on attitudinal, rather than political or legal,
reform that has won him the hearts of his Japanese readers. Who,
after all, can resist his call for acceptance and understanding? His
story is not one that fundamentally challenges the state of Japanese
disability policy; indeed, his refusal to ask for accommodations in
the classroom reinforces rather than confronts the central premise
of the Japanese educational system: everybody works under the same
rules and expectations for success, despite varying amounts of talent
and energy required to master the curriculum. As an example, consider that Ototake, despite being a gifted student, had to work hard
to offset his low grades in physical education. To him, this proves
that mainstream education does not need to be modified to include
students with disabilities and that the same rules can be applied to
everybody. Ototake's experience in education endorses the terms of
the educational meritocracy.[42]

A "barrier-free heart" paves the way toward a better society. And
it is people with disabilities who are coming "to the rescue" of a
society that has become increasingly competitive, self-centered, and
individualistic. As Ototake's experience demonstrates, regular education not only benefits the child with a disability but also "enlightens"
the entire class. Nondisabled children become aware of differences
and the need to be considerate of others. Just as academically gifted
students in Ototake's class were expected to help struggling students,
and the "kids who could do a backward somersault on the high
bar taught the ones who couldn't," so, according to Ototake, should

nondisabled students be expected to help out their disabled peers: "If there's a hearing impaired child in the class, then it's enough if her neighbor shares his notes. That's all it takes for people who are grouped together as 'the disabled' to receive a regular education too."[43]

The contention that "this is all it takes" to integrate people with disabilities has been criticized as simplistic and naïve, and some assume that Ototake's sunny outlook might darken with maturity.[44] But this cheerful and optimistic demeanor appeals to people who are otherwise uncomfortable around disability. As Ototake explains, "In today's competitive society where one is always expected to excel, we are losing sight of what's obvious—when you see someone having trouble, you lend a hand. We've been hearing for a long time now about the breakdown of communities whose members used to help one another. It could be that the people who come to the rescue, the people who can rebuild a more fully human society, will be people with disabilities." Ototake demonstrates valued Japanese traits, such as believing that hard work is the only path to success, and rejecting self-pity. With the exception of one bleak episode in which Ototake's recovery from surgery deprives him of his friends for two months, Ototake's story is devoid of anger and bitterness. Most important, his vision for change asks for very little social and political capital and calls for something that nobody can refuse to endorse: a "more fully human society."[45]

Notes

1. Hirotada Ototake, *Gotai Fumanzoku* (Tokyo: Kodansha International, 1998); *No One's Perfect*, trans. Gerry Harcourt (New York: Kodansha America, 2000). All citations refer to the English language edition.
2. Simi Linton, *Claiming Disability: Knowledge and Identity* (New York: New York University Press, 1998).
3. Jennifer Hanawald, "Armless (and Legless) in Japan," *Salon Online*, September 11, 2000, http://www.archive.salon.com/books/feature/2000/09/11/ototake.index.html (accessed May 5, 2006).
4. Murakami Mutsuko, "Handicap? What Handicap?" *Asiaweek Online*, July 9, 1999, http://www.pathfinder.com/asiaweek/99/0709/feat2.html.
5. Katharina Heyer, "Rights or Quotas? The ADA as a Model for Disability Rights," in *Handbook of Research on Employment Discrimination: Rights and Realities*, ed. Bob Nelson and Laura Beth Nielsen (New

York: Springer, 2005); Heyer, "Rights on the Road: Disability Politics in Japan and Germany" (Ph.D. diss., University of Hawai'i, 2002); Heyer, "From Welfare to Rights—Japanese Disability Law," *Asia-Pacific Law and Policy Journal* 1 (2000): 1–21.

6. Geraldine Harcourt,"Walls? What Walls? A Translator Breaks Down Barriers," http://web-japan.org/trends01/article/020109fea_r.html (accessed April 24, 2007).

7. Ototake, *No One*, 9.

8. Ibid., 10.

9. Miho Iwakuma, "Intercultural Views of People with Disabilities in Asia and Africa" (unpublished paper, 2000), n.p.

10. Stephan Salzberg, "Japan's New Mental Health Law: More Light Shed on Dark Places?" *International Journal of Law and Psychiatry* 14 (1991): 145.

11. See Heyer, "From Welfare to Rights," passim.

12. Iwakuma, "Intercultural Views," 10.

13. Catherine Lewis, *Educating Hearts and Minds: Reflections on Japanese Preschool and Elementary Education* (Cambridge: Cambridge University Press, 1995), 8.

14. Ototake, *No One*, 14–16.

15. Toshihiko Mogi, "The Disabled in Society," *Japan Quarterly* 39 (1992): 135.

16. These categories are vision impaired, hard of hearing, physically disabled, mentally disabled, ill and weak, behavior impairment, and speech impairment. Students with learning disabilities (*gakushû shôgai*) are not yet recognized as disabled by Japanese disability law, although awareness of "LD," as it is commonly referred to, is certainly growing in schools. See Yoshihisa Abe, "Special Education Reform in Japan," *European Journal of Special Needs Education* 13 (1998): 86–97.

17. Mogi, "Disabled," 443.

18. Ototake, *No One*, 18.

19. Jeffrey Maret, "An Inauspicious Birth: A Physically Impaired Child's View of Japan's Educational Meritocracy" (unpublished paper, 2000).

20. Ototake, *No One*, 21.

21. See Anne Imamura, *Urban Japanese Housewives* (Honolulu: University of Hawai'i Press, 1987).

22. See Mariko Fujita, "It's All Mother's Fault: Childcare and the Socialization of Working Mothers in Japan," *Journal of Japanese Studies* 15 (1989): 67–91; Mary Brinton, *Women and the Economic Miracle: Gender and Work in Postwar Japan* (Berkeley: University of California Press, 1993).

23. Individuals with Disabilities Education Act, U.S. Code 20 (1997), Section 1400 et seq.

24. Ototake, *No One*, 28.

25. Ibid., 33.
26. See Susan Stainbeck and William Stainbeck, eds., *Inclusion: A Guide for Educators* (Baltimore: Paul H. Brookes Publishing, 1996).
27. Lewis, *Educating,* 32.
28. Ototake, *No One,* 44.
29. Ibid., 210–11.
30. Yoko Nakanishi, "Independence from Spoiling Parents: The Struggle of Women with Disabilities in Japan," in *Imprinting Our Image: An International Anthology by Women with Disabilities,* ed. Diane Driedger (Toronto: Gynergy Books, 1992), 25–30.
31. See Heyer, "Rights on the Road."
32. See Heyer, "From Welfare to Rights."
33. See Nakanishi, "Independence."
34. Atsuko Kuwana, "Korei: Satogaeri Sutoresu (Homecoming Stress)," *Fukushi Rodo* 76 (1997): 118, as cited in Iwakuma, "Intercultural Views," n.p.
35. Ototake, *No One,* 56.
36. Ibid., 57.
37. Ibid., 61–65.
38. The shift to people-first language is not universally accepted in the disability community. For example, the National Federation of the Blind rejects people-first language for related reasons. See C. Edwin Vaughn, "People-First Language: An Unholy Crusade," http://www.blind.net/bpg00006.htm (accessed April 24, 2007); cf. Kathie Snow, "People First Language," http://www.disabilityisnatural.com/peoplefirstlanguage.htm (accessed April 24, 2007).
39. Nanette Gottlieb, "Language and Disability in Japan," *Disability and Society* 16 (2001): 983.
40. Ibid., 985–86.
41. See Heyer, "Rights on the Road."
42. See Maret, "Inauspicious," 10.
43. Ototake, *No One,* 77–78.
44. See Hanawald, "Armless," n.p.
45. Ototake, *No One,* 81.

Abbreviations

ACT American College Test
ADA Americans with Disabilities Act
ADD/ADHD Attention Deficit Disorder/Attention Deficit Hyper-
    activity Disorder
ADFL Association of Departments of Foreign Languages
APH American Printing House for the Blind
ASD Autism Spectrum Disorders
ASL American Sign Language
ASLTA American Sign Language Teachers Association
CAST Center for Applied Special Technology
CDI (Modern Languages Association) Committee on Disability
    Issues in the Profession
CRISS (Project for) Creating Independence through Student-
    Owned Strategies
DISFL listserv for disabilities and foreign languages
FL foreign language
IDEA Individuals with Disabilities Education Act
IEP Individualized Education Plan
IYDP (United Nations) International Year of Disabled Peoples
L2 second language
LD learning disability / learning disabled
LESCO Costa Rican Sign Language
MIUSA Mobility International U.S.A.
MLA Modern Languages Association
NCDE National Clearinghouse on Disability and Exchange
NIMAS National Instructional Materials Accessibility Standard
PACE (Project for) Postsecondary Academic Curriculum
    Excellence

RID Registry of Interpreters for the Deaf
UDL Universal Design for Learning
ULE Universal Learning Edition

Contributors

Michelle N. Abadia is originally from Caguas, Puerto Rico. She has taught both Spanish and French at Framingham State College and Roxbury Community College, and various adult education programs. She currently teaches modern languages at Babson College and Massbay Community College in Wellesley, Massachusetts.

Donalda Ammons is Professor of Spanish at Gallaudet University in Washington, D.C. In addition, she currently serves as the first female president of Deaflympics, a quadrennial Olympic-equivalent event exclusively for Deaf athletes and the world's oldest sports organization for the disabled. She also serves as field editor for *Palaestra,* a professional quarterly journal on sports for the disabled.

Salwa Ali Benzahra is a Tunisian professor currently teaching American and British literature in the English department of la Faculté des Lettres et des Sciences Humaines, University of Sousse, Tunisia. Her interdisciplinary interests include disability studies, body theory, postcolonial literature, Middle Eastern and North African cultures, films, and fiction, including Francophone Maghrebian literature.

Tammy Berberi is Assistant Professor of French at the University of Minnesota, Morris, where she teaches French language, literature, and culture courses, and disability studies. She has published articles on universal design in foreign language courses as well as representations of disability in French literature. She served as the first student member of the Modern Language Association's Committee on Disability Issues in the Profession and is the cofounder, with Elizabeth C. Hamilton, of disfl@lists.umn.edu, a listserv devoted to disabilities and foreign language learning.

Brenda Jo Brueggemann is Associate Professor of English, women's studies, and comparative studies at Ohio State University, where she also serves as co-coordinator for both the ASL program and the disability studies undergraduate minor and graduate specialization. She is the author, coauthor, editor, and coeditor of several books in disability studies and deaf studies.

Teresa Cabal Krastel is an independent consultant for private companies and is currently developing educational content for local and national school language curricula for learners of Spanish as a foreign language and Heritage learners of Spanish.

Elizabeth Emery is Associate Professor of French at Montclair State University and the author of numerous essays devoted to medieval and nineteenth-century French literature and culture, as well as *Romancing the Cathedral: Gothic Architecture in Fin-de-siècle French Culture* (SUNY Press, 2001), coauthor of *Consuming the Past: The Medieval Revival in Fin-de-siècle France* (Ashgate, 2003), and coeditor of *Medieval Saints in Nineteenth-Century France* (McFarland, 2004).

Tracey Hall is a senior research scientist and instructional designer at CAST, the Center for Applied Special Technology, where she directs CAST's initiatives to create and evaluate digital supported writing environments across content areas. She has also served as director of curriculum for the National Center on Accessing the General Curriculum (1999–2004) led by CAST.

Elizabeth C. Hamilton is Associate Professor of German at Oberlin College, where she teaches German language, literature, and cinema courses. In addition to several articles that address pedagogical developments for teaching disabled students, she has published studies of contemporary portrayals of disability in German fiction and film.

Katharina Heyer is Assistant Professor of Political Science with joint appointments at the School of Law and the Center for Disability Studies at the University of Hawai'i. Her research focuses on the expansion of disability rights law and rights consciousness to countries across the globe. She is currently working on a federal grant developing faculty training in disability issues to ensure that students with disabilities receive equal opportunities in the postsecondary classroom.

Rasma Lazda-Cazers teaches German at the University of Alabama and is the coauthor, with Helga Thorson, of a German cultural reader entitled *Neuer Wein und Zwiebelkuchen* (McGraw Hill, 2005).

Anne Meyer is co–founding director and chief of educational design at CAST, where she has played a leading role in defining the principles and practices of Universal Design for Learning. She is coauthor, with David Rose, of *Teaching Every Student in the Digital Age: Universal Design for Learning* (ASCD, 2002) and *Learning to Read in the Computer Age* (Brookline Books, 1998), and has published numerous journal articles. She is also coeditor, with David Rose and Chuck Hitchcock, of *The Universally Designed Classroom* (Harvard Education Press, 2005).

Melissa Mitchell serves as the National Clearinghouse on Disability and Exchange Outreach/Training Coordinator and has developed trainings based on the Clearinghouse's disability and exchange publications. Ms. Mitchell, who uses a wheelchair, can relate her trainings to her experiences studying and teaching abroad in France. She has also served on Washington State's disability council, youth leadership projects, and disaster preparedness training for people with disabilities.

Facundo Montenegro (1966–2005) taught at Gallaudet University and devoted himself to mentoring a new generation of Deaf video- and filmmakers. He coproduced two videos with his students, "Resurrecting Sound: A Deaf Perspective on Cochlear Implants" and "Signing the Body Poetic," in addition to *Audism Unveiled*, a film that won first prize for Best Documentary at the 2005 Deaf Rochester Film Festival.

Pilar Piñar is Associate Professor of Spanish at Gallaudet University. Her research explores issues of literacy development and foreign language teaching methodologies for Deaf students. She is the author of a Spanish textbook and DVD entitled *Español en Vivo*, published by Yale University Press, which features a sociolinguistic approach to language teaching.

C. Patrick Proctor is a research scientist at CAST, where he applies his expertise in bilingualism, biliteracy, and education to the development of universally designed learning environments for English language learners.

Michele Scheib is Project Specialist for the National Clearinghouse on Disability and Exchange, which is sponsored by the U.S. State Department and administered by Mobility International USA. She has contributed to numerous publications on disability and exchange.

Nicole Strangman is a member of CAST's research and development team and has contributed to numerous journal articles and book chapters on a variety of subjects, including Universal Design for Learning.

Ian M. Sutherland is Associate Professor of Latin and Italian at Gallaudet University. He has presented papers and published on Roman architecture and archaeology, and on disability studies. He excavates annually at Pompeii and is field director for the Restoring Ancient Stabiae Foundation.

Helga Thorson teaches German at the University of Victoria in British Columbia, Canada. In addition to disability studies, her research focuses on early twentieth-century women writers, foreign language writing processes, and foreign language pedagogy. She and Rasma Lazda-Cazers have collaborated on a German cultural reader entitled *Neuer Wein und Zwiebelkuchen* (McGraw Hill, 2005).

Index